COLOURS TO THE CHAMELEON:

Canadian Actors on Shakespeare

ESSENTIAL ESSAYS SERIES 72

Canada Council Conseil des Arts for the Arts du Canada

**ONTARIO ARTS COUNCIL
CONSEIL DES ARTS DE L'ONTARIO**
an Ontario government agency
un organisme du gouvernement de l'Ont

Canadä

Guernica Editions Inc. acknowledges the support of the Canada Council
for the Arts and the Ontario Arts Council. The Ontario Arts Council
is an agency of the Government of Ontario.

We acknowledge the financial support of the Government of Canada.

KEITH GAREBIAN

COLOURS
TO THE
CHAMELEON:

Canadian Actors on Shakespeare

GUERNICA
EDITIONS

TORONTO – BUFFALO – LANCASTER (U.K.)
2019

Michael Mirolla, editor
Cover and Interior Design: Errol F. Richardson
Cover photo: Tom Rooney (Richard II) and Graham Abbey (Bolingbroke)
in *Richard II*. (Photo: David Hou)
Courtesy of the Stratford Festival Archives)
Guernica Editions Inc.
1569 Heritage Way, Oakville, (ON), Canada L6M 2Z7
2250 Military Road, Tonawanda, N.Y. 14150-6000 U.S.A.
www.guernicaeditions.com

Distributors:
University of Toronto Press Distribution,
5201 Dufferin Street, Toronto (ON), Canada M3H 5T8
Gazelle Book Services, White Cross Mills
High Town, Lancaster LA1 4XS U.K.

First edition.
Printed in Canada.

Legal Deposit – Third Quarter
Library of Congress Catalog Card Number: 2019930423
Library and Archives Canada Cataloguing in Publication
Title: Colours to the chameleon : Canadian actors on Shakespeare / Keith Garebian.
Other titles: Canadian actors on Shakespeare
Names: Garebian, Keith, 1943- author.
Series: Essential essays series ; 72.
Description: Series statement: Essential essays series ; 72
Identifiers: Canadiana (print) 2019005249X | Canadiana (ebook) 20190052538 | ISBN
9781771833936
(softcover) | ISBN 9781771833943 (EPUB) | ISBN 9781771833950 (Kindle)
Subjects: LCSH: Shakespearean actors and actresses—Canada. | LCSH: Shakespeare, William,
1564-1616—
Stage history—Canada. | LCSH: Shakespeare, William, 1564-1616—Dramatic production. |
LCSH:
Theatre—Canada. | LCSH: Acting.
Classification: LCC PR3109.C3 G37 2019 | DDC 792.02/8092271—dc23

For Michael Garebian
who saw his first Stratford Shakespeare when he was 9
and
Matt Mackey
a friend with sharp intelligence

"I can add colours to the chameleon,
Change shapes with Proteus for advantages …"
Henry VI, Part 3, (3.2.191-192)

Contents

Preface   1

Nancy Palk:
Text as Iceberg   23
Joseph Ziegler:
Trusting the Play   45
Albert Schultz:
Provocations   67
Ben Carlson:
Speedy Clarity for the Shakespearean Lift   81
Moya O'Connell:
Living the Human Inside of It   105
Tom McCamus:
"I Ended Up Loving Shakespeare"   121
Juan Chioran:
Making a World We All Understand   143
Chick Reid:
Gladly Does She Learn and Gladly Teach   159
Tom Rooney:
The Riddle of It Is Never-Ending   175
Graham Abbey:
Seeking the Middle Ground   193
Lucy Peacock:
Language Through the Chaos of the Heart   215

Appendix A: List of Interviews Conducted for This Book   235
Select Bibliography   235
Acknowledgements   241
About the Author   242
Selected Books in Print   243

Tom Rooney as King Richard II in Breath of Kings: Rebellion *(Stratford Festival, 2016).*
(Photo: David Hou. Courtesy of the Stratford Festival)

Preface

Why Shakespeare? Why does it matter so much to actors (especially Canadian ones) how to act Shakespeare? These are the two radical questions at the very basis of this book. Taking the questions in order, I need to dispense immediately with anticipated objections from rabid ultra-nationalists who would have us believe that Shakespeare is simply a foreigner and, therefore, not especially relevant to Canadians. Shakespeare easily transcends their misconceived, misdirected choler because his works are a living legacy to be read, performed, and adapted by creative professionals and lay enthusiasts the world over. He has a kind of wisdom about human contradictions, and an empathy for some of the most conflicted beings. Shakespeare covers just about every subject in our human journey: circumstances of birth, family (with betrayals), personal humiliation and indignity, suffering, and death. He sifts reality from illusion, truth from falsehood. In his book of personal essays on outstanding and prolific creative figures, Paul Johnson writes of Shakespeare:

> During his lifetime his plays were already being performed abroad as well as all over Britain, and even at sea off the coast of West Africa; they have since been translated into every known language and acted all over the world. They have become the basis for over 200 operas by composers great and minor, including Purcell, Rossini, Verdi, Wagner, and Britten, and have inspired works by Mendelssohn, Berlioz, Tchaikovsky, Prokofiev, and scores of other masters. The 103 songs that dot his plays have been set to music by all the composers of art songs. Shakespeare's works have inspired over 300 movies and thousands of television adaptations, and have provided material or ideas for most professional playwrights from Dryden to Shaw and Stoppard. His poetry is a mainspring of imaginative English literature and a formative influence on its foreign equivalents, especially French, Italian, German, Spanish, and Russian (Johnson 49).

Tina Packer has asserted that Shakespeare wrote on three levels simultaneously (the personal, contextual, and macrocosmic), and because of this, "his stories speak to many cultures, can be performed anywhere in the world, are as much about the colonized as the colonizers, the repressed as the repressors, the workingman as the aristocrat, the woman as the man, and the potential in all of us" (Packer 112). But there is no single Shakespeare: He is an expert shape-shifter who can have more colours than a chameleon. His immense curiosity about life generates enormous plays with significant questions that cut across all generations and cultures.

So, it is understandable why he is, as Susannah Carson claims, "the most widely read author in English; his *Complete Works* are second in popularity only to the Bible" (Carson xv). I would not go as far as Harold Bloom in considering Shakespeare God ("On Heine's model, I again remark: there is a God, there is no God but God, and his name is William Shakespeare" (Carson viii).), but that is because I am an agnostic. If we discount his excessive reverence, we can agree with Bloom about Shakespeare's genius in taking "literature beyond its limits": "Ralph Waldo Emerson said that Shakespeare wrote the text of modern life, which means that we are all of us, each in turn, a kind of amalgam of various Shakespearean roles, though I would prefer to call them people" (Carson ix).

Shakespeare is probably the most performed playwright internationally, especially among people who do not measure art primarily by nationality or passport and who do not continue to fight outdated battles in some post-colonial twilight. Indeed, there was a World Shakespeare Festival in 2012 that formed part of the Cultural Olympiad of that year and that boasted over 70 productions from India, Turkey, Georgia, Afghanistan, Japan, Wales, South Sudan, Lithuania, Mexico,

Argentina, Serbia, Albania, Macedonia, Spain, Italy, Armenia, Belarus, Poland, Russia, Israel, Kenya, South Korea, France, Greece, Scotland, Palestine, China, Brazil, Iraq, Pakistan, Germany, Hong Kong, New Zealand, South Africa, Nigeria, the United States, and England—but none, strangely, from Canada (for speculative reasons that invite cultural embarrassment).

One of the common misconceptions that contaminate discussions of Shakespeare concerns the nature and style of Shakespearean acting. It is not at all rare to see disparaging remarks about old-style acting or "ham" acting. As actor John Bell has noted:

> Most people, when they think of Shakespearean acting, think of something old-fashioned—actors adopting heroic postures and declaiming in fruity voices. It's the sort of acting Shakespeare himself hated, mocked and roundly criticized, whether it's actors 'out-Heroding Herod' and 'sawing the air' with their arms, or Bottom declaiming:
> 'The raging rocks and shivering shocks
> Shall break the locks of prison gates;
> And Phoebus' car shall shine from far
> And make or mar the foolish Fates…'
> And then sighing contentedly:
> 'This was lofty' (Bell 66).

Shakespeare was himself an actor at a time when the profession was borderline disreputable, when actors were lumped together with rogues, vagabonds, and thieves.[1] Mary Z. Maher points out that even his lead actor, Richard Burbage, was mostly documented in an epitaph,[2] even though many of the major roles (Hamlet, Lear, Macbeth, and Othello, for example) were written for him (Maher xiii). Though he was not held in the same high regard as Burbage, Will Kemp, Henry Condell, and John Heminges, Shakespeare was an astute critic of other actors, as his Hamlet demonstrates in a memorable lesson to the travelling players who visit Elsinore:

> Speak the speech, I pray you, as I pronounc'd it to you, trippingly on the
> tongue, but if you mouth it, as many of our players do, I had as live [sic]
> the town-crier spoke the lines. Nor do not saw the air too much with
> your hand, thus, but use all gently, for in the very torrent, tempest, and,
> as I may say, whirlwind of your passion, you must acquire and beget a
> temperance that may give it smoothness (3.2. 1-8)[3]

One of the first things to note is that the passage is in prose; another is that it is Hamlet, a troubled prince, counselling professional actors; a third is the punctuation (usually a ticklish issue for critics and actors because of variations between Folio and Quarto). Ironies abound in this passage and the entire speech: One of Shakespeare's most poetic tragic heroes uses prose (heightened only occasionally by metaphor or figurative language or, a little later in the same speech, a range of allusion) to make his instruction sound pragmatic. Hamlet is also being technical in his examples of bad acting: He refers to physical gestures, pace, clarity, vocal emphases, and quality of characterization—all in negative ways.

He could well have made a fine Danish theatre critic with a sharp psychological underpinning. I jest but only just. He makes theatrical performance the crucial centre of the scene, because he is intent on using playacting as a means to unmasking the fratricidal guilt of Claudius. Hamlet accentuates the importance of truth in acting, and while his prescription about the "modesty" of nature is open to dispute, he makes other useful points about acting. Of course, he also makes an important point about the age in which he lives, with phrases referring to the "body of the time" and its "forms and pressures" (3.2.16-23).

Little wonder, then, that Bell can claim that "Shakespeare redefined the art of acting," leaving behind guild actors (models for the "mechanicals" in *A Midsummer Night's Dream*) and medieval charismatic villains, while writing huge roles for Richard Burbage that could replace the old-style acting of Ned Alleyn (Bell 66).

Unlike Christopher Marlowe or other of his contemporaries, Shakespeare "never stopped experimenting, breaking up the iambic pentameter to make it more natural and psychologically truthful, switching back and forth between verse and prose, inventing an individual voice for each character" (Bell 74). Yet, despite his awesome reputation, Shakespeare did not leave many clues about *how his actors really performed his plays.*

As someone who has had virtually a lifelong passion for Shakespeare and theatre, I would love to find documentation of how major actors of his day interpreted the great roles, just as I read with great relish accounts of contemporary actors (Anthony Sher and Ian McKellen, for instance) of how they have fashioned their interpretations of Richard III, Falstaff, Lear, or Macbeth. I would wager that many contemporary actors share my interest, though there seems to be a split in opinion of the Canadian actors in this book.

On the one hand, Nancy Palk, for instance, remarks in our interview that she would rather read books such as *The Year of the King, Will in the World,* and *Clamorous Voices* ("where you get what was going on at the time that would have made Shakespeare write about that") than "finding out how Judi Dench played Lady Macbeth. As much as I love Judi Dench, I didn't see it."

On the other hand, there is Lucy Peacock who is curious about the men/boys who played women in Shakespeare's day: "That would be a very interesting story, much like what Timothy Findley explored in *Elizabeth Rex.* I would be very curious to know who they were—who played Rosalind, Queen Elizabeth in Richard III, or Volumnia. As far as the manner in which it was done, I don't particularly care about that."

There is abundant evidence that many present-day actors come to Shakespeare cold, because for them, as for most of us, the first encounter with Shakespeare is in the classroom, perhaps with a dry pedant who mines every line for similes, metaphors, alliteration, and allusion. Few first encounters, alas, are through the stage, where it is easier to slide into his plots, experience his registers of language, and range of heroes, heroines, comic rogues, villains, brilliant fools, ghosts, and star-crossed lovers.

In my own case, though born on the Indian subcontinent to an Armenian father and an Anglo-Indian mother, I had English as my mother tongue, and my earliest experience of Shakespeare on stage was in my teens in the late 1950s, through Geoffrey Kendal's travelling troupe, Shakespeareana Company, later memorialized in the 1965 Merchant-Ivory black-and-white film *Shakespeare Wallah* that provides a vivid picture about the nature and travails of touring players.

Kendal's troupe "pounded the highways and byways of India, taking versions of Shakespeare to schools, convents, village squares, maharajas' palaces; anywhere that would cover their costs, from the North-west Frontier Province in what became Pakistan down to Travancore in the south" (Dickson 175).

All I remember of their version of *The Merchant of Venice* in an auditorium at St. Mary's High School in Bombay (now Mumbai) were some wan drapery, tacky painted sets, florid acting by Kendal who played Shylock, and the mocking raspberries some cynical students sounded during the Jessica-Lorenzo moonlight duet. One of the British cast members dared to bray back at the hecklers, raising even more laughter in the student audience. I do not remember if Kendal's daughters, Jennifer and Felicity, acted in that production. They probably did, but at that time we teenage students did not know the cultural significance and implications of Kendal's itinerant troupe, though I was fascinated by the English performers and their actor-manager.

It is only by looking back at the fictionalized story of the Kendals (their surname changed to Buckingham in the film) that I can see (what Andrew Dickson calls) its "unrepentant nostalgia" and the extent to which "Shakespeare's name is inscribed deep into this narrative of loss—lost ground, lost culture, lost empire. Just as India has shaken off the British yoke, so it is attempting to shrug off Britain's National Poet" (Dickson 177).[4]

Perhaps, but not at our school and not till at least after the early 1960s.[5] My peers and I were headed for the Cambridge GCE, and Shakespeare was on the curriculum: first, *The Tempest*, and then *Henry V*. Actually, my interest in Shakespeare was passionate from the time predating these years in high school. When I was around ten or twelve, I memorized and performed (often for myself) soliloquies or monologues, and virtually all the roles in the Pyramus and Thisbe play-within-the-play from *A Midsummer Night's Dream*. And at our all-boys school, I played Antonio in *The Merchant of Venice*, without knowing at the time that this play was one of the most popular titles to be adapted in India.[6]

Later, at St. Joseph Teachers College in Montreal, where I adapted, acted, and/or directed scenes from various Shakespearean plays, I was nicknamed "Shakespeare" by a colleague, a tag I accepted with a mixture of embarrassment and pride. Blissfully free (because of my young age and inexperience) of political correctness or of any militancy about cultural appropriation, I knew instinctively that Shakespeare was an artist of the highest degree, who had the absolute right to create or appropriate whatever character of whatever colour, race, or religion he wished in whatever country of a map or mind, because the ultimate journey of any real artist is the journey into the human heart and soul.

His plays "bestride the world," with characters in them hailing "from Tunisia, the Levant, Algeria, India; his dramatic imagination roams restlessly across France, Denmark, Austria, Turkey, Greece, covering a veritable gazetteer of far-flung destinations"

(Dickson xviii). In fact, a survey of his plays would show that "he seems actively to have avoided writing about the Britain of his own lifetime: The plays Shakespeare does locate in the British Isles are either distanced by time (the English histories) or by theme (the ancient Britain of *King Lear*, feudal Scotland in *Macbeth*, the Roman invasion-era *Cymbeline*" (Dickson xviii).

His cosmopolitan geography and history did not matter as much to me as his other facets. Although I did not know the full connotations or resonances of his language, I felt the rhetorical force of Shakespeare's verse, and when I did get the opportunity to see Laurence Olivier on screen—first as Richard III, then as Henry V, and only later as Hamlet, I knew that an essential part of my core had changed forever.

There is, of course, a world of difference between acting for the screen and acting on stage. Scale and technique vary, and the screen actor is at the mercy of the director and cameraman who can destroy the credibility of a performance by choosing to use a close-up when a medium shot is more desirable during a vocal climax and by an editor who can alter the dramatic or comic rhythm or cut out moments that are deemed vitally important by the actor.

However, even on screen (where he had to restrain the full force of his stage acting) Olivier was thrilling: He had a plasticity of appearance, voice, and movement. Every action of his seemed to have poetry of some sort, and to this day he remains my favourite Richard III, Henry V, Hamlet, and Othello—all for different reasons, but all related to conception and technique.

Olivier was in the line of Edmund Kean—part of a world of super-actors—and to see him perform Shakespeare (even if only on screen) was to witness thunder and lightning in the blood. His Othello (disparaged only by those who could not abide its stunning all-out vocal pyrotechnics and physicality) was strange, bizarre, awesomely daring, with howls, screams, crying, catatonia, and gestures that no other actor had ever dared perform. It was a great flourish of charismatically heroic acting, praised by actors as different as Michael Redgrave and Steven Berkoff.

Where his great contemporary, John Gielgud, claimed to "study the shape, sound, and length of the words themselves [in a role], and try to reproduce them exactly as they were written" (Trewin 194), Olivier went for bold cogency—as in his stage Richard III that expressed "the marriage of intellect and dramatic force, bravura and cold reason ... mind and mask" (Trewin 193). According to the same critic, "His speech, flexible and swift, was bred of a racing brain. If, outwardly, he was a limping panther, there was no lameness in his mind" (Trewin 193).

I did get to see my idol perform brilliantly on stage in Montreal during glorious Expo 67 in three totally different plays (by Strindberg, Congreve, and Feydeau), but not in Shakespeare, and, alas, for all his bravura on stage, his reflections on acting in his two books, *Confessions of an Actor* (1982) and *On Acting* (1986), though interesting and not without value, unfold only partial layers of a metaphorical onion.

Olivier was one who believed that it was foolish to explain how an actor built or executed a role, because this would detract from the mystique or magic of performance. The acting spell would be broken. It would be tantamount to taking apart an expensive watch merely to find out how the little cogs and wheels fit together. And, so, it is not uncommon to find even the greatest stage actors either reluctant or unable to describe what they do in performance. James Earl Jones once recalled a confidence shared with him by Geraldine Page: "I don't know what I'm doing. Do you?"[7]

Perhaps, so, but all the same, I wish to know how a role is created at least in broad outline, how a particularly difficult speech is delivered, how a gesture defines a character, et cetera. This is why stage production histories can be useful, and I confess to reading, for example, David Selbourne's eye-witness account of Peter Brook's *A Midsummer Night's Dream* and Tirzah Lowen's equally detailed record of Peter Hall's direction of Anthony Hopkins and Judi Dench in *Antony and Cleopatra* with considerable pleasure, and, best of all, Tynan's rehearsal record of Olivier's Othello with supreme relish.[8]

Even Olivier ultimately succumbed to the lure of publication (and financial compensation), though he couched his submission very astutely by suggesting that his remarks on acting were not "the usual boring theatrical gossip—he's sleeping with her, she's sleeping with him stuff—but discussing in detail this wonderful business of ours from the right angle. Searching for origins, discussing beliefs, trying to explain what it was like for me to be up there inside the Shakespearean greats" (Olivier, 1986:2).

Indeed, his shrewd remarks run parallel to my own curiosity about Shakespearean acting. Theatre schools and literary critics all have their uses, but many wish to have truths or beliefs or hints directly from the actors—and especially so in Canada, where Shakespearean acting has now reached a level that can be compared to English or American Shakespeare without embarrassment, indeed, with justifiable pride.

My encounters with Canadian actors performing Shakespeare in Canada have been mainly at Stratford, Ontario, though I have also seen his plays performed professionally in Vancouver, Toronto, Kingston, Barrie, Montreal, and Niagara-on-the-Lake.[9] But it was the Stratford Shakespeare Festival that gradually made me aware of what I call Canadian Shakespeare—Shakespeare performed by Canadians in ways that are different from how he is performed in other English-language countries. As in the cases of William Hutt, Christopher Plummer, Kate Reid, Martha Henry, Seana McKenna, Yanna McIntosh, Maev Beaty, et cetera.

And when an especially inventive or creative Canadian director is at the helm of a production—a Robert Lepage or Chris Abraham, for example, the national stamp can become even more impressive. But to state this is not to exclude the "Canadian" aspects of immigrant British directors, such as Robin Phillips, who find contexts for Shakespeare that are closer to our own post-colonial history, or of Brits who use the best of their "foreign" resources (as in the cases of Michael Langham or David William or Brian Bedford or Tim Carroll) to strengthen the techniques and styles of Canadian actors.

My first visit to the Stratford Festival was in 1969, when I became aware of Kenneth Welsh, Leo Ciceri, Eric Donkin, Powys Thomas, Mervyn Blake, Kenneth Pogue, Pat Galloway, Jane Casson, and, of course, William Hutt—some of whom were not born in Canada. (I had passed foolishly on Christopher Plummer and Zoe Caldwell's Antony and Cleopatra in Montreal in 1967 because I was put off by the *Montreal Star's* review headline: "Comedy on the Nile.")

But it was only with the onset of the 1970s, and the beginning of my professional theatre reviewing career in 1976 (for such print outlets as *Scene Changes* and *Performing Arts in Canada*, before adding *Canadian Theatre Review*, *Canadian Forum*, *Queen's Quarterly*, *Journal of Canadian Studies*, *Theatrum*, and various newspapers and international anthologies to my resume) that my cultural enrichment in classical Canadian theatre really began. I saw productions by Michael Langham, John Hirsch, Jean Gascon, Robin Phillips, John Neville, John Wood, and Richard Monette, and learned how they interpreted the plays and guided performances in ways that put an indisputable Canadian stamp on Shakespearean plays.

It would not be inaccurate for any reader of this book to call me a disciple of bravura acting. I am that, without apology. Nevertheless, I am also a disciple of closely observed characterization on a narrower scale of subtlety. I have treasured memories of Christopher Plummer, William Hutt, Brian Bedford, Douglas Campbell, William Needles, Nicholas Pennell, Kenneth Welsh, and Peter Donaldson (many now deceased)—actors of very different temperaments and skills. I also admire Tom McCamus, Colm Feore, Stephen Ouimette, Tom Rooney, Benedict Campbell, Brent Carver, Geraint Wyn Davies, Graham Abbey, Jonathan Goad, Joseph Ziegler, Ben Carlson, Juan Chioran, Evan Buliung, Scott Wentworth, and Peter Hutt who follow in their footsteps though not necessarily in identical manner or scale of acting.

On the female side, I have admired (among the dead and the living) Kate Reid, Amelia Hall, Frances Hyland, Domini Blythe, Susan Wright, Jennifer Phipps, Martha Henry, Pat Galloway, Patricia Collins, Moya O'Connell, Nancy Palk, Susan Coyne, Deborah Hay, Yanna McIntosh, Lucy Peacock, Seana McKenna, Maev Beaty, and Sara Topham, at their best.

Like most long practising critics, I have seen the entire Shakespearean canon on stage (most of the plays many times) and I have experienced Shakespeare in French, Russian, Japanese, Italian, Spanish, Romanian, and Hindi, though not necessarily on stage. But as my mother tongue is English and because most of my theatre-going experiences are in this language, I shall not draw comparisons and contrasts with Shakespearean performances in French (especially in Quebec)[10] or other foreign languages. I am an unabashed collector of great acting performances, especially of the Shakespearean sort. All these players have been superb in roles other than Shakespearean, of course, but because Shakespeare is the supreme poet-playwright of all time, his roles are prime challenges for actors, and, therefore, my book focuses on how some contemporary leading Canadian stage performers deal with his distinctive challenges and lures.

My book is not concerned with academic theory or loads of learned lumber. There is an over-abundance of scholarly books that expose the vital, radical difference between the library and the stage. Literary criticism is not usually actable, to put it bluntly. Or to quote Nicholas Hytner: "The literary critic reveals the text and the circumstances that gave birth to it. The actor reveals the play, for which the text is only the starting point" (Hytner 170). My goal is to explore actors' perceptions and comments in relation to performing Shakespeare in order to offer a sense of what these actors mean by "the work."

I am not so much interested in theory as I am in theatre practice. Accordingly, the various essays reveal the extent to which this book is steeped in the contributors' working experiences, professional histories, current projects, technical skills, and dynamic engagements with Shakespeare. Following the model of Mary Z. Maher's *Actors Talk About Shakespeare* (which concentrated on British, American, and only three choice Canadian performers), my book is a series of profiles (with generous quotations from the interviews) that focus on specific roles, resulting in a compendium of observations, insights, and opinions about acting (and sometimes directing) Shakespeare.

It necessarily encompasses shifting trends in Shakespearean acting, especially as guided or shaped by vastly different directors, such as Michael Langham, Robin Phillips, John Hirsch, Richard Monette, Robert Lepage, Chris Abraham, Antoni Cimolino, and Tim Carroll, all of whom have re-envisaged Shakespearean acting, and four of whom, Canadian-born, have made distinctive contributions to strengthening the very idea of Canadian Shakespeare.

I want to disabuse any reader of the notion that there are rules that govern acting, especially Shakespearean acting. One of the fallacies of acting theories is that a particular method can be the definitive one. In actual fact, every good actor has his or her own method or way of approaching, rehearsing, and playing a role. If we could watch the Hamlets of, let us say, Colm Feore, Paul Gross, Stephen Ouimette, Albert Schultz, Ben Carlson, Brent Carver, and Jonathan Goad, we may be hard pressed to know which theory of acting was applicable to each actor, particularly because acting has nothing to do with theory.

Each of these excellent actors took ownership of the role in his particular way. Each was subject to the vision of his director, the ensemble and context, as well as the size and quality of the auditorium in which he offered his Prince. Moreover, each actor's performance probably varied nightly in some subtle way. First-rate actors know how to make a performance grow and fill out in the course of a run, but even great actors realize that audience reaction can affect performance. So, any discussion of acting has to make allowances for factors beyond the actor.

Nevertheless, this book is not meant to be a critical *evaluation* of performances. Instead, it is meant to explore various actors' processes in the hope of discovering what skills are foundational, what the components are of an acting process, and how the actors layer technique into their own onstage realities. If my book helps bring professional theatre insights into the public arena, it would be an opportunity to understand and appreciate the customarily private world of the actor. However, no matter what these actors say or reveal, there is always something inexplicable and mysterious about acting, and nowhere more so than in Shakespearean acting.

There are many good actors in this country, and the best are in the front ranks of classical acting in the English-language world. It wasn't that long ago that as eminent a critic-academic as the late Ronald Bryden (also a Stratford Festival Board member) was brash enough to pass a sweeping opinion on Robin Phillips' Stratford Festival acting company during an era that Bryden called "a Camelot": "After Maggie [Smith], Brian Bedford and Canada's one great home-grown actress, Martha Henry, [Robin Phillips] was working with a middle level of character stalwarts who would have seemed slightly over-parted in the Old Vic of the 1950s, and below them a ruck of young Canadians of uneven natural talent and almost uniformly inadequate training" (Coveney 169).

What is stunning about this generalization is its blind side. Bryden overlooks William Hutt, Douglas Rain, Kate Reid, Patricia Collins, Domini Blythe, William Needles, Pat Galloway, Mervyn Blake, Nicholas Pennell, Jackie Burroughs, Barry MacGregor, Richard Monette, Brent Carver, Marti Maraden, et cetera. None of these actors or actresses would have seemed over-parted in any Old Vic company of any era. Perhaps, Bryden was betraying his own special brand of colonial romanticism, but, nonetheless, his opinion deserves critical pushback. In terms of acting, Canada is no longer the poor cousin of any international theatre. It has had a very short professional theatre history in relation, let us say, to England or the United States, but it has progressed very quickly on the acting front.

This book does not pretend to be a *definitive account* of contemporary Canadian actors and actresses at the highest reaches of their craft and art. It offers a *sampler* of different voices, attitudes, practices, and, perhaps, even cultural politics. I have dealt only with living stage performers of the first magnitude in whom I see special talents, who were *available* to me within the time-frame I had to begin and complete the book,[11] and who were willing to share their insights in print. My choices are mainly those who made their biggest marks at the Stratford Festival because that is, indeed, our national theatre when it comes to classical acting and Shakespeare in particular.

The single exception is Moya O'Connell, an extraordinary actress who should, by all rights, be part of any classical acting company. I was fortunate to see her Lady Macbeth at Bard on the Beach in Vancouver, and the experience consolidated my admiration for her grace, visceral force, technical skill, and stage charisma. There are at least half a dozen or more Canadian actors who belong in any sampler, but the eleven on my list make a compelling case for creative vitality as they share their discoveries about Shakespearean acting.

Because I was granted interviews by directors Tim Carroll and Chris Abraham that provided significant material on such diverse subjects as verse speaking, soliloquies, theatrical interpretation, gender bending, et cetera, I have made use of their insights within several essays. Many of the actors supplied their own comments on other directors, such as Michael Langham, Robin Phillips, John Hirsch, David William, Richard Monette, Martha Henry, Antoni Cimolino, and Robert Lepage.

The interviews (conducted in Toronto, Stratford, Mississauga, Vancouver, and Niagara-on-the-Lake) occurred between January 2017 and September 2018. Done in person (the only exceptions were two phone interviews, one with director Chris Abraham and the other with Lucy Peacock who generously granted me a second interview after our face-to-face one in Stratford), they were not managed as rigid inquisitions but as probing explorations, leading off with some general questions or some weightier ones and then following the conversation wherever it went, but always striving to keep it on track in relation to themes or subjects I wished to explore.

The actors were allowed free rein of ideas and opinions, but if I felt a need to question or lend further support to their beliefs, I would offer my own as point or counterpoint. This resulted in lively, respectful exchanges, and some of the most fruitful I have ever had the privilege of experiencing.

After completing my transcriptions, I drafted eleven essays, making revisions of expression and removing sound effects or emphatic casual repetitions that work on a voice recorder but not necessarily in print. I allowed the participants to vet what I had written, not to censor but to correct factual inaccuracies or smoothen phrasing.

The resulting essays cover an extensive area of Shakespearean acting. Some of the most significant roles are explored in various ways and to various degrees: Hamlet, Rosalind, Volumnia, Timon, Lady Macbeth, Macbeth, Juliet's Nurse, Beatrice, Benedick, Petruchio, Kate, Don Armado, Angelo, Richard II, Henry V, Jaques, Lear, King John, Richard III, Iago, Philip the Bastard, and Malvolio. There are, of course, overlaps in these explorations—Lady Macbeth, Hamlet, and Jaques, for example, are the subjects of several actors' discourses—but these are enrichments rather than redundancies because the players speak from their individual sensibilities and from their particular experiences.

The players describe how they developed an interest in Shakespeare, their training, preparation for roles, special mentors, actor-director relationships, the difference between verse speaking and verse acting, production style, the text as metaphorical iceberg, text as fact versus acting as truth, the actor's "double consciousness," gender bending, et cetera. For example, Tom Rooney explains how hard he works to move the text from his brain into his heart and nervous system, whereas Lucy Peacock records how she thrills to the language as she applies it to the chaos of the heart.

Significant directors get their nods from the actors, some of whom have become directors of note themselves. Albert Schultz recalls how Robin Phillips was intensely averse to poeticising, and both Schultz and Nancy Palk describe Phillips' rehearsal and directorial methods, especially when guiding them to play Romeo in Schultz's case; Rosalind and Juliet's Nurse in Palk's. Tom McCamus shares what Tim Carroll teaches about verse speaking, and how Martha Henry allows actors to exploit a new discovery in rehearsal. Joseph Ziegler pays tribute to Phillips, Brian Bedford, and Michael Langham, while Juan Chioran speaks especially highly of Brian Bedford. Ben Carlson and Moya O'Connell praise Chris Abraham for resisting received theatrical conventions for Shakespeare. Graham Abbey carries discussion into the provocative area of gender-bending, while seeking the middle ground in other issues.[12]

All the players discuss the importance of technique and imaginative creation, but when it comes to the issue of actual actor training, Chick Reid is a unique source as she describes how she teaches courses at Queen's University on Acting Shakespeare. She is important for a second reason: She is the only one who discourses on the peculiar function, nature, and scope of an understudy—a subject that is not usually discussed in books of interviews with actors.

Documenting these actors for whom Shakespeare is a generous inspiration has been a pleasure because they have shared their insights, helping enlarge my own understanding of what Shakespearean acting encompasses. None of their statements was presented as dogma or doctrine or theory, and each player's passion was eminently palpable. They were catalysts for my own passion in this area, and I hope they can be similar catalysts for many readers who can re-visit Shakespeare in the theatre with re-opened minds and hearts.

Keith Garebian
September 2018

Notes

[1]As Camille Paglia phrases it in her inimitably assertive manner, free of reticence: "Shakespeare was a popular entertainer who knew how to work a crowd. His daring shifts in tone, juxtaposing comedy with tragedy; his deft weaving of a main plot with multiple subplots; his restless oscillations from talk to action to song and dance: this fast pace and variety-show format were the tricks of a veteran actor adept at seizing the attention of chattering groundlings who milled around the jutting stage of open-air theaters." (Qtd. in Carson 26-27)

[2]The epitaph reads:

Hee's gone and with him what a world are dead,

Which he reuiud, to be reuiued soe.

No more young Hamlet, ould Heironymoe.

King Leer, the greued Moore, and more beside,

That lived in him, have now forever dy'de.

As quoted by Olivier in *On Acting* (London: Weidenfeld and Nicolson, 1986), p. 18.

[3]All direct quotations from Shakespeare are drawn from *The Riverside Shakespeare, Vols. 1 &2.* ed. G. Blakemore Evans. Boston: Houghton Mifflin Co., 1974.

[4]According to Kunal Kapoor, whose mother was Jennifer Kendal and whose grandfather was Geoffrey Kendal, India has not abandoned Shakespeare. He has explained that the Indian connection to Shakespeare was strengthened by education in mission schools from the 19th century onwards when students were forced to learn by rote. But the connection was really based in the fact that Indians read the plays as stories about themselves: "The love, the jealousy, the loyalty, the melodrama, the sense of family—they're such identifiable Indian values. In some ways the plays make more sense here. Tybalt and Juliet are cousins—the intensity of that relationship, I'm not sure it makes sense instinctively in Britain or America. Put them in an Eastern setting, India or wherever, and it all starts to be much more real." (Qtd. in Andrew Dickson, *Worlds Elsewhere: Journeys Around Shakespeare's Globe* (New York: Henry Holt and Co., 2015), p. 239.

[5]Indeed, even Dickson was compelled to admit that "Shakespeare hadn't evaporated when the British slipped away on liners bound for foggy Tillbury: on the contrary, there were plentiful modern adaptations of the plays. Indeed, an entire festival near Chennai was dedicated to Shakespeare translated into Indian languages—proof of the vibrant life of Shakespeare on the subcontinent" (Dickson 179), and in the 21st century, "there are now estimated to be several hundred adaptations of Shakespeare plays into nearly all of India's twenty-plus official languages, and more versions of Shakespeare in Indian cinema than anywhere else on the globe" (Dickson 181).

[6]See Dickson, p. 219.

[7]Jeremy Gerard, "Tribute to Geraldine Page fills Neil Simon Theater," *New York Times*, June 18, 1987.

[8]David Selbourne, *The Making of 'A Midsummer Night's Dream.'* (Methuen); *Peter Hall Directs 'Antony and Cleopatra.'* (Limelight Editions); and Kenneth Tynan, ed., *'Othello':*

The National Theatre Production (Rupert Hart-Davis).

[9]In 2018, the Shaw Festival did a version of *Henry V*, set in a WWI trench for Canadian soldiers, and co-directed by Kevin Bennett and Tim Carroll.

[10]See Jennifer Drouin, *Shakespeare in Quebec: Nature, Gender, and Adaptation* (Toronto: University of Toronto Press, 2014). While useful for its scholarship, this book is concerned primarily with sociological, political, and taxonomic issues, and its primary focus is not on acting in general or on Shakespearean acting in particular.

[11]This book was contracted in December 2016 by Guernica that aimed for publication in 2019. My first interview was with Nancy Palk in Toronto on January 17, 2017, and my final interview was a phone interview with Lucy Peacock on August 25, 2018, more than two months after a face-to-face with her in Stratford.

[12]Harriet Walter makes an interesting case for gender-bending in her book *Brutus and Other Heroines*: "The classics are revisited for what they can tell us about our world today, and the world today is much more feminised than in Shakespeare's lifetime. Women, in the West at least, have access to perform in any and every field of public endeavour, in theory at least. Could we not play the male leaders in our national playwright's canon? And if it looked or felt wrong, wouldn't we have to ask ourselves useful questions as to why? We are continually broadening the definition of what a man or a woman is, so couldn't we be holding Shakespeare's mirror up to the nature of a more current world?" (p.157). Of course, the modern trend for actresses to play male Shakespearean roles has antecedents dating back to the 19th century. In London, Charlotte Cushman played Romeo, while her sister, Susan, was Juliet (1846). Sarah Bernhardt played Hamlet in 1899, claiming she was better suited to the role than any man, and winning acclaim (from fans, though not from many critics) on both sides of the Atlantic for her daringly energetic and volatile interpretation. In the silent film era, Danish actress Asta Nielsen played the melancholy Prince in 1921, though her performance could hardly be called Shakespearean for its being sans any spoken sound. The role of Hamlet has long attracted actresses, but even the role of Falstaff was taken over in the United States in 1990 by Pat Carroll, who first came to popular fame in television situation-comedy, variety shows, and a recording of her award-winning one-woman show as Gertrude Stein. The 20th and 21st centuries have been marked by at least two waves of feminism in which contemporary English actresses (such as Fiona Shaw, Michelle Terry, Maxine Peake, Harriet Walter, Tamsin Grieg, Vanessa Redgrave, Janet McTeer, Pippa Nixon, and Glenda Jackson) played leading Shakespearean roles.

Nancy Palk as Lady Macbeth, from Macbeth *(1989), directed by Nicholas Mahon for the Theatre for a New Audience, New York. Used by kind permission of Nancy Palk. Inset: Nancy Palk.*

(Photo: Tim Leyes)

Nancy Palk
Text As Iceberg

I interviewed tall, willowy Nancy Palk on a remarkably warm but damp January morning at her home in Toronto.[1] Hers is a two-storey, four-bedroom house, embellished with theatre posters, oil paintings, photographs, and a piano that boasts sheet-music by Cole Porter. It has been home since 1998, "literally days before we premiered *Don Carlos* for the launch of Soulpepper." She is referring to the golden first season of what has become the premier actor-run company in Canada, founded by Palk, her husband Joseph Ziegler, and other Robin Phillips' "kids" from his Stratford Young Company, such as Stuart Hughes, Susan Coyne, Martha Burns, Michael Hanrahan, and Albert Schultz.

Phillips directed the Schiller (headlined electrifyingly by Brent Carver in the title role and Palk as Queen Elizabeth of Valois) to overwhelming acclaim in the company's first home in the waterfront district, before the company found its permanent home at the Young Centre in the historic distillery district. Her shoulder-length brown hair, streaked with grey, she is a gracious hostess in her black long-sleeved turtle neck and slacks. Long and happily married to Joseph Ziegler, she is the mother to three grown sons, Timothy, Charles, and Henry.

Nancy has recently opened at Tarragon Theatre, in *Sequence*, a new Canadian work by Calgarian Arun Lakra who divides his time between ophthalmology and creative writing. She plays Dr. Guzman, a virtually blind genetics professor with a vehement, almost unhinged commitment to her research, yet a character with snappily ironic wit. "It's all language and a lot of props," she comments, subtly suggesting that the props detract from the language that is really the crux of the play. Husband Joe is about to open in Kate Hennig's *The Last Wife* (about Katherine Parr, Henry VIII's sixth and final wife) at Soulpepper Theatre. He extends a New Year's greeting to me, gives Nancy a quick goodbye kiss and dashes off to rehearsal.

I have known the couple for a great many years, having first seen them act together in production of *The Importance of Being Earnest* at the National Theatre School in Montreal, where both were studying for a professional career. Nancy was playing the formidable Lady Bracknell, and Joseph was Algernon. Although she was much too young for her role, she was a striking young actress of real stage presence, authority, and comic sense.

The youngest of three siblings in Winnipeg whose parents gave her a choice between piano lessons and theatre school on Saturdays, Nancy opted for theatre. Her parents took her to great plays, and she decorated her bedroom with "fantastic posters" from the Manitoba Theatre Centre that the late John Hirsch ran at the time. The Manitoba Theatre School quickly became part of her life, where, given a choice of poems to work on, she (then in Grade 5) was fascinated by a speech that began "All the world's a stage," without really knowing its author or its context.

When the family moved to London, Ontario, she auditioned at the Grand Theatre for an amateur production of *The Prime of Miss Jean Brodie*, but she didn't get cast because she was too tall to be one of Brodie's schoolgirls. Her high-school peers included Tom McCamus and Alicia Jeffries, but the only Shakespeare she did were scenes from *King Lear* in lieu of a Grade 13 essay. Later, at Queen's University, Kingston (where Fred Euringer and Gary Wagner were teachers, and Judith Thompson a classmate), she played Luciana in *The Comedy of Errors* while Wendy Crewson (who would later become a film star) played Adriana.

After her B.A. (Drama) in 1976, she successfully auditioned for the National Theatre School, Montreal. Her audition was conducted by highly respected actor Douglas Rain, who was "very intimidating" but who would become a dear friend to her and Joseph. Rain's wife at the time was Martha Henry who also did some teaching, though not in Shakespeare, and whose instinctive acting Palk admired. She later got to act opposite Rain in *The Dining Room*, which toured across Canada, with Leon Major, Marti Maraden, and Barbara Gordon in the cast.

One of her NTS teachers was Louis Spritzer, a Renaissance man, who had studied guitar, Chinese medicine in China, Reichian therapy recognizing the essential functional identity of mind and body, sang tenor, and was an accomplished equestrian jumper. Spritzer taught his budding thespians how to relax on stage and be free. His teaching was similar to what she would later learn from her greatest teacher, Robin Phillips at the Stratford Festival, where colleagues included Stuart Hughes, Susan Coyne, Albert Schultz, and Peter Donaldson: "Robin never wanted anything in your face, in the audience's face. He always wanted people to be drawn in—which is a wonderful thing for actors, yet so difficult to do."

While receiving a firm grounding in acting, she also found herself subject to the mysterious but gratifying workings of real-life romance. Tall, handsome, Minnesota-born Joseph Ziegler performed the balcony scene with her from *Romeo and Juliet*—surely one of life's dramatic ironies, given the fact that they fell in love for real, though Ziegler had a fiancée back home in the U.S. "I'm not sure exactly what happened," Ziegler remarked with shy bewilderment during an interview with David Berry for the *National Post* (August 21, 2014).

"I set you straight," Palk jokes. "As I recall, I fell into tears and demanded an explanation." Well, he did explain and ended the other young woman's dreams. Nancy and Joe's mutual obsession with theatre helped, as did their general openness to reality, a trait that is surely an asset for actors. The pair launched a marriage, parenthood, and long, distinguished careers that make them theatre royalty, but such status, unfortunately, doesn't mean much in a country without real royalty.

Palk has acted in theatres across Canada, though mainly in Toronto, where she has appeared in new Canadian work (by Judith Thompson, John Murrell, George Walker, Joanna Glass, Andrew Kushnir, et cetera) at NDWT, Canadian Stage, and Tarragon. I reviewed several of those performances, in particular her portrayal of Dee in Judith Thompson's *I Am Yours* at Tarragon in 1988, where she "worked her willowy way into an area between ritual and naturalism, illuminating the character's inner contradiction, revealing her neurotic fears of psychic disintegration, and creating an image of a character quaking with insecurity."[2]

At Soulpepper, she has played in Tennessee Williams, Edward Albee, Henrik Ibsen, William Shakespeare, Eugene O'Neill, Thornton Wilder, Arthur Miller, Tony Kushner, and Sam Shepherd. Her range is impressively wide: a true, deep Paulina of piteous laments, red-hot tirades against Leontes (*The Winter's Tale*, 2002); a shimmering, incantatory, insulting, erotic Solange (*The Maids*, 2002); a vulpine Goneril (*King Lear*, 2006); an Elizabeth I of stunning bravura (*Mary Stuart*, 2007); Martha in Albee's *Who's Afraid of Virginia Woolf?* (2009), who was not just a sloppy, foul-mouthed harridan, but a boozy woman of outrageous spontaneity, as well as periods of cleverly vile strategy—a bruising and bruised battler, a raving predator with a tender, ravaged soul; and an Amanda Wingfield fundamentally bewildered by life (*The Glass Menagerie*, 2010).

Two performances at Soulpepper bolster her status as one of Canada's best actresses. As Phedre (2003) in Jean Racine's neoclassical tragedy, her bony frame and face vibrated with emotion as she made a thrilling spectacle of the woman's frenzy, cool depravity, mania, and masochism. Her performance was boldly operatic in dimension as she sank into self-lacerating mournfulness, flashed with deep-down gulfs of liquid fire, or, in Phedre's dying moments, became an awful ghostly apparition.

And in 2013, she outstripped Meryl Streep's trio of performances (including a gender-bending one) in *Angels in America*, when she limned an Ethel Rosenberg of blissfully serene Schadenfreude, a blind male Jewish Bolshevik, and a sensible Mormon mother that added immeasurably to a mind-stirring, heart-wrenching canvas. She has received numerous Dora Award nominations but has never won, which is certainly more a reflection on the quixotic nature of awards than on her talent. Although she takes pride in her contribution to new Canadian plays, she realizes the limitation:

> It's a different job being an actor doing new Canadian work because you are part dramaturge, you're creating something new. The focus is on the play—as it should be. I've always enjoyed working on new Canadian plays but then to work on the classics, to do something of Shakespeare, where the play just works fine, rather than your trying to dig around the moguls of something that doesn't quite work. How many times actors have been called upon to hide the mistakes in new Canadian work. So, it is a glorious opportunity to do the classics as much as you can, and to have it be about the acting.

Her first professional Shakespearean role was Katharina in *The Taming of the Shrew* at the Globe (Regina), opposite Vancouverite Tom MacBeath's Petruchio. Subsequent Shakespearean credits include Gertrude, Goneril, Paulina, Rosalind, Lady Macbeth, Viola, Elizabeth in *Richard III*, and the Nurse in *Romeo and Juliet*, directed variously by Nick Mahon (only once), Ziegler, and Robin Phillips. In Canada, it is rare for an actor to get more than a single shot at a Shakespearean role. Palk has been lucky. She has played Gertrude and Lady Macbeth twice, each time for a different company and production.

Her first attempt at Lady Macbeth came in New York in a production by Theatre for a New Audience, directed by Nick Mahon: "Unfortunately, I found myself not breathing but pushing because you have this image in your head of the ball-buster. The second time around—and that's the great thing about the second time around—is a gift to play the part without the nervous tension of the first time." She played the sleepwalking scene with eyes wide open, and the "perfumes of Arabia" hand washing was modelled after the way raccoons clean their paws.

Did she work out how to chart Lady Macbeth's descent into madness? "The beginning of the madness is much earlier than when you actually see it. But there are a lot of scenes where you're so much a part of the action at the beginning and then you're watching him leave—which, I suppose, is very female in a way. The male is at the heart of the politics of it, and you realize that you're supposed to just retreat because you are a lady. So, what was meshed between the two of them so strongly actually turns out to be about the man." There is a sharp truth in her viewpoint. English actor Brian Cox points out:

> [Lady Macbeth] functions best when she's pragmatic and efficient. Any imaginative awareness she has comes when she's unconscious, through sleep. In her conscious life, she has no idea what she's doing to Macbeth. It's Macbeth himself who has all the imagination. He knows what the consequences are, but she can't see it through. That's one of the great human dilemmas. The Macbeths function as a duo, and together they're a dream team, but when you split them up, you split up imagination and pragmatism, and a form of chaos ensues (Carson 214-15).

Although Lady Macbeth invokes and strikes a bargain with the dark spirits ("murdering ministers") to unsex her, Palk sees the role as being fundamentally feminine in a visceral way. Lady Macbeth could switch off her mind (the instrument of sense) and abandon caution, logic, and conscience in order to further her plan of assassinating Duncan and securing the crown for her husband. The best Lady Macbeths are the ones who work from the groin and their sex. Vivien Leigh was probably the first literally beautiful Lady Macbeth, whose sexy glamour easily made her erotically desirable to Laurence Olivier's Macbeth. But other beautiful actresses (such as Sinead Cusack, Janet Suzman, Alex Kingston, and (on film) Marion Cotillard) have followed Leigh in the role.

Because of their physical appeal, they are the ones who could exert a sexual power over their Macbeths, and who thereby are able to use their bodies, instincts, and emotions to give them sway over their lords. But there is another important angle to the best Lady Macbeths: the sense of maternal loss for which is substituted a murderous drive and commitment. Only once does Lady Macbeth talk of being a mother (or, perhaps, a wet-nurse):

> I have given suck, and know
> How tender 'tis to love the babe that milks me:
> I would, while it was smiling in my face,
> Have pluck'd my nipple from his boneless gums,
> And dash'd the brains out, had I so sworn as you
> Have done to this (1.7.54-59).

The lines speak to Lady Macbeth's feeling for the child, who is never mentioned again. Shakespeare's purpose is to add conviction to Lady Macbeth's assassination plot against Duncan. She would have happily killed the child she loved than break her word about dispatching the king.

However, Palk also showed a frightened Lady Macbeth—a woman who could see in her mind what her husband was doing. In other words, a wife with such a vivid imagination that its intensity leads to mental disintegration: a determined woman who is capable of ruthlessness, yet who suffers a panic attack when she sees the blood-stained daggers in her husband's hands. The reality of this sight is like a blow to her stomach, and in this highly charged scene, the pair perform an electrifying duet of nervous terror that is dramatically expressed in Macbeth's spontaneous torrent of torment culminating in "Sleep no more!/ ... Macbeth shall sleep no more" (2.2.40).

It is clear that husband and wife are speaking two different languages because they are in two different emotional or psychic zones. As Sinead Cusack (who played the role in 1986) points out: "She realises he's gone somewhere that she doesn't understand; she can't bring him back. It's as if she's seeing him drifting, drifting, she's trying to pull him back, but he won't come" (Rutter 65). Eve Best (who played Lady Macbeth in 2001) contends that "it's this separation which is the real tragedy, for it felt to me at the time that even though the spur for the murder is on the surface to do with ambition, with power, for her, at root, it is about their relationship. It is about love" (Carson 382).

All softness has gone from Lady Macbeth, though not the regal glamour. But her disintegration is internal, as in the Banquet scene where she maintains a façade of composure and control. She does not see Banquo's ghost that terrifies Macbeth, but she does see a man who is now totally outside her control. She realizes that she has unleashed a monster. When Macbeth speaks later of more killing, hinting at the murder of young Fleance, she becomes increasingly frightened, perhaps because her husband is planning on child-murder. Now, he is completely gone from her, and her feeling is that of absolute hopelessness.

Perhaps, a female director would help strengthen an actress's journey to points of maniacal fervour and despair. But Palk's only experience, so far, with a female Shakespearean director was Susan Furley at the Grand when the actress made her second essay at Lady Macbeth, with Oliver Becker playing her Macbeth. An astonishing paucity that only substantiates the common feminist complaint about women directors being neglected or even ignored. Jane Laportaire has commented: "I've been in the business for twenty-five years and, in all that time, I have only worked with three women directors" (Schafer 3). Till 2000, only six women ever directed Shakespeare on the Royal Shakespeare Company mainstage at Stratford-upon-Avon (Schafer 3), and at the Stratford Festival, the record was not much better until quite recently.

In England, too, the situation has improved rapidly of late—as Elizabeth Schafer's book on female directors of Shakespeare shows by featuring the work of Joan Littlewood, Jane Howell, Yvonne Brewster, Di Trevis, Deborah Paige, Jude Kelly, Gale Edwards, Jules Wright, and Helena Kaut-Howson. Schafer's book provides evidence of how women directors have often been marginalized in Shakespearean theatre, working in provincial theatres rather than in large, establishment ones where arts grants are more generous, and these directors often face the hostility of establishment critics who assume that "the 'correct' way to present Shakespeare's tragic heroes is to endorse their heroism, not question it" (Schafer 161).

Given the fact that many of the ideas and characters in Shakespeare are "profoundly problematic for modern women—the ending of *The Taming of the Shrew* being the most obvious example" (Schafer 6)—what does a female director bring to Shakespeare? Palk doesn't believe that all female directors are necessarily good for Shakespeare. Of course, not all male directors are good for Shakespeare either, but given the small number of their opposite sex who direct Shakespeare, the flops are more visible.

However, there is a female way of looking at things. The sensuousness of theatre suits women, and directors (like actors) bring their gender history into the work. In Shakespeare, we are dealing with a male construct and male political choices. But Palk agrees with Jules Wright's comment: "Feminism is about saying 'What is the meaning of this moment?' … If you're going to deal with misogyny then you want the men in the cast to take on the violence, to acknowledge the journey those characters go on" (Schafer 36). And Palk feels at one with someone such as Gale Edwards who recognizes that she is made a better director because of Shakespeare: "Every time it's like going into this tunnel of exploration; you have to do so much detective work, technical work, historical work and *thinking* and I love that" (Schafer 51).

Palk, who has herself directed playwrights other than Shakespeare, does not believe in the supremacy of the director. She is critical of directors who see their primary function as being that of directing a concept rather than actors, of making theatre "such a visual palette." She insists that directors who allow actors to rehearse themselves and wait till the set is ready so that they can prepare "a feast for the eyes," ignore the problem of the clear text they really need to direct. "I think they have to do a lot more homework before they come to the first day of rehearsal so that the focus can then be on the conversation and the relationships in a scene rather than how guys move furniture. I can't tell you how many directors have you rehearse the transitions more than you rehearse the scenes."

Her view can find wide support from fellow-players because the primacy of the director is a relatively new phenomenon, dating back to the second-half or later in the 20th century. (Does anyone remember or care to remember who directed David Garrick, Edmund Kean, Henry Irving, Sarah Siddons, or Ellen Terry?) Zoe Caldwell once declared that there are "only three things that are necessary in the theater: the playwright—someone to write the text—the actor, and the audience … Everyone else is an appendage. Each of the three had better serve the play, or each will become an unnecessary appendage. That includes the director" (Maher 104).

Like Palk, Caldwell complains that the tendency of the modern director is to serve his own concept rather than serving the needs of the playwright and actor. Palk recalls something Stuart Hughes once reported: "One of the last things Michael Langham ever said to him was 'Don't let go of the word.' That generation, and Robin and Douglas Rain included, would always make certain that the play was the focus, so it was always about the play. You're not gaining anything by having it all be about computers and digital things. That's fine—only if it enhances the text."

Kevin Kline has contended that "an interpretation cannot be circumscribed by an idea. When a director says he has an idea about Henry V, it must be a *large* idea that can embrace the scale of just about any of Shakespeare's characters, because they're full of paradox, of contradiction and ambiguity" (Maher 9), and Palk immediately agrees with him. But I follow this with a question about the "double consciousness" of an actor that operates during a performance where there is a kind of split in the actor's mind where a part of him is watching and monitoring his own performance, virtually as his own director. Derek Jacobi calls it the "third eye," which is "looking at the performance from inside the actor"—an example being "Ouch, I did the wrong thing," or "*That* sucked" (Maher 11).

Palk declares that there is a method where an actor is always looking for new ways to play a part: "I don't know that I *exactly* disagree with that, but I always want it to be fresh, to be true to that night. I would say that is an absolute conflict in yourself—where you're outside the scene while at the same time as being inside the scene. And all we long to be is inside the scene. You don't want to be observing it or directing yourself. But if you don't have a good enough director, you're always having to direct yourself instead of being able to let go." She adds: "Hopefully, your director is a comrade enough to know that. The director should know that sometimes you will just quietly take the note and then try to ignore it. Eventually you do have to learn how to direct yourself as an actor—but not while you are training. In your training you need to learn what it is to be free and open and clear and receptive. Acting requires an awful lot from you."

How aware should a performer be of the audience? "Well, that's very interesting," she says. "I think it depends on every play. It does vary. I always see monologues as being assuring, for the most part, when the actor feels there's someone out there who empathizes with what you're going through. If you were playing Richard III, that would not necessarily be the case. I think that if Hamlet is speaking a monologue, even though it's definitely inside himself, I would prefer to see him trying to work it out with the audience rather than have him thinking it as though he were by himself."

This, of course, brings up the issue of handling language in performance, and Kline is once again a good springboard for discussion, as he virtually paraphrases Hamlet's advice to the players: "Don't mouth it. Be not too tame, neither. Don't overdo it. Don't underdo it. Let the language be there. The French say *juste*. Give it its due, no more and no less. Rather than making a meal of it, clobbering it over my head and shoving it down my throat, let the audience get the goose bumps and the orgasms as opposed to watching the actor do that" (Maher 16).

The notions of language change with the times, as do notions about speaking Shakespeare, which are subject to convention, public taste, the actor and director's sensibility, and the shifting quality of mass media. But it is always critical to recognize and stress the importance of language in Shakespeare—something that Robin Phillips emphasized, as Palk recalls:

Robin was always so great. He would sometimes close his eyes and listen. He was not really an academic in any way. If he couldn't understand a passage, he would stop and question the meaning. "If that's what it means, then what is it that you (the character) wants?" It was about the text rather than about an interpretation of a role ... Robin would say "I don't want to see your muscle. I don't want to see the strain in your neck. I don't want to see you pushing to get to them (the audience)." The thing about Robin is that ultimately it was about conversation. So, if you get to a particularly purple passage, you can't pretend it's not a purply passage. You have to approach it with more muscle at that moment because you, at your best game, you on your best day, are the most articulate and you could come up with a way of articulating yourself if you were that charged emotionally and your brain and body were working in the moment. It was always as though he used to describe it as an iceberg. The text is just the iceberg, and down below is the body of emotion and intellect. The purply passage is actually not what you wanted to say because what is more important is what the thought is underneath. This amazing text is actually miniscule next to what I'm actually feeling—the unspoken.

When she played Rosalind for Phillips at the Tom Patterson theatre, Stratford (after his acclaimed main stage production with Maggie Smith), she learned an important but painful lesson. "Rosalind is such an extraordinary character, so if you ride the wave of what he's written, it tells you so much." After receiving a generous round of applause after a showy scene with Orlando, and feeling pretty chuffed, she came off and passed by Phillips who had been listening backstage. "My, my, weren't you clever!" he remarked softly, but not without irony. "Why?" she asked. "Oh, you had it all at the tip of your fingers."

Basically, what he was saying was: "Don't get showy with this part." So, she retreated to her dressing room and cried. However, when she returned to the stage for her next scene, she felt vulnerable—which was exactly what he wanted her to be. She came to see the point of Phillips' lesson: the minute the actors enjoy themselves too much or play to the audience, they are superficial and not fully committed to their roles.

"Quite rightly, he put me in my place. You felt you were on a bigger mission than just being showy."

Phillips wanted clarity of text so as to enable the audience to understand the story. He stressed verse-acting as opposed to verse-speaking. It was a value that the late Kenneth Tynan considered a requisite for Shakespeare: "A golden voice, however angelic, is not enough. Whenever a climax looms up, the actor faces a choice between the poetry and the character, the sound and the fury, because you cannot rage mellifluously or cry your eyes out in tune. The answer, now as always, is: Take care of the sense, and the sounds will take care of themselves" (Tynan 1976: 119).

Phillips scorned self-conscious poeticizing. When an actor fell into bad habits, he would groan: "Oh, please! I can't stand the crap! Let's go to the next scene!" When I interviewed Susan Coyne while she was in rehearsals as Juliet for Phillips in 1987, she commented: "Robin often talks about needing the words—that you need to say those words at that time. You need to say, 'Gallop apace, you fiery steeds.' It is demystifying in a lot of ways. You stop thinking about the great poet and start thinking about the great characters he's created."

Phillips had a gift for enabling his actors to feel free with their bodies because, like all good theatre practitioners, he understood that acting (especially in the classics) is about the text and the performer in a specific space. Given her natural height, Palk had a disadvantage as Rosalind as to how to make the character vulnerable in her yearning for love and how to move around the stage with freedom of her body, while speaking Shakespeare's verse with seeming ease. Phillips had a brilliant solution: He added a dock and imaginary water to a scene she had with Orlando that made the sequence physically romantic and erotic. As she and her Orlando (Nigel Hamer) mimed swimming and some romantic byplay, their youthful bodies seemed somehow more tangibly sensual by the connection to water. And given this context to relax physically and be playful, her body showed no tension and she found no barrier to conversational speech.

Phillips was very much an actor's director in the sense that he was against anything that interfered with stage truth. At the first dress rehearsal for *As You Like It*, the young cast got only three scenes in before he yelled: "That's it! Stop! Stop! Everybody out of costumes! It's just awful. I can't see you." The cast was to return to the Third Stage auditorium in rehearsal clothes. Phillips was protesting their preening and posing with their wigs, hats, and costumes. He declared to Palk: "You will never be as *free* and as *beautiful* as you are in your little pink T-shirt, your rehearsal skirt, and your ballet flats. With all that frou-frou, it's taking away from the truth."

Phillips expected total commitment from his cast, to the point of having them leap willingly into a rehearsal, trusting their instincts as much as their technique. On the very first day of rehearsal, he asked her and Melanie Miller (Celia): "Would you please start." Which took both of them by surprise as the play actually opens with males. Palk was a bit thrown by this. She had worked like a demon at home, where Tim, her firstborn, could entertain himself with toys while she studied her role fastidiously, preparing questions for her director. Phillips had filled her up with information and images for the role, but when he quietly told her "Go" at that first rehearsal, she said shyly: "I just have a couple of questions. How long has it been since my father was banished?"

Without missing a beat, Phillips reacted: "Right. We'll start with the boys." She was, of course, devastated, but she recognized the fundamental error. "I would never do that again. What was unimportant was whether it was two months or weeks or days. We didn't need to talk about that. What he had been doing was creating something for the whole room and for myself, but I was scared of leaping in. So, I wanted to go heady and intellectual—which is sometimes a problem I can have."

Phillips enabled Palk to trust the text in a special way. Phillips was able to impress on the actress a very significant point that he would later articulate for Ralph Berry: how theatrical communication is "not, *in truth*, the text; in *fact*, but not in truth. The text is a means to the end. The end is a spontaneous communication of whatever lies beyond the text, beyond the subtext, the cumulative effect of thought and feeling" (Qtd. in Berry 1989: 152). This version of *As You Like It* described an entirely different relationship between Rosalind and Orlando than had Phillips' earlier version with Maggie Smith.

Because Smith was much older than Jack Wetherall's Orlando, Phillips believed that an audience could pick up on the point that a wise, mature Rosalind was "leading a less experienced Orlando towards love, teaching him, guiding him towards experience and understanding," whereas Palk's Rosalind "discovered freedom in disguise, personal freedom" just as the same actress's Viola in *Twelfth Night* was "in disguise for her life." Because it was the same actress in the same company, "one saw very clearly the suffocating covering that disguise created for Viola and the pain she experienced of having love held in and controlled by Cesario. She [was] unable to express herself as she would wish" (Berry 153-54).

Phillips seemed to know exactly what a specific actor required as a hint or suggestion to enhance interpretation. When he asked Palk at the first reading of *Romeo and Juliet* for his Young Company at Stratford to make the Nurse Greek, there was no reason given. In fact, there was no discussion ahead of rehearsal about interpretation or directorial concept. This was yet another instance of Phillips throwing something at a performer at the first reading, thereby requiring the actor to leap in daringly.

By reading the play closely, she figured out his motive: She was 31 at the time and playing someone older or someone, at any rate, who was usually played as an older woman—as in the cases of Edith Evans, Edna May Oliver, Flora Robson, or Miriam Margolyes. Moreover, her height and figure were not in keeping with the customary silhouette of the Nurse. "What he believed was that she was an outsider. I thought it was a really good decision. It allowed her to have some sensuality rather than be a crusty old crone."

The text reveals the character's bawdiness, and it is clear that the Nurse gave birth at a very early age to a daughter whom she lost prematurely. Lady Capulet was only 14 when she gave birth to Juliet, who is purportedly the same age as the Nurse's Susan who went to God prematurely. So, the youthfulness of the acting company, far from being an impediment to authenticity, was really well suited to the ages of many of the characters. To find a Greek accent, Palk remembered the wonderful Russian-born librarian Asya DeVries at the National Theatre School who spoke multiple languages fluently, was "a real mama," a lover of Scrabble, and most generous to students. After consulting her, Palk wound up imitating her mimicry of a Greek accent. "Robin just wanted the sound of it at the first read, and after that, it didn't matter. She played the role in a black dress and carried black knitting.

Phillips had devised a *context* rather than a concept for the play. The long blonde pine stage looked bare. No canopies, balconies, no marketplaces or Mediterranean streets. There was a sense of a military academy nearby. The males wore white undershirts, black trousers, and white half masks. It was therefore difficult to tell a Montague from a Capulet, which was a deliberate strategy because, as Phillips explained: "I don't find it more interesting or exciting when you have the Montagues in blue and the Capulets in red. The horror is when you don't know which is which, and you don't know who is doing what to whom."[3]

The production was harsh-edged, masculine, and percussive. Drumbeats marked changes in mood or gave edge to staccato moments. The ill-fated young lovers (Albert Schultz and Susan Coyne) were impetuous, vehemently, candidly carnal, capable of headlong rushes of passion but incapable of knowing the price to themselves of concupiscence. All the characters were real people in real situations, and what an audience witnessed was a very human story, illuminated by flashes of insight into the errors and disposition of young love and clan animosities, as well as of the fateful generation gap between parents and their headstrong children. And Palk's Nurse, being closer in age to the young generation than to the old, seemed to have special empathy for her Juliet.

Palk relished the Nurse's earthiness and spoke the realistic colloquial prose with ease, enjoying the character's frankness in sexual matters, presenting in context a welcome contrast with the artifice and prissiness of Lady Capulet. She pretended insult when Mercutio cracked a sexual innuendo ("the bawdy hand of the dial is now upon the prick of noon"—2.4.112-13), but she quivered with titillation, her sexual candour allowing the audience to forget for a while that the Nurse is really a static character who does not change in the course of the drama.

Palk likes to call herself a working actor. She looks back at her experience in New York in 1990 when she and husband Joe were directed by Phillips at the Delacorte Theater in Central Park in *Richard III*, where Denzel Washington essayed the title role. Although the production was faulted for being disappointingly muted, with Washington being cramped in voice and movement, Palk recognized that New York actors in general were more concerned about staying in the city, waiting for their big break in TV and film. By contrast with them, Palk accepts work wherever it is offered, and she carries this attitude into her own teaching.

When she runs acting classes, she promotes her idea of a working actor: "It doesn't matter where you go, if you get to play Juliet. You go to Regina or to Sudbury, if need be, to play Lady Macbeth. You do it so you can get the opportunity to play those great parts." She believes in the "Olympian aspect of Shakespeare" where "your body and your brain and your heart all have to be pumping for the same purpose, and there's no kitchen sink and very few props. It's an actor on a bare stage a lot of the time, and it is the best kind of training."

But she certainly subscribes to the idea that being a member of a permanent classical company has some of the best advantages: "I can look around me and see Diego Matamoros, Joe Ziegler, Stu Hughes, Michelle Monteith, Susan Coyne (when she was here), Martha Burns (when she was here), Gregory Prest, Oliver Dennis, et cetera. These are people that I can really admire, and get the chance to have layer upon layer upon layer of experience with them, and friendship with them. It can only be good for the work. That's at its best. What Soulpepper was twenty years ago has changed formidably, but what I love about it are my colleagues."

Her view is probably shared by a great many professional actors, and it is certainly echoed by Carey Perloff, Artistic Director of San Francisco's legendary American Conservatory Theater, who argues for actors investing not only in their own performances but in "the health and direction" of an entire organization (Perloff 71). The practical life of an actor requires acceptance of transient, temporary work, of course, but this can make the performer feel devalued because as Zelda Fichandler puts it: "A 'gig' can only be followed by another 'gig.' You may be moving along but only from here to there—moving but not evolving." (Qtd. in Perloff 71)

Returning to the subject of work, I bring up the issue of a playwright's original intention. Is it ever possible to determine this, or is it even necessary? Unless one were a Deconstructionist, one would know that an author is always present in his text. But in Shakespeare's case, the text itself can be unreliable in the sense that there are discrepancies between Folio and Quarto versions. Moreover, the English language itself has changed, and one needs the help of academics in order to discover the meanings of even simple words such as "honour," "honest," "reason," or "virtue." Then there is the question of historical context. What, for instance, was behind Shakespeare's use of witches in *Macbeth*, or is *Henry V* an anti-war play or a play that glorifies war?

"Well, one trusts Shakespeare much deeper than one might any other playwright," she comments. "But there are times when I have felt that my job is not necessarily to be true to the playwright. My job is to be true to the character." And this necessarily means using every clue from the text, and being fully in the moment because it is moment by moment that a character is revealed. The true personality, grain, and colour of a character, his or her face of life, is found only in these moments, which are always in the present tense. In other words, the moment is the present, the present is the scene, and the scene, with text and subtext, is part of a metaphorical iceberg.

Notes

[1] Our interview was conducted January 17, 2017.
[2] Keith Garebian, rev. of *I Am Yours, Queen's Quarterly*, Vol. 95, No. 1, Spring 1988, 234.
[3] Keith Garebian, "Robin Phillips Reascendant," *A Well-Bred Muse: Selected Theatre Writings 1978-1988*. Oakville: Mosaic, 1991, 10.

Joseph Ziegler as Timon in Timon of Athens *(Stratford Festival, 2017).*
(Photo: Cylla von Tiedemann. Courtesy of the Stratford Festival)

Joseph Ziegler
Trusting The Play

Before our interview[1] at Toronto's Green Beanery Café, I skimmed over an archive of my theatre reviews, and a pattern emerged regarding the acting quality of Joseph Ziegler: a low-keyed restraint, building in detail and truth, so that nothing seems forced or artificially contrived. In other words, he is always securely grounded in every stage moment, and he never seeks to steal attention to himself. Of course, because he is so truthful, so real, he can't help but shine in an ensemble. His Soulpepper performances make for a memorable album. In William Saroyan's *The Time of Your Life* (2007), he was a world-weary, quixotic, bar sage; in Miklos Laszlo's *Parfumerie* (2009), as the owner of an elegant perfume store, he invested even the tiniest moment with deep feeling, delivering a fine study of painful heartbreak rather than mere choleric distemper over his wife's infidelity; and in Turgenev's *A Month in the Country* (2010), he and wife, Nancy Palk, did a marvellous acting duet—she as a spinster, coquettishly shy but eager and teary-eyed, and he as a doctor of shambling, physical awkwardness and curvilinear but clear-sighted realism.

More recently, Ziegler has done outstanding work at the Stratford Festival. His Joe Keller in Arthur Miller's *All My Sons* (2016) was a strong patriarchal figure, warm, caring, and firm until hidden moral cracks showed nakedly, and then his desperation and collapse translated into a powerful emotional disintegration. In Henrik Ibsen's *John Gabriel Borkman* that same season at Stratford, he etched an unforgettable portrait of a man who combined grand delusion with pathos-inflected seedy reality.

But these were little gems. There were much larger ones in leading roles. His Willy Loman in *Death of a Salesman* (2010) for Soulpepper was a performance worthy of being included in any list of great acting. Moving almost throughout with slumped shoulders, and using his hands like organic semaphores of broken or desperate thoughts, he ensured that attention was paid to Arthur Miller's low man of empty dreams. Ziegler was not the aggressively grandiose figure that Lee J. Cobb portrayed in the original Broadway production, but his Loman was a fresh creation of incurable self-doom and flawed love.

Ziegler worked miracles that were transfigurations of the ordinary. His voice husky and at times exhausted with his sense of moral failure, he paid scrupulous attention to the text, changing a thought or emotion in the same breath to capture Loman's contradictions. His boasts were immediately followed by self-deflations ("I'm very well liked, the only thing is people don't take to me"), and, so, the character became falsely self-glorifying as well as cuttingly self-deflating. Thus, through such anomalies, Ziegler built a devastating portrait that was heartbreakingly real and pitiable. His Loman agonized over his small life, ever dwindling with crushed hopes and dreams, and then crumpled before his wife and sons.

Ziegler knows exactly where his role fits in a text, and though he hits very high peaks of emotion, he never seems to manufacture passion. In Reginald Rose's *Twelve Angry Men* (2014), an old-fashioned jury room drama (first written for television in 1954), he played Juror Three, a role that Lee J. Cobb had performed with vivid power on film. This is the role in which a middle-aged man proves to be a vehement antagonist because of a terrible personal secret whose weight burdens him with violent anger. Ziegler's occasional flashes of impatient outrage turned into a towering display of explosive anger. Mounting the jury table and striding like an avenger hell-bent on asserting his moral rights, he seemed uncontrollable, but he eventually broke down into lacerating moral self-recognition that was raw yet devoid of self-pity.

His guiding credo is something he learned from Robin Phillips: "Trust the play, and just have a conversation." Ziegler's theatrical "conversations" were inspired by expatriate directors. Born in Minneapolis, Minnesota, he was drawn to professional theatre in his late teens. His family never attended theatre, except to see him in a play, and he appeared in five or six plays in high school and university before he ever saw one himself.

The first play he remembers seeing was *Love's Labour's Lost* at the Guthrie Theatre, with some guest Canadian actors, directed by legendary British director Michael Langham. "I had never seen anything like it. My eyes were opened. I understood every moment. I felt every moment of that play. It was funny but terribly moving, and then years later, when I was in my first year at Stratford, I was in *Love's Labour's Lost* (with Michael Langham directing), and when I began to read the play, I couldn't understand any of it." The irony was not lost on him.

What made Langham such a great director? "He understood that the greatest of Shakespeare is *beyond* words. We pay all the attention to the words because the words are so amazing. But Langham said (and this is something Robin Phillips talked about too) that it is the thought behind the words that is so earth-changing and shattering. That is what you have to aim for. What is it that makes you feel what you are feeling? Both these directors were incredibly important in my life."

But before his direct experiences with Langham and Phillips, there was his B.A. in theatre from the University of Minnesota, where he took a course in Shakespeare, as literature rather than as theatre. "They took you into the play. They didn't talk about it as theatre people; they talked about it as literature. When your eyes are opened to what's really in there and what's behind the writing, it's pretty startling."

His theatre degree courses didn't tell him much about acting Shakespeare, but he was very keen on such actors as Kenneth Welsh, Blair Brown, and August Schellenberg, and he was good enough to be accepted into the National Theatre School of Canada in Montreal. He was 22 at the time of his audition, for which he had prepared two speeches, one from *Romeo and Juliet* and the other from *Love's Labour's Lost*.

Douglas Rain, then Head of the Acting Program, ran the audition. After watching Ziegler do one of Berowne's speeches from *LLL*, he said: "Could you just do your speech again, and stick your hands in your pocket?" Ziegler's hand gestures were proving to be such distractions that Rain could not hear what he was saying because focus was being drawn to his moving hands. Ziegler was quick to adapt to the suggestion, and Rain remarked: "Yeah, now I can hear it." It wasn't long before Rain became a valued friend and acting guide to both Ziegler and Nancy Palk, his classmate of outstanding talent, who became the love of his life and mother to their three sons.

After graduation from the NTS in 1979, he was immediately hired by Theatre Passe Muraille for *October Soldiers* (about the terrifying FLQ crisis) and for the CBC radio version of Thornton Wilder's *Our Town*, starring Lorne Greene and Nonnie Griffin, a play he would later direct to much acclaim for Soulpepper. Engagements with mid-size Toronto theatres (especially Tarragon Theatre) followed in quick succession, and it was no surprise when he joined Christopher Newton's first Shaw Festival acting ensemble (1980-82), and Stratford's Young Company under Michael Langham (1983), before becoming part of that festival's main company (1984-87), in which he played such major Shakespearean roles as Berowne (*Love's Labour's Lost*), Hotspur (*Henry IV, Part One*), Edgar (*King Lear*), Sir Andrew Aguecheek (*Twelfth Night*), Claudio (*Measure for Measure*), and Posthumus (*Cymbeline*).

He would also become a director, one of his significant credits being the production of *Hamlet* at the Stratford Festival in 2000, starring Paul Gross in the title role. His audition for Langham has stayed in his mind because it was a signal lesson in speaking and acting Shakespeare. He had selected a speech by Berowne from *LLL*, without knowing that the festival would be doing the same play that season) and the molehill speech from Henry *VI, Part 3*. It was the latter speech that provoked Langham's instructive lesson:

> This battle fares like to the morning's war,
> When dying clouds contend with growing light,
> What time the shepherd, blowing of his nails,
> Can neither call it perfect day nor night.
> …
> Here on this molehill will I sit me down.
> To whom God will, there be the victory!
> For Margaret my queen, and Clifford too,
> Have chid me from the battle; swearing both
> They prosper best of all when I am thence.
> Would I were dead, if God's good will were so;
> For what is in this world but grief and woe? (2.5. 1-4, 14-20)

After he concluded the lines, he heard Langham say: "Yes, that's very clear, very clear. I don't get anything from it. I don't know what you're feeling. What's happening to this man? What does he feel? What is his problem? Why is he giving this speech?" Ziegler realized: "He opened up the speech for me by saying: 'This man is falling apart. This man is at a crisis point.' I had understood the speech in an intellectual way, and he was asking for emotion." Langham's comment was also a director's shrewd way of determining whether Ziegler was open to suggestion, if the young actor could take direction and adapt.

But how does an actor deal with long expository passages? "You have to find your way through it as a human being. First and foremost, what is it that makes you *want* to say this? What is it that you are talking about? Often, it's just the attempt to put into words what you're feeling. It's as simple and as complicated as that." Ziegler uses Hamlet's "To be or not to be" soliloquy as an example:

> To be, or not to be, that is the question:
> Whether 'tis nobler in the mind to suffer
> The slings and arrows of outrageous fortune,
> Or to take arms against a sea of troubles,
> And by opposing, end them. To die, to sleep—
> No more, and by a sleep to say we end
> The heart-ache and the thousand natural shocks
> That flesh is heir to; 'tis a consummation
> Devoutly to be wish'd. To die, to sleep—
> To sleep, perchance to dream—ay, there's the rub (3.1.55-64).

"When Hamlet is putting his thoughts together, the thoughts are amazing, perfect. But he's still trying to figure out how to express what he feels. If 'To be, or not to be' was really the question, the speech would be over much earlier than it is. But that doesn't quite say it for him. He needs to find a way to get it out of himself." Ziegler points out the difficulty for an actor speaking the soliloquy to everybody in the audience while Hamlet the character must be alone with his own complex thoughts.

Robin Phillips (who directed him in the role at the Citadel Theatre, with Domini Blythe as Gertrude and Martha Burns as Ophelia) helped with insights into how the soliloquies should be handled, suggesting that of course, these speeches were to an audience but that Hamlet was not talking to them as if they were present in the same room as he was. Hamlet would have to project the feeling of being alone.

Ziegler caught on: "He's there and he's available, and so are his thoughts. He's not holding anything back but he does not get comfort from the audience in any way. If we even subconsciously feel that Hamlet has somebody to talk to, it ruins the play. So, the actor playing Hamlet has to make his words and thoughts available but at the same time be completely alone."

Phillips had done the play many times earlier—none of these productions seen by Ziegler—and he had his own take on the story. Ziegler recalls:

> When we began rehearsing it, I had done a number of plays with Robin by that time and I trusted him like I had never trusted anybody else. If he had said 'Take off your clothes and jump through that window,' I would have agreed, because I trusted him absolutely. He directed me in *Hamlet* in a way that I found I didn't totally understand. I felt that what he was asking for was something a bit more aggressive than I would have come up with. And then we did a dress rehearsal, and I did my best. After that rehearsal, he took me apart from the beginning of the play to the end in front of everybody. He just destroyed me, but that didn't matter. I kept thinking 'Yeah, he's right. That's absolutely right. That's what I'm doing.' He said Hamlet does not come on stage to attack people. He comes on stage for a different reason—whatever that reason may be. He had wanted me to be aggressive, and then that all changed in an afternoon, and he was right. I agreed with everything he said. It made all the difference in the world. I cried all night, but I trusted him absolutely.
>
> It was not unusual for Robin to direct an actor a certain way for a long time and then suddenly change it. I think what happened was he saw the play in one way and that was affected by the productions he had been involved with in the past. And then for some reason, he saw it completely differently in the rehearsal and changed it in an afternoon. And he couldn't understand why I was literally doing what he had asked me to do earlier.

It takes a special actor to adapt to a special director, and Ziegler is a special actor. He applied Phillips' critique to his performance, altering it radically by finding motives for each of Hamlet's speeches. When he came out for his first scene with the "O, that this too, too sullied flesh would melt" soliloquy, he fell apart. "That was what Robin wanted. He didn't say 'Please fall apart there.' He said the world is changing. The world starts changing as of tomorrow. You have a new head of state, you have a new marriage. You have a new father. Buck up. What Hamlet doesn't really understand is how the world can go on, how things can continue. He's absolutely devastated. He doesn't have anything to fall back on."

As he recounts the moment and recites the soliloquy, Ziegler becomes the devastated Prince, his eyes filling with tears. And they are not glycerine tears. The actor becomes the character, even for a moment of brief retrospection. But rather than putting the emphasis on himself, he credits Phillips for the revelation or insight. "He was like no other."

I have heard his remark mouthed by other Canadian actors, who also had extraordinary experiences and lessons under Phillips' tutelage. Nancy Palk has mentioned how Phillips had suddenly ordered the doffing of all costumes after a bad rehearsal of *As You Like It*. And Ziegler recalls a similar experience when Phillips mounted David Hirson's *La Bête* at the Citadel. The pastiche Moliere had beautiful 17th century costumes, but at the dress rehearsal, Phillips summoned Stephen Ouimette, Ziegler, and William Webster and said: "I need to talk to you. We're going to cut the costumes." The beautiful costumes were colourful and perfectly cut, but they were detracting from the play. Audiences were watching the costumes rather than the performers. Ziegler remarks:

> We came in with versions of modern dress, and he was right. It wasn't about his ego. He just realized that what he was seeing on stage were moving costumes. The thing about Robin is that you would be in a rehearsal hall with fluorescent lights, no props, no music, no costumes, and the actors watching, totally transfixed by what they saw. That's how *brilliant* it was in the rehearsal hall. That's what he aimed for. Then he would take it into the theatre, and suddenly there was lighting, there was sound, and he always had a hard time with that transition. The actors were changing their performances as soon as

they got into costume. But it's up to the actor to hold on to the truth.
You've got to keep the relationship alive with the other characters.

One way of keeping this relationship dynamic is to understand
how to make the language available to everyone in the audience.
Lovers of Shakespeare tend to pay attention to the words because
they are amazing, but as Michael Langham understood (and as
Ziegler phrases it) "the greatest of Shakespeare is beyond words. It
is the thought behind the words that is so earth-shattering." This
is what an actor should aim for, according to Ziegler: "What is it
that makes you feel what you are feeling?"

He draws other examples from *Macbeth*, the first being the
title character's dagger vision, which begins this way:

> Is this a dagger which I see before me,
> The handle toward my hand? Come, let me clutch thee:
> I have thee not, and yet I see thee still.
> Art thou not, fatal vision, sensible
> To feeling as to sight? or art thou but
> A dagger of the mind, a false creation,
> Proceeding from the heat-oppressed brain? (2.1. 33-39)

Ziegler expands:

> Macbeth is solitary. I try to get it in my head as human thought and
> speech. The important part of that question ('Is this a dagger which
> I see before me') is I am seeing a dagger and I know there's no reason
> for a dagger to be suspended in mid-air. It's not how I phrase it. What
> the audience sees at that point is a man who has been very inward
> looking:
>
> > My thought, whose murther yet is but fantastical,
> > Shakes so my single state of man that function
> > Is smother'd in surmise, and nothing is
> > But what is not (1.3.139-142).
>
> The beauty of the construction of language is not mine. I don't take
> ownership of that. But I cannot get in its way. I'm not going for
> beauty of language. The author is. I think what happens sometimes is
> that we go for the sensational in the play. And that's where we make

our mistake. It's an identifiable human being up there, not a super hero, but an identifiable human being who wonders what is going on. You could make a thriller without all those soliloquies, but what's great about the play is that it is more than a thriller. It gives you a peek inside a human being who is faced with extraordinary circumstances, and it shows how he copes.

Ziegler has played the role twice (once in theatre school and once in New York), and he is aware of current practice to strip the language down to make it feel contemporary. "They forget they're still speaking Shakespeare. You've got to have the tools. You do. The big thing is that you can't get in the way of what Shakespeare did. Scholars figure that an audience ought to be able to hear and actors ought to be able to say 1,000 lines in an hour. The only way that's possible is if the iambic pentameter is realized. The reason it's written that way is not just because of the beautiful sound, it's also to help you understand. It's easier to understand a thousand lines of Shakespeare in an hour if it is properly spoken—not if I'm breaking every half line, interrupting, changing, making a shift. All this gets in the way. There are breaks in Shakespeare. There are also changes in thought, but he wrote them. We have to find them rather than impose."

In his youth, Ziegler was most impressed by William Hutt, Brian Bedford, Douglas Rain, and Martha Henry for being models of Shakespearean acting. He got to act with Hutt in 2004 at Soulpepper in *Waiting for Godot*, and earlier with Bedford at Stratford in A *Midsummer Night's Dream*. He watched Bedford night after night, marvelling at how true and real he was as Bottom. "I couldn't believe how natural he was. He was just talking. Everybody else, including myself, were getting our character stuff going, but not Brian. He was playing a character, certainly, but he was human and bringing a lot of humanity to it. There were times when he was goofy, but most of the time it was so fresh."

Bedford was a master of verbal architecture. He could take daring pauses without ever losing the shape of a speech. Whether he was playing Jaques, Benedick, Richard II, or Angelo, he inhabited the characters. "Everything was so human, and I say that because all around me—and probably including me—there were people who were super-sizing everything they did in order to try to be impressive or interesting. But the really good ones—such as Hutt and Bedford—just went out and spoke."

Ziegler's comments often return to the theme of size or scale. When I remark that I sometimes miss the bravura in modern Shakespearean acting, he counters: "I'm not sure about that, but I think that speech has to do something *in* you. If you attempt to do the speech without anything going on inside you, it's empty. Unfortunately, actors are not always in the heart of the matter."

Having performed the role of Macbeth twice, he maintains that the play would work best in a small room, such as the space used for the Ian McKellen-Judi Dench *Macbeth* for the Royal Shakespeare Company. Ziegler himself goes for an intimate quality in his own acting. "As soon as it becomes too big, it loses because it's about a guy wondering about what is happening to him." Although he has models of acting, he does not study his predecessors in a role. "I don't like to know what they did. It's better if I can discover for myself."

In the course of our interview, he articulates some of his discoveries, and these span subjects as diverse as the witches, the central bedevilled marriage, and Lady Macbeth's madness. One of the key difficulties in this play is the question concerning witches and the supernatural. How does one approach these subjects? I complain that I never feel a real sense of witchcraft and the supernatural in the stage versions I see. "I think it has a lot to do with things that the modern actor does not control—such as production or concept. So, I have to commit myself to believing in it."

Ziegler feels that Macbeth has never experienced anything in his life that prepares him for what he sees. Banquo wonders about the first apparition: "What are these/So wither'd, and so wild in their attire/That look not like th'inhabitants o' th'earth,/ And yet are on't?" (1.3.39-42) Macbeth doesn't understand the witches. "This supernatural soliciting/Cannot be ill; cannot be good" (1.3. 130-31).

> And that's one of the fascinating things about the play. A man of the earth, of the here and now, is grappling with that which is not here and now, that which is other. He is freaked out by it, and he knows this. In the banquet scene, when the ghost of Banquo shows up, Macbeth can't understand why nobody else sees it:
>
> 'You make me strange
> Even to the disposition that I owe,
> When now I think you can behold such sights,
> And keep the natural ruby of your cheeks,
> When mine is blanch'd with fear '(3.4.111-15).
>
> He can't understand why his wife is so calm. I think it's important that she's not mad. She is observing something that she fears is mad. There's a line where he says: 'So, prithee, go with me' (3.2.56), and another: 'Come, we'll to sleep' (3.4.142). That's a very telling moment in the play, where after everything has happened, he still needs her. But, then, he goes off before her, not wanting her to follow—which is different from the other scenes where there is a need.

But, I point out, Macbeth returns to the witches in Act 4:

> I will tomorrow
> (And betimes I will) to the weird sisters.
> More shall they speak; for now I am bent to know,
> By the worst means, the worst (3.4.131-34).

"He comes to accept them," Ziegler remarks. How does he, the actor, internalize this change? "Really, it's moment by moment—like any acting moment."

One of the most fascinating things in this tragedy is the relationship of Macbeth and his wife. "I think it's probably the happiest marriage in all of Shakespeare," Ziegler says, laughing, without sticking his tongue in cheek. "Rosalind and Orlando get married. So do Jessica and Lorenzo. Their plays are over. But Macbeth and Lady Macbeth love each other passionately. At the end of the play, when he hears that she is dead, his world changes completely and he becomes an animal. Not long after that, he says: 'I'll fight, till from my bones my flesh be hack'd' (5.3.32) because he is pure animal."

Knowing that his wife Nancy Palk played Lady Macbeth opposite him, I ask if it helps matters when your spouse is playing the lady. "For sure. Absolutely, because you can do anything," he contends. "She could hit me, choke me, or I could choke her, anything—not that it ever happened—but there's an absolute trust. That's how we got together in the same theatre school class. In those days, you were given a scene to rehearse, and you would go up to a room and rehearse. You didn't know any better, so you would tell each other what to do. I would say, 'I don't know why you're doing that. You should do this!' And she would tell me what to do, she would boss me around. We don't do that anymore, although we're pretty open with each other. We've acted a lot together. We attempt to be on the same page in terms of what we're going for."

They won't actually direct each other, however. That is the right of the production's director. But having this real-life couple performing stage duets has produced some very memorable moments in Canadian theatre, because though you can polish technique, you cannot manufacture chemistry—something this couple has in spades when they act opposite each other.

Moving to a technical matter, I ask him about the difference between verse speaking and verse acting. "Wow, what a good question that is!" he exclaims softly. "I think you have to let the verse inform you what the scene is about. All the good directors talk about going to the end of the line. Don't stop in the middle, except occasionally. Follow the thought all the way through because if I have a thought felt halfway through a line, that won't be as complete as if I spoke the text all the way through. Our thoughts are too short. I remember doing *The Voysey Inheritance* at the Shaw Festival, and Neil Munro (the director) would be after me, saying: 'The thought is much longer than you're making it. You're breaking it up too much, I can't follow the thought.' He was right. Once I clued into it, it made a lot of sense. It made it easier to follow the story and the character."

He provides Posthumus' line from *Cymbeline* as an example: "Is there no way for men to be, but women/Must be half-workers?" (2.5.1-2) Posthumus' thought is a criticism of women in the sense that it is suggesting that the normal, acceptable way for men to be themselves is not possible without having women as collaborators in some sense. Ziegler spoke it as a rant, and Phillips (who was directing the production) remarked on this. "I said, 'Yeah, it feels like he's really angry,'" Ziegler countered, to which Phillips retorted: "Have a thought about the pain that he feels that got him to this point. He thought he was in love forever. He thought this woman (Imogen) was going to be true to him forever and now he hears that she has betrayed him. It's more about his pain than his anger." When Ziegler, considered the remarks, he saw the lines in a clear, new light:

> Could I find out
> The woman's part in me—for there's no motion
> That tends to vice in man, but I affirm
> It is the woman's part: be it lying, note it,
> The woman's; flattering, hers; deceiving, hers;
> Lust and rank thoughts, hers, hers; revenges, hers;
> ...
> For even to vice

They are not constant, but are changing still:
One vice but of a minute old, for one
Not half so old as that (2.5.19-24; 29-32).

Pain more than anger. The very same emotion bubbling within Timon of Athens, Ziegler's starring role, directed by Stephen Ouimette in a modern-dress version for the 2017 Stratford Festival season. "We know very little about *Timon of Athens*. It has only been produced very rarely so that very few people have seen it," claimed the late Malcolm Muggeridge with some validity, before going on to other shaky, if not totally false generalizations: "There are no long, exciting parts in it to attract the attention of famous or aspiring actors and no parts for women at all. It's also a hard read. The truth is that, but for a tenuous connection with Shakespeare, it would probably have got forgotten like many another Elizabethan play" (qtd. Sales 1984: 250).

Ziegler's dissent is prompt: "There may be a lot of people who feel that way. Our society has such a problem with plays that are not easily put into categories." I concur, referencing Polonius' amusing catalogue of genres for actors of the time: "tragedy, comedy, history, pastoral, pastoral-comical, historical-pastoral, tragical-comical-historical-pastoral, scene individable, or poem unlimited" (2.2.396-98). The Elizabethan Age encouraged flexible genres, and Shakespeare was never one to blindly follow tradition. Ziegler expands on the topic:

> At the beginning of the 17th century, everybody was writing revenge tragedies. Shakespeare was not writing revenge tragedies. Arguably, the last thing he wrote as a revenge tragedy was *Hamlet*, which was at the beginning of the century. But Hamlet does not understand revenge the traditional way. 'Now might I do it pat, now 'a is a-praying;/And now I'll do't—and so 'a goes to heaven,/And so am I reveng'd' (3.3.73-75). What Shakespeare was writing were what we call problem-plays. We call them that because basically we don't understand them. The big thing that these plays all seem to have in common is that their level of human-ness or humanity is constantly

being talked about or looked at. If you take *Measure for Measure*, *All's Well that Ends Well*, *The Winter's Tale*, *Pericles*, *Cymbeline*, or *The Tempest*, every single one of them ends in forgiveness. And we don't understand forgiveness as well as we understand revenge.

Timon of Athens complicates things by its central mysteries about the eponymous character and his wealth. The English actor Richard Pasco, a notable Timon in Britain, has commented: "The character of Timon is at once a mystery. Shakespeare gives us no hint of his background or his forebears. We know something at least of the character of the leading protagonist in most of the great tragedies: Hamlet's life at Elsinore, Lear's court and his three daughters, Julius Caesar and the state of Rome. But we know nothing of Timon. We don't even know whether he acquired his vast wealth and lands by inheritance or gift. We know nothing of his family. He is, of all Shakespeare's major figures, the most isolated" (qtd. Sales 257).

"I think that's closer to the truth," Ziegler says. "I don't know how he got his money. I think in our production it must look like he's in business or finance—or maybe it was inherited. He's always had money. It doesn't really matter. He knows what it feels like not to have money, so when somebody's in need, he wants to take care of that. It's a very important aspect—his capacity for empathy or his capacity to feel for other people. Money may be a jumping-off place for a couple of scenes, but it's about what people do to people."

Shakespearean scholar Marjorie Garber argues that the play is about "philanthropy and misanthropy, but also about the use and abuse of patronage" (Garber 2005: 647)—an interpretation that can be linked to Ziegler's view that the play offers a critique of society. After all, Shakespeare uses an artist, poet, and philosopher as leading beneficiaries of Timon's patronage. But why not a tradesman or financier, for example?

Ziegler explains: "I think because if there is humanity, they should be leading the way. Instead, they join in and wonder how to get something out of Timon. He lives his life under the assumption that if he's good and decent, if he takes care of people around him, they'll take care of him if that's ever necessary—although he doesn't even think that far. He's completely gob-smacked when everybody turns their back on him. Now, we may say that this is naïve of him, but I don't like to think that it's necessarily naïve. I think he's right in being disappointed. He's right in wondering what we have done to one another, what we have meant to one another. He's shattered."

But why, then, does he brush off his servant Flavius who warns him against false flattery and extravagant generosity? "He has no idea of his financial state. He eventually says: 'You make me marvel wherefore ere this time/Had you not fully laid my state before me,/That I might so have rated my expense/As I had leave of means' (2.2.124-27). I don't know if he is blaming the servant, although it sounds like that to me, but eventually he says in the same scene 'No blame belongs to thee' (2.2.222).

"So much of Timon is a rant and rage but a lot is because he expected people to be decent and reasonable. What he is shocked at and changed by is how indifferent people have been to him. In his moment of need, he expected people to be there for him, but they weren't."

Paul Scofield, who played the role at Stratford-upon-Avon in 1965, commented that "The play is that of a man mentally and spiritually scarred by a betrayal of trust, and Timon's experience of such a betrayal is the most bitter and painful denunciation of man's cupidity and cruelty and faithlessness" (qtd. *Introductions to Shakespeare* 176). Given these facts, does the role require the actor to be out-sized, I wonder aloud to Ziegler. "I'm not going to decide now. I'm going to wait till I'm in the rehearsal room and see what I'm getting from other actors. There are times when he loses it. He prepares a banquet where he serves warm water and stones. He is punishing them. He wants to hurt them as much as they have hurt him. So, that calls for rage, and that won't be a problem. The world is not what he thought it was."

Ziegler does not watch other actors' interpretations of the roles he himself is attempting. "I want to be schooled by the *play* I'm in. Let it speak to me so that I can find out how it moves me. The other way can actually be a problem because it can get between you and the play. If you have a preconception based on how amazing an actor was in the role, it doesn't help. Once you get into the text, once you find yourself unlocking little messages in the text, it doesn't really matter what anybody did before you."

His words would be signal ones even for a director—something Ziegler often is at Soulpepper, Stratford, and elsewhere. "When I directed Hamlet at Stratford, I went to see my friend Douglas Rain. He gave me a cassette tape, which had Tyrone Guthrie talking about directing. He was very funny, very witty, saying, in effect, 'I have been asked to talk to you about the role of the director. The first job of the director is to read the play.' His audience laughed, and he said, 'Yes, you can laugh but you'll be surprised how many times that is not the case. The second job of the director, after having read the play, is to read the play. You want the play to tell you, you want to be informed by the play.'"

Ziegler takes Guthrie's instruction to heart. "When I read a play, I try to figure out how we got from A to B." He looks up the meanings of words such as "honour," "virtue," "noble," "reason," et cetera. He consults variorum editions, taking great pride in the fact that he owns every such edition of Shakespeare's plays. In this way, he doesn't play a speech; he plays a character.

Is the play unfinished? Ziegler doesn't think so: "What is a little unsatisfying is that someone comes on at the end and says

Timon is dead. You didn't see that happen. Does he kill himself? I don't think so. Timon's last line is: 'Sun, hide thy beams. Timon hath done his reign' (5.1.223). He doesn't have the will to go on, so he just lies down and doesn't get up again. He doesn't have the will to go on anymore."

Considering Timon's heartbreak or utter disillusionment, I wonder if benevolent Timon is really aiming at our better natures or if he has a motive of self-glorification. Ziegler answers:

> I think that is a way to play it. I tried not to go down that road because I don't understand what the payoff would be. I think the play is not about a freakish man or a bizarre one. I think it's about society and the world. Timon says near the beginning at one of his dinner parties: 'O, what a precious comfort 'tis to have so many like brothers commanding one another's fortunes!' (1.2.104). He feels that we are all in this together. Wealthy people are here to help each other and help those who need it. Of course, that's not true, but that's what he believes. He's quickly disillusioned. He is alone. By the end of the play, he wants to be alone. He doesn't want anybody to see him, he doesn't want to be seen, he doesn't want anyone to talk to. He doesn't want anything. He just wants to die and forget he ever lived.

What sort of preparation does he do before each performance of this play? "There's a group warm-up before every performance, led by a voice and movement coach. It has a lot to do with breathing, relaxation, and resonance. It's usually at about 6:30 p.m. for an 8 o'clock show, and it lasts about half an hour. I never miss a warm-up. I do my best to keep fit. In order to perform these plays, you have to be present, you have to be in [a scene] at that moment. We have to be able to come up with whatever it takes to achieve that." Given the difficulty and intricacy of the text, Ziegler runs his lines several times before a performance:

> The text is so complicated, and it was important to Stephen Ouimette (the director) that it be spoken as it was written. We didn't make a lot of cuts. I say to Apemantus late in the play:

> Hadst thou like us from our first swath proceeded
> The sweet degrees that this brief world affords
> To such as may the passive drudges of it
> Freely command, thou wouldst have plung'd thyself
> In general riot, melted down thy youth
> In different beds of lust, and never learn'd
> The icy precepts of respect, but follow'd
> The sug'red game before thee (4.3.252-59).

That's *half* a thought, and it's a paragraph. I love that, but it's extremely challenging. The challenge is to somehow pull the audience through it image by image. [In Shakespeare] people have big thoughts, and as you begin to speak the thought, it is qualified by something else you've just thought of, and it changes. Then it changes again, and you still have to keep it going. It is a difficult text to just illuminate, to let it be heard.

With Ziegler at the helm, the difficult text is not only heard, it is clarified in such a palpable manner that an audience experiences a Timon who is taking in all the persons he is listening to or speaking with. Ziegler allows us to see and hear whatever has affected Timon, as well as the degree to which these things produce and deepen his misanthropy and soul devastation.

Notes

[1] I interviewed Joseph Ziegler twice: the first interview was conducted on January 31, 2017. There was a follow-up interview in the Playwrights Circle Lounge, Festival Theatre, Stratford on July 20, 2017.

Albert Schultz as Hamlet (Soulpepper Theatre Company, 2004)
(Photo: Sandy Nicholson. Courtesy of Soulpepper Company)

Albert Schultz
Provocations

Former Artistic Director of Soulpepper (the most famous actor-run theatre company in Canada), Albert Schultz has a personality as impressive as his credentials. Standing 6' 1," he has a full flush of dark brown hair, and a beard to match (at the time of our interview).[1] His bass-baritone voice is rich and supple, and he can break into the warmest smile and be utterly charming when he wishes. Offstage he is all business, but his signature charm never deserts him. There are massive demands on his time from every quarter: actors, directors, staff members, corporate poohbahs, theatre students, journalists, et cetera.

The fact that he has proved to be one of Canada's most successful producers and artistic directors, while remaining a highly-respected actor, director, and singer, is a miracle of successful artistic husbandry. One of Robin Phillips' "kids," he helped found Soulpepper in order to give fellow-actors opportunities to explore lesser known classics—by Friedrich Schiller, Friedrich Durrenmatt, William Saroyan, Brian Friel, Miklos Laszlo, Gotthold Ephraim Lessing, Mikhail Bulgakov, Ferenc Molnar, et cetera—though later in his tenure, the company branched out into modern American, European, and Canadian plays by such playwrights as Alan Ayckbourn, Harold Pinter, Tony Kushner, Caryl Churchill, Sam Shepard, David Mamet, Suzanne-Lori Parks, David French, John Murrell, Sharon Pollack, Judith Thompson, and Michel Tremblay, even making room in the company repertoire for neophyte Canadian writers.

Though Schultz toured the country performing a cabaret repertoire of Sinatra songs, he never forsook his personal interest in Shakespeare's poetry or in great language. The roots of this passion reach back to his boyhood and adolescence. Born in Port Hope, Ontario, he lost his father prematurely (which accounts for his earlier fear that he himself might die young), but not before he sang as an Anglican choirboy at the age of six, using the 1662 *Book of Common Prayer*. His Anglican faith also meant an exposure to the King James bible. For his entire childhood, three days a week, he would sing the Psalms and other sacred music while also reading the liturgy. This developed an ease with language and ritual, but the boy also had another special resource and inspiration.

His godfather, Ron Gasch, was the one who introduced him to Shakespeare. Gasch would spread a book on the floor and make young Albert read a passage to his applause and encouragement. Then Gasch would play Gielgud's *Ages of Man* recording and make the boy repeat the passages in imitation. So, the process was read, listen, recite, but instead of being dreary, it was a friendly, easy apprenticeship without the boy's knowing what it was. "The language was as much of my childhood as anything else. That's where the facility or ease or interest came from," claims Schultz. By the time he encountered Shakespeare in high school, he suffered no impediment of language the way most of his peers did. The text seemed native to him and there was nothing foreign about the "distance" of language.

His mother remarried after the death of Albert's father, and the family moved to Alberta by the time he was 12, where in his parents' library he discovered three ground-breaking books about the first three seasons of the Stratford Festival (collaborations by Robertson Davies, Tyrone Guthrie, and Grant Macdonald). He was hooked:

Those books helped create this mythology for me. I then decided in high school to study at theatre school [York University], and though I had a wonderful time, there wasn't much opportunity to do Shakespeare. At the end of my second year, I applied to the London Academy of Music and Dramatic Arts (LAMDA) to do a course in the classics (particularly Shakespeare) at the Master's program level. At 21, I was the youngest. I saw everything I could see in English theatre. I discovered old BBC recordings of Shakespeare and fell in love with Derek Jacobi, who had done *Hamlet* and *I, Claudius* (which was on television at the time). I ran into Jacobi, Sian Phillips, Brian Blessed, John Hurt, Claire Bloom, Patrick Stewart, and all these amazing actors. I saw rep at the RSC, in which Jacobi was playing Cyrano de Bergerac, Prospero, and Benedick. I saw him in shows several times and went backstage, and he was so generous. He even talked to our acting class, at my invitation, which was really sweet.

England gave him a glorious opportunity to see and do Shakespearean acting. Just the proximity to Stratford and to that history was enough to deepen his appetite. He encountered some amazing teachers: Glynne Macdonald (later Head of Movement for Mark Rylance at the Globe) taught the Alexander Technique; and guest director Chris Sandford taught him valuable lessons in rigour. When Schultz recited "Let's sit upon the ground" from *Richard II*, Sandford remarked that the sense wasn't clear, and when Schultz repeated the speech over and over, he felt that Sandford's repeated criticism was beastly. But a month later, Schultz realized the sense of it:

> He just rode me and rode me, but it gave me courage to be rigorous with myself as actor, director, and teacher, because this stuff needs rigour. And what Bill Hutt and the best people do—Joseph Ziegler, Nancy Palk, Susan Coyne—is terribly impressive. Bill was the master at it, which is to do all the rigorous work and then throw it away and just think. There's an awful lot of actors who give the impression they are thinking because they can speak very quickly and they can turn a phrase, but they aren't really thinking with the depth that Sandford made me do, and which Robin made me do later.

Of course, he had not yet seen anything by Phillips yet, though he knew him by reputation by reading about him. When Schultz returned to Canada in 1984, within a year he found himself performing Tybalt in High Park, where Lady Capulet was Diana Leblanc, and the director Guy Sprung. Shortly after, R.H. Thomson did Hamlet and Schultz played Laertes.

Phillips was rumoured to be returning to Stratford, and there was buzz that he was conducting a national search for actors. Schultz was recommended to him by colleagues Sheila McCarthy and Barbara Budd. Wearing a T-shirt and suspenders to hold up very baggy pants coming up to just below his rib-cage, he created a spectacle that provoked Phillips' curiosity.

Schultz performed a scene from *Amadeus* and Hamlet's "How all occasions do inform against me" soliloquy as Phillips threw prompts at him, expecting him to respond in order to demonstrate his creative flexibility. At the end, Phillips came up to him and asked: "Is your body all right?" Schultz was taken aback momentarily: "Yes, what do you mean?" "If I asked you to play Jesus on the cross, would you be comfortable? Because the pants, you know, don't give me that impression."

A week later, he was offered Romeo, Touchstone, and Stanhope in *Journey's End*, (a role Olivier had played in his youth). Like almost all young actors who were guided by Phillips, Schultz learned a great deal from the director (whose accent and speaking manner he imitates brilliantly):

> Robin was so great. His ear was attuned to what he called the *acting* of theatre. Robin would say, 'That sounds like theatre, darling.' You can sound like good theatre and be impressive to a lot of people, but they haven't felt anything listening to you or thought anything. I won't name names, but they're all over the place. Robin had an unerring ear for the substitution of actual thought or desire by the *sound* of it. And it happened to me with Romeo. When I recited 'But soft, what light through yonder window breaks,' he would say: 'Darling, that's

beautiful, beautiful poetry. I really think you're good at the poetry. Could we have some humanity instead? I think you want [Juliet]. Don't you want her? Doesn't sound like you want her, darling. Sounds like you've put her on a pedestal.'

Phillips did very little table work, and Schultz approved of this.

My feeling is the work that gets done at the table is all important work but I much prefer to do it on my feet. Too much table work deadens the impulse and you make decisions before you get up, so you tend not to discover anything. It can help you formulate thoughts, but in terms of the creative process and moments of inspiration, those are harder to find at a table setting. Robin would get a scene quickly on its feet, whether we were doing *The Music Man* or Romeo or Feste, and he would give me provocations. I will tell you the best one.

The first time we staged the balcony scene from *Romeo and Juliet*, there was no balcony. It's a scene that's got every trap known to man. I remember being terribly disappointed when at the first design presentation he said there was no balcony: 'I'm so tired of looking at the back ends of Romeos reaching up. I don't know *what* we'll do, but there'll be no balcony.' Susan [Coyne, his Juliet] and I had disappointment in every pore. We were on a rostrum in the centre—a funky YMCA building on Waterloo Street, where there may be condos now. Creaky gym floor and windows with chain mail on them so no birds would enter. Chilly day in April, Laura Burton on piano. Susan and I were going through, off book. Robin sent me outside: 'Go outside. Get her through the window.' My job was to actually make her fall in love with me from outside the building and through the window and cage.

Schultz improvised with the text and tried to communicate desperately with her. Because of the cold, his breath frosted the window and he drew an arrow-pierced heart with the initials R&J on it. Phillips laughed, putting his hands on his heart. So, he brought back Schultz into the room, and made him reach for Juliet with a palm as if touching glass in order to find warmth in Juliet's palm. In the actual production at the Third Stage, Phillips created the sense that Juliet was encased in a glass cube, so that the lovers could literally play "palm to palm" against that glass. Schultz would move around in a full circle, only three inches from her but unable to penetrate the glass. Of course, this was incredibly erotic because it was as if Romeo could feel Juliet's breath without being able to touch her. It also had a kinetic quality sprung out of Phillips' improvisation. Schultz adds:

> I don't think people talk much about Robin's improvisation. They talk as if he were some master who passed down pearls or nuggets. He wasn't. At his best, he was in the moment, and his best work as a director was when he would provoke the actors to explore and thereby find something. All my most delicious memories of working with him came from those actions. I can think of ones that weren't as delicious, when he didn't feel as free. It would depend on the play or the mood or the cast.
>
> He had two kinds of actors he could work really well with: those who wanted to do his very bidding; and those he could throw provocations at and who would respond in a way on which he could build. He never sat me down and analyzed the text. He would never block me. It would always be fluid until he set it, and then he would be incredibly rigorous.
>
> *Twelfth Night* frustrated him more, although he and I had a great collaboration on that. He didn't know what to do with me as a 24-year old Feste, and his last Feste had been Bill Hutt. But he knew that I loved jazz and that I was musical, so he started me off once by saying, 'What if he has Duke Ellington's mind?' He did let me try for about two weeks where I was a jazz Feste, and would do bop, bop, bop and scat. But both of us felt that this wasn't going anywhere because my Feste was very facile. Then one day I remember him coming up to me and saying, 'I think he shakes. Doesn't he? Doesn't he shake? Who's that terribly clever man who writes about black holes?' 'Stephen Hawking?' 'Yes.' Then he would walk away. That's how Robin would provoke me. He put in my mind an image of a man with a physical infirmity and a genius brain. So, I started looking at Lou Gehrig's disease and what that might do to a body.
>
> When we were singing the songs, he didn't want me singing them in my natural voice. He said, 'What if we pitched them from your head?' So, I used a higher pitch and microphone for 'When that I was a little boy.' It created a kind of ethereal ending, and we produced something that I can say to this day is one of the richest performances of which I am most proud.

Of course, Schultz also learned a great deal from acting with William Hutt in Phillips' extraordinary production of *King Lear* with the Young Company, in which he played Edgar:

> That, to me, was a remarkable lesson and a remarkable gift. I'll never forget [his Lear] seeing the mouse on his hand and giving it a bit of cheese. And how alive he was constantly! How he would find such specific reality for the text! Probably there was a time in his career when he himself would say he was guilty of making the *sound* of things. When he met Robin, that changed significantly, and when he played that Lear, it was a very special situation. I think that was Bill's greatest Lear—a great Lear in a really great production. The Lear that he did with Jordan Pettle later [produced] a gorgeous relationship. His Lear was that much older, but the production wasn't nearly as revelatory as in Robin's, where you had a great actor meeting a great director with a really strong company around him. That was the one I got to witness every day, and if I wasn't on stage, I would watch and listen to him.

Schultz also got to observe closely how Phillips interacted with Hutt:

> I remember one day in rehearsal—it might have been dress rehearsal. We were all sitting on stage as Robin would go around and give his notes. He'd look at Bill and seem confused about what to say, and he'd move on. He'd give notes to others, look at Bill, seem confused and move on. This went on and we could all feel something coming. Finally, he looked at Bill and said, 'Bill, darling, you *are* old,' and moved on.
>
> Robin knew that remark would cut Bill, but this was his genius. He knew that Bill wanted nothing more than to excel. He was a thoroughbred. Robin knew that the truly great have the ability to be tasteless. This was certainly true of Olivier, and Bill could be tasteless. We've all seen it, but when he was on top [of things], that greatness was unbelievable.

Schultz offers another instructive example of how Phillips handled Hutt with subtle shrewdness that the great actor used to his own advantage. In the same production when Hutt had to utter Lear's pathos-inducing lines "You think I'll weep./No, I'll not weep"

(2.4.282-283), Hutt had a tendency to milk the situation simply because he could. Hutt would never carry it to the point where an audience wasn't with him, but he would take an inordinate amount of time forcing pathos for Lear—until Robin gave him a strong note. What had lasted 34 seconds was swiftly cut down to a mere 8, teaching Schultz that even a great actor needs someone like Phillips to put a lid on unnecessary histrionics and self-indulgence. It wasn't that Phillips was against enlarging a moment; it was just his wisdom that such enlargement could be put to better use elsewhere in the play.

Schultz articulates the qualities necessary for a great actor. First is Self: "You need to know who you are, and where you came from. You need to have voice, the mind, the sexuality, and understanding of your gender." The second is Source: "How deeply do I understand the text? And in Shakespeare, this is really important. You have to understand it on so many levels: intellectually, structurally, theatrically, and emotionally. Then down below, we have two others. One is awareness of and responsibility to the audience. In there I would put taste and communication. And the fourth is the Other." He expounds:

> The Other is whom am I on stage with? Who am I working with as my designer, my director, my fellow actors? Where do I fit inside this multi-bodied organization that will create not only the show but my performance? I can't do it on my own.
>
> For some actors, some strings are tighter than others. Bill is the first actor I've ever worked with who sits right in the middle in his relationship to the audience, and his relationship to others on stage. Never have I worked with anyone more generous than William Hutt. He knew who he was, he had the facility, and he understood the text profoundly. Bill had all of those four qualities. Robin understood that too. Robin was the quintessential director; Bill was the quintessential actor.

Schultz's own acting (especially in Shakespeare) can be as rugged, muscular, and agile, but it is also capable of extraordinary grace notes of soft vulnerability. It gained immensely in quality from Phillips' rehearsal methods. When he eventually got to perform Hamlet (under Joseph Ziegler's direction) at Soulpepper, he gave a performance that was compulsively clear without being superficial or hollow. The outline of the performance was rugged and muscular; its details often sharp and coloured by an emotionality that felt like a flagellant. There were some crude brushstrokes at times, and moments (especially in Act 5) when his stamina flagged, but he had the right sadness, the right irony, and the right anger. Physically, he loomed large, powerful hands at his side, his bearded face looking darkly leonine, his long legs moving in easy strides, his baritone voice taking the soliloquies swiftly.

He acted on and through the lines, rather than over or under them. His first soliloquy ("O, that this too, too solid flesh would melt") was played directly to the audience as a dramatic aside, bleeding passion. He was smarter than Claudius and the interchangeable spies Rosencrantz and Guildenstern, and his choleric disillusionment with Ophelia registered in a voice that sounded like an anvil receiving heavy hammer blows. He was altogether a mocking and self-mocking prince, intimating something dying within himself. He was a man who had lost faith in others and even in himself. He seemed to see Gertrude and Ophelia in two dimensions—the way he seemed to view others. Perhaps he was so burdened by his avenging mission that they appeared to him like figures in a dream to whom he could not connect.

Intellectually agile but neurotic, his Hamlet demonstrated the actor's talent to explore questions in an unpredictable way. It was a clearly spoken, clearly thought, clearly felt interpretation, but it was evident that this Prince was a questioning being, his most famous soliloquy ("To be or not to be") sounding slightly pedantic. Reacting to my use of the word "pedantic," Schultz explained his motive and method:

Why Hamlet was revolutionary can be summed up in the question mark. We know that Shakespeare will have read William Cornwallis' essays in 1598 or 1599, when he was writing this play. The thing that separates Hamlet from anyone who's come before is the same quality that happens in a Montaigne essay or in a Cornwallis: essay as questions. It's about questions and the journey towards answers. The mistake that we make too often and, in particular, with Hamlet is making soliloquies statements of emotional fact when they need to be explorations of a given problem.

You look at how many question marks are in his soliloquies—an extraordinary number. 'To be or not to be, that is the question.' It is not the 'is' that is important. It's not the answer; it's the fact of the question. When he says 'Whether 'tis nobler in the mind to suffer / The slings and arrows of outrageous fortune,/Or to take arms against a sea of troubles,/And by opposing, end them. To die, to sleep—/No more, and by a sleep to say we end/The heart-ache and the thousand natural shocks/That flesh is heir to; 'tis a consummation/Devoutly to be wish'd. To die, to sleep—/To sleep, perchance to dream—ay, there's the rub.' et cetera. to the end of 'With this regard their currents turn awry,/And lose the name of action' (3.1.55-87). It's an epiphany, and it needs to demand that the audience come with us because it's only by the end that I am going to understand the metaphor of the eddy.

Conscience is the only thing that makes cowards, not of me, but of all of us. 'And thus the native hue of resolution/Is sicklied o'er with the pale cast of thought,/And enterprises of great pitch and moment/With this regard their currents turn awry,/And lose the name of action.' It's not until then that he understands what's going on—as opposed to a recitation. As Hamlet, I don't know when that speech starts what's going on. I have to figure out why I can't do this thing. What is it? It's not laid out as poetry. It's someone saying, "Think this through, people, and think it through with me." It's pedantic to himself. He's actually in the process of learning (as he's thinking aloud with you) why he is where he is. And when I did it, every time was different. So, what Joe [Ziegler, the director] encouraged me to do—Joe having played it himself—was to think that stuff aloud, and joining you (in the audience) in thinking this through.

I had an Armenian woman from Egypt who met me on the subway and said, "Thank you so much. I don't know why you chose to, but I want to thank you for choosing me to help you in your soliloquies. I've never been so engaged.' She thought I had picked her out of the audience to go through them with me. I'm not saying that happened that way every night or that everyone felt that way, but I was very pleased to hear that because we made a concerted effort to ensure

that the speeches never became set. When they become set, they lose
the name of action.

Schultz's Hamlet expressed the interiority and consciousness of the
Prince, in accord with Marjorie Garber's essay on the play and this
soliloquy in particular. Noting how the speech is "almost entirely
composed of questions, conditionals, infinitives, and passive con-
structions" (Garber 2005: 502), Garber reads the speech as one that
"has come to define modernity and modern self-consciousness, the
birth, in effect, of modern subjectivity itself" (Garber 475). She
explains how it draws a vivid picture of an anguished mental process: "The diction—the single string of relentless monosyllables, the
repetition of the infinitive 'to be'—draws a verbal picture of the
anguish of thought. And this almost unbearable moment of full
consciousness—*too* full consciousness—is what we think of as the
condition and the tragedy of modernity" (Garber 475).

But just as significant as the diction, verbal style, rhythm, and
tone, is Hamlet's relationship to an audience—that in effect has
an intriguing dualism: actor to role, actor to audience. Hamlet
assumes an "antic disposition" with two notable features: "his mask
of modernity, his costume of the fool" (Garber 492), and "finds an
electric gaiety and release with the players." And both Prince and
play are from the first concerned with playing, with Shakespeare's
play itself offering its spectators "not only a series of nested plays,
but a series of nested audiences."

As Garber demonstrates, we can draw up a list of what an
audience at the play watches: the sentries observing the Ghost
(1.1); Claudius and Polonius hidden behind a curtain, watching Ophelia "loosed" to Hamlet (3.1); Polonius spying on
Hamlet's interaction with Gertrude in her closet (3.4); Hamlet
watching *The Mousetrap* while keeping even closer watch on
Claudius' reactions (3.2); Hamlet eavesdropping on Claudius
praying (3.3); and Hamlet watching the funeral procession and

interment of Ophelia (5.1). The overall effect, it seems more than likely, is that an audience joins with Hamlet in seeing his world "peopled by pretenders" and in which "only those who know they are actors are 'real'" (Garber 498).

The psychological, epistemological, and metaphysical complexity of the play, in concert with a vivid interpretation of the title role, came through in the Schultz version. And the very best things in that interpretation owed at least as much to Phillips as to director Ziegler. In fact, having seen some of Schultz's best productions he has directed to date (*Of Human Bondage, Spoon River Anthology, The Time of Your Life, Death of a Salesman, Angels in America*), it is eminently clear that he has taken many of Phillips' teachings about directing, as well, to heart.

His productions have not elected elaborate décor or special technological effects; they gleam with ensemble work and some imaginative impressionism, as if (like his Stratford *guru*, Phillips, a directorial pointillist of the first order) he was an oil painter passionately dedicated to small detail, well-wrought texture, and accurate tone rather than huge canvases of thick impasto or inordinately quirky brushstrokes. His best productions never force significant moments, there is not any irrelevant ostentation, and the ensembles tend to be tightly knit and totally at the service of the particular play. And whether they are proscenium arch productions or environmental/immersive cases, they shed light on existential points of view, joining art and craft to philosophic wisdom.

Notes

[1] Our interview was conducted in a Soulpepper Administration office on April 24, 2017.

Ben Carlson as Petruchio in The Taming of the Shrew *(Stratford Festival, 2015)*.
(Photo: David Hou. Courtesy of the Stratford Festival)

Ben Carlson
Speedy Clarity for the Shakespearean Lift

Ever since his ne'er-do-well Eustace in St. John Hankin's *Return of the Prodigal* at the Shaw Festival in 2002, Ben Carlson has proved himself to be one of the fastest speakers of prose and verse anywhere in the English-language theatre world. He is also one of the clearest in enunciation, ensuring that the lines carry their implicit meaning with utter clarity. In Shaw's *Man and Superman* at the Shaw Festival in 2004, his John Tanner (a modern Don Juan ironically reconceived) was praised fulsomely by normally acerbic John Simon in *New York* magazine: "Long and convoluted speeches are tossed off with machine-gun speed and bull's-eye precision, with unparalleled elocution and infectious humor, not to mention Carlson's immaculate timing and endearingly boyish looks." Simon claimed: "It was a performance to chortlingly remember one's entire life, however long."

Carlson would five years later toss off Oscar Wilde's epigrams as John Worthing in *The Importance of Being Earnest* at the Stratford Festival with silken aplomb, sounding wonderfully natural while being comically priggish yet charming, and suggesting that he was the sanest character (as Charles Isherwood described in his *New York Times* review) in a "decorous madhouse, the lone character in the play whose feet are on the ground, at least intermittently." And he did so in the distinguished company of Brian Bedford (no mean speaker himself) in outrageously flamboyant cross-dress as Lady Bracknell.

But celerity and fluency of speech are not Carlson's only acting virtue. He has a clear-headed, unsentimental perspective on roles, whether these be amoral Charteris (*The Philanderer*), coldly calculating yet humane Octavius Caesar (*Antony and Cleopatra*), urbane but neurotically distempered, astral bigamist Charles Condomine (*Blithe Spirit*), or dangerously cynical Cusins (*Major Barbara*). As Moliere's Alceste, that relentlessly unflattering eponymous misanthrope, he balanced comedy on the edge of heartbreak, using his superb sophistication of speech and the character's phlegmatic temperament to create romantic passion before discovering painfully that "reason doesn't rule in love."

More recently, as De Flores in *The Changeling*, the facially disfigured man who seduces Beatrice ("the deed's creature") who has recruited him to murder her fiancé, he showed a wary suspicion evolving into an ecstasy of carnal expectation and then into sheer psychosexual bravado, chilling audiences merely with his silences.

No wonder Carlson is a border-crosser, in demand not only in Canada but in the United States as well, particularly in Chicago, where he and his actress-wife Deborah Hay have been viewed as Canadian Lunts, though their acting (individually or combined) is never Old-School or as genteel as that famous American couple's. Reviewing the couple in a 2012 radically updated version of *The Misanthrope*, Chris Jones of the *Chicago Tribune* wrote: "He has total ease with language of any stripe and yet always conveys a contemporary insouciance at the same time. Few can match him. Hay, meanwhile, is a charmer with a very un-Canadian sting in her tail—and in her voice box, which emits a great boom whenever she needs to call some miscreant soul to order or land a laugh."

On November 19, 2017, I got to interview Carlson (bearded at the time) at the Toronto Reference Library and experienced his rapid volubility directly in conversation. He is not one to mince words about virtually any subject that intersects with his life, though in this case the subject was almost always theatre. Born to Les Carlson (from South Dakota, who had come to Canada to marry, after having served in Korea) and Patricia Hamilton (from Saskatchewan, who had received her acting training at Carnegie Tech), he inherited but resisted the acting gene. His parents divorced when he was 2, so he grew up alternating between their separate households and theatrical ventures.

When he was fourteen, his mother urged: "Come into the TV room, I want you to watch something." However, he was immersed in a comic book, so did not want to bother. "I want you to watch twenty minutes of *King Lear*, with Laurence Olivier. This is one of the greatest actors alive, and this is one of the greatest plays." He reluctantly agreed to watch twenty minutes but ended up watching the entire production.

"I certainly didn't understand everything, but I caught the gist of it, and it was completely captivating." He was hooked and subsequently started reading and watching anything he could of Shakespeare. (Years later, he would agree with Tony van Bridge's dictum: "You don't choose the theatre; it chooses you!") At one point, at the age of 20, he memorized all of Hotspur "just for fun—just because it seemed like a good idea," even though he never got to play the role.

After he graduated from Leaside High School, he studied music at McGill University in Montreal, splitting his time between classical and jazz performance, doing the best he could to keep up on both of these on the double bass, but after two years, he found himself seeking out theatre wherever he could find it in Montreal, and knew that he wanted to make the transition to study acting. He enrolled at the George Brown Theatre School, where his voice teacher was Susan Stackhouse, his movement coach Leslie French, and where Paul Lampert, Sharry Flett, Denise Ferguson, and Rodger Barton conducted him in scene study.

Barton led "a really intensive study" on controversial British playwright Howard Barker, once described as a foe of literalness and a champion of imagination. And it is easy to see why Barker's provocative perspective on theatre would appeal to Carlson, who delights in upsetting traditionalists. What did his teachers think of him? "They kept their cards pretty close to their chests, and understandably so. I was always smart, but that is sometimes a detriment, particularly in the initial stages of actually just being present on the stage. Intelligence can be a liability. It was for me for awhile. And my mom always says: 'It's a lifetime study.' I haven't finished studying."

His acting class had thirty people, but he thinks he could be the only one who is still working consistently. "But that's the story of the business," he adds, revealing how a week ago, a 45-year-old colleague who was a year below him at George Brown, had quit the business at 30, after becoming a father and taking a year off because he realized: "Oh, my goodness, I'm happy." Carlson thinks that "basically a lot of people stick it out till they're 30 or 35 years old, and then they feel they've had enough rejection and decide to choose another career."

He himself never entertained any romantic or unrealistic ideas about acting. He knew from his parents' experiences that theatre "is brutally difficult, very unforgiving, and filled with rejection and heartbreak. That's why my parents encouraged me not to be an actor—until I showed real interest—even before aptitude. When I showed a little aptitude, they were very relieved." Did they see all his shows? "Yeah, for a very long time they did, until I was working as much as they were, and then they said: 'Okay, maybe we can miss the odd show. We don't need to see everything he does.'"

In response to my question whether they were candid or diplomatic in their reactions to his acting, he says: "One of the benefits of being the next generation of actor is that you get a lot of what some people won't tell you. I certainly had fewer illusions going into the business than a lot of people in my peer group had. [My parents] were intelligent, sensitive people, and the big thing is that they had good timing. They were just smart that way."

His mother demonstrated this when Ben was singing the part of Amahl in Gian Carlo Menotti's one-act opera *Amahl and the Night Visitors* for the Canadian Children's Opera Company (affiliated with the Canadian Opera Company).[1] There was a point where Amahl, who is handicapped, plays the flute, and young Ben danced and mimed playing the flute as much as the character's disability allowed. His mother remarked after the performance: "That was pretty good, but I wonder what it would really be like if you were actually playing that flute." Not wanting to hear that, her son complained: "Oh, mom what do you mean? What are you talking about?" However, the next day, he was much more contained in his acting, causing his mother to comment: "Yeah, that was much better."

Carlson's musical training has been of real benefit to him in some stage roles, such as Feste in Des McAnuff's *Twelfth Night* at Stratford in 2011. Although rather young for the role that is usually played by a much older actor, Carlson (in a salt-and-pepper wig) sang the ballads with rare style and musicality, expressing through his own innate lyricism the comedy's anxieties, follies, and resolutions. I ask if a good actor is also someone who has a musical voice, to which he replies:

> Well, that would certainly be true of Laurence Olivier. It seems to be an older concept. I think I understand why. As film and television have taken over and our acting style has changed—especially with regard to American film and television—there's a kind of realism that is associated with a lack of musicality. I think it's a trap. I think it's a dead end because I don't think the technical question of the music of the text or the music of the poetry is incompatible with so-called realism or, even worse word, naturalism. They go hand in hand. One benefits from the other. Ultimately, it's all about storytelling.

So, Carlson would approve of anything that helps the storytelling. "That usually is a freedom of expression, which is maybe a better word than musicality of expression because if you can have the freedom to use your voice, you at least will be a lot farther towards actually embodying the monumental, incredible works of many playwrights, including William Shakespeare."

When questioned about the distinction between verse speaking and verse acting, Carlson believes one incorporates the other because one is "at the service of the other. But verse acting is just acting. The difference is that you're speaking verse. You should know how to handle verse. But if you're not speaking verse, what are you speaking? Prose? Well, you should know how to handle prose. So, there's not much of a difference." But isn't there a greater technical challenge to handling verse? He acknowledges the probability:

> I guess *that* is the difference. There is a challenge to it because it is poetry, and because you have to put it into context. What am I doing? Why is it poetry? What is he getting at? How can I present this in a way so it doesn't sound like a poem but, rather, like dramatic action so as to keep people interested, without my having to ignore the music of the poetry? I don't think it's actually a hard job, but it's a job that needs to be addressed. You could say it's a hard-enough job that you can spend your whole life doing, but that's just acting. You spend your whole life acting. It's a lifelong pursuit.

Carlson's first professional Shakespearean role came after his second year at George Brown when he played Demetrius in *A Midsummer Night's Dream* for the short-lived Ottawa Shakespeare Festival. It was performed in a tent, where the set was simply sand and a few rocks, but the simplicity appealed to him, as did the director, Brigid Panet from RADA, later the author of *Essential Acting*, a practical handbook for actors, teachers, and directors. "Brigid was very good at making it active," making sure that he, who "could sit in the poetry and just *bathe* in it," did not indulge himself at merely the sound of it. She challenged: "What's your action? What are you doing?" It was her way of getting him to make his acting real and not mannered.

After he graduated from George Brown, Carlson freelanced, then joined the Shaw Festival company in 1995 and stayed for 11 consecutive years, making headlines in a number of roles. Before he transitioned to the Stratford Festival, he played Hamlet at the Chicago Shakespeare Theater in 2006, under the direction of Terry Hands (who had run the Royal Shakespeare Company for 13 years).

"They had a director before they had a Hamlet—which was the case both times I did the part. I auditioned for him, not thinking I would get it but thinking it would be good to make an association with Terry Hands." He had prepared the "To be or not to be" soliloquy and Hamlet's address to the Players as his audition pieces. He had thought that the first selection "would probably be professional suicide on many occasions," but he said to Hands: "Clearly if you're going to consider me for this role, at some point I am going to have to speak these words, so I thought why not have a look at this one."

"That's very interesting," Hands replied. "Why don't you give it a go?" He did, and then Hands made him do it faster. Next came the "Speak the speech, I pray you …" that Hands made him repeat extremely quickly, as if to test his speed and clarity of enunciation and thought. He got the part in a production that was "very bare bones in terms of set" (at one point, just a flat with virtually a hand-drawn mountain on it), in costuming that was essentially Edwardian. Carlson felt the rehearsal period for him was like painting a Jackson Pollock. "I was basically throwing everything at the wall and seeing how it would jell and stick. It was absolutely an exhausting thing to do."

He knew that he was in control of certain aspects of the performance and he knew he would get through the night and would still be standing. But it took him a long time to get to that point of security. The production, like Carlson, raced through the text. Charles Isherwood of the *New York Times* noted: "A Canadian actor with 20 productions at Canada's Shaw Festival behind him, Mr. Carlson is superbly trained, so at ease with Shakespeare's language that at times he rattles through the verse with such speed that there isn't time to absorb any nuance." However, Isherwood also noted: "Even when Mr. Carlson leaves us straining to catch up, his Hamlet is clearly the smartest guy in the room." So, fluency was aligned to speed of language and intellectual wit—enough to win the actor a Joseph Jefferson Award for Best Actor that season.

Thinking back to that production, Carlson recalls he was a melancholy prince "but in the sense of the word 'crazy.' I am still of the opinion that while flirting with madness, he decides to go mad." What was his director's guiding concept? "I don't know if he had a guiding concept, but he certainly did have a guiding hand. He was certainly very good with text. He had never directed the play before in English. He had directed it in French at the Comédie Française, but he had only given it to other directors while he was running the RSC. He knew all the lines, and could quote them to you and would, if you got them wrong. He was very helpful to me in textual and verse analysis."

Did the director keep the lid on him or allow him to enlarge his acting? "He was very encouraging. At a certain point he said: 'It's all there. Now you must be Hamlet. You've done the work, now you must let the work go and be flamboyant, take the centre of the stage.' That was very helpful because Hamlet can be a terrifically lonely part, and terrible and scary to play. He helped me feel somehow that I was supported."

He got his second chance at the role at Stratford two years later, under the direction of Adrian Noble, one of the world's leading stage directors, and former Artistic Director of the Royal Shakespeare Company (1991-2003). On this occasion, he had more time to put his characterization together piece by piece: "I had the luxury of knowing the part and the lines, and not having to feel that I was having to make decisions all the time. Those parts [like Hamlet] are great to play more than once because there's a certain amount of terror involved the first time, and slightly less the second."

One of his big consolations was his already having worked with David Leyshon (Rosencrantz) and Patrick McManus (Guildenstern) at the Shaw Festival, and his Stratford Horatio was none other than Tom Rooney, the actor who had done Hamlet in 2004 at the National Arts Centre in Ottawa, with Carlson playing Horatio. "So, we actually got to do Hamlet and Horatio for each other, which is great because when you play Hamlet, you need to have a Horatio that you feel close to. Horatio is his only friend, and you need to be able to look into his eyes and have him look back at you."

Is it more beneficial to be working with actors you've already worked with? "Yes, it absolutely is. When I did it in Chicago, I knew nobody there, except Melissa Veal, the wigs lady, who is now back at Stratford as Co-ordinator of the Birmingham Conservatory. You develop a shorthand with everybody—designers, directors, and certainly fellow actors. That's one of the reasons I stayed at the Shaw for so long because I got to know those actors intimately and they knew me. I'm all for repertory companies. It's great training."

What makes a great Hamlet? Carlson answers: "A lot of endurance, a really good mouth [he laughs], musculature, which is weird because the part is one of an intellectual. He is definitely an intellectual. It does not help to be stupid. I think it probably helps to be quite smart. He doesn't hesitate when he thinks he has Claudius behind the arras. He just makes a huge mistake."

Carlson's prince was a man smart enough to know the world and to be apprehensive of it. Unafraid to speak his mind, he understood himself, though not necessarily understanding his motivation or blind spot. He saw through Gertrude, Claudius, Rosencrantz and Guildenstern, Polonius, and even Ophelia. He saw through himself but with such rue that he could be ironic about it. A convincing scholar, hands buried deep in pockets, face registering introspection and some disgust at the rotten state of Denmark, he exercised a sardonic humour, his comic irony sometimes coming in unexpected places—one being Claudius's prayer scene.

In the graveyard scene, where he held Yorick's skull high aloft, he reflected on man's mortality with sober gravity. It is possible that in his offstage remarks about Hamlet's reasoning, Carlson is over emphasizing the prince's intellect. He wouldn't be the only actor to do so. Sir John Gielgud (once considered the greatest Hamlet of his time) played the Prince as one marked by sharp intelligence, curbing emotions, even fear and apprehension, though not to the extent that he was *without* passion. Paraphrasing this particular review of one of Gielgud's Hamlets,[2] Anthony B. Dawson explains that "Hamlet's delay is the result not of fear, nor of weakness, but of intelligence: he knows the *futility* of action, he has read and assessed the situation, plumbed its depths. Had he been less intelligent, he would have acted" (Dawson 104).

Another point of contention for critics and actors alike is the issue of madness. Is Hamlet mad? Dawson expounds: "The old questions about the extent of Hamlet's madness have generated a wide range of answers; audiences have been witness on the one hand to the sanest and stateliest Hamlets (like John Phillip Kemble's or Ben Kingsley's) and on the other to the most mercurial and even demented (like Kean's or Pryce's)," whereas "[Michael] Penington rendered Hamlet's madness ambiguous, a sort of comment on the whole critical tradition. Was it a theatrical ruse, or was it genuine?" (Dawson 167-68).

Carlson is reluctant to expand on the subject: "I don't want to say too much because it's almost ten years since I did it, and any answer I give would be glib. I think there's so much at work in the man that to say he's sane at this moment or crazy at that moment doesn't actually inform my appreciation of the part." He is unable to provide a definitive explanation of how his interpretation of the role changed.

> I know it changed, and it changed a lot in a physical way because of the demands of the spaces that were so different. There were a couple of things that were probably constraints, and the biggest thing is they changed entirely in terms of whom I was acting with. They were all different actors, and they brought different energies, so I tried to respond to the energies that were brought. You can make all the decisions that you want about a character. It doesn't matter until you get in the room with the other actors because real acting happens between two actors and the audience—in the shared space between them.

Our conversation turns to the subject of acting philosophy, and I quote Kevin Kline on this topic: "The author of the play is Shakespeare, but the actor has to own the character he is playing. Olivier aptly said you marry yourself to the character" (Maher 4). This remark is just common sense to Carlson, who is adamant about never taking Shakespeare for granted simply because he was Shakespeare, the world's greatest playwright. He recalls commenting to director Peter Hinton while they were rehearsing *The Taming of the Shrew*: "You know, Peter, if we just comfort ourselves with the knowledge that this play is by William Shakespeare and therefore it will take care of everything, we're fucked." Hinton agreed: "You know, you're absolutely right!"

Carlson recognizes that the plays are superb, but it is important not to take them for granted. "Someone once remarked to me that it's not good enough to take the character and collapse it into yourself. What you must do is look for the character and then bring yourself into it to inhabit it, to look up and out, not to contract it but to expand out and into it. Stanislavsky talks about the lift. In Shakespeare that lift is very important." I ask if that lift is achieved primarily through the language.

> You could say that because it's verse. The funny thing is that even within the verse there are great long passages that are entirely banal, as in the staccato opening of *Hamlet*. The mood is entirely tense because what we don't know (if we don't know the play) is that there's a bloody ghost on the ramparts. There's something walking from beyond the dead. Another example is from *King Lear*: 'I thought the King had more affected the Duke of Albany than Cornwall.' 'It did always seem so to us' (1.1.1-3). They're talking about immensely important things in a very banal way. That's not an accident.
>
> So, it is important that the language be understood. At the same time, you can't be so lifted that the people stop listening to you. I don't believe that Shakespeare wrote in verse in order to heighten his own poetry. I think he wrote verse in order to make poetry more accessible and more like everyday speech. That's why he wrote plays and not books.

Robin Phillips used to say that an actor has to say the lines as if there aren't enough words in a long speech, that there is much more to say. "Of course," concurs Carlson, "because ultimately the words are only there because of what you need." But I wonder how an actor handles big passages of declamation or expository verse in a way that would make them interesting. "On a case by case basis," insists Carlson. "It always depends on the situation, the structure of the scene, the character. It depends on a million things." Does he work in units of thought?

> Well, sure, of course, but those units of thought are always in service to the character arc, and the character arc is always in service to the

arc of the play—the spine of the play—what the play is trying to do. I believe in all that kind of work: the analysis of what a play is actually about. I don't think there's a single answer but you should have some inkling as to what the playwright is trying to get at. Sometimes that is very hard with Shakespeare because Shakespeare disguises himself. He keeps himself in the background. His characters are more important than he is, or so you might believe when you see Hamlet or when you see Falstaff or when you see Macbeth. The characters are so strong, they take on lives of their own and you forget that there is a play-wright. There are not too many playwrights that are that good.

Hamlet is a problem play for anyone who is unwilling to engage with Shakespeare's unique sensibility and genius, or with the Prince's apparent inconsistencies and ambivalences. But there are other Shakespearean plays that are considered problem plays for other reasons. One such is *The Merchant of Venice* because of sensitivity to the presence of anti-Semitism in the story; another is *The Taming of the Shrew* because of Petruchio's brutally abusive tactics deployed to "tame" Katherina. Carlson identifies the problem more in the mind of the audience or critic than in the play itself:

I certainly understand why it's considered tricky. I've always wanted to play Petruchio, particularly if I had a great Kate. I think the play is fantastic. It's an absolutely extraordinary piece of writing from his early period, so much of which is presentational. *Richard III* is a great example. *Titus Andronicus* and all the early plays are touch and go. I'm not crazy about *The Two Gentlemen of Verona* or *Henry VI, Part 1*. There are some plays I could miss, but not *Shrew*, which is fantastic because it's all action from the very beginning. Even the stuff that's goofy—and there's clown, *buffo, commedia*, and stock character types—and there's this crazy love story in the heart of that. Yes, it's a problem because it exists in a world where women have no agency. Therefore, some people think the play is a reactionary piece of pre-feminist feminism, and some say it's a misogynistic piece of garbage. It's none of those things, in my opinion. It is an example of human behaviour, and a great one of how a woman attempts to survive and be herself in this world.

You can say that world is different from our world, but is it really? We are attempting to make our world different but I don't know that

> it is all that different. Anyway, it's one of the proudest things I ever
> got to do, and particularly because I got to do it with Deborah [Hay].

There is a scholarly view that perception is a central factor in this play, as well as performance. In the Induction, which features a joke played on the drunken tinker, Christopher Sly, one of the key words of the Lord is "persuade": "Persuade him that he hath been lunatic" (1.63). Bartholomew (a page) impersonates Sly's wife, and Sly is to be told that he has slept and dreamed for fifteen years. As Marjorie Garber explains, the play proper, is structured as "a series of performances within performances, or plays-within-the play, from the Induction to the masquerades of Bianca's suitors to Kate's shrewishness to Petruchio's devices. The final, much-debated scene in which Kate delivers her speech about women's obedience is itself a performance, staged—at Petruchio's request and command—for an onstage audience of husbands and fathers, who are watching the responses of their wives and daughters" (Garber 60).

After informal remarks to the audience by Tom Rooney in pumpkin pants for his role as Tranio, broaching the topic of perception and performance, Chris Abraham's Stratford production in 2015 opened with Deborah Hay introducing a 17th century song, "A Virgin's Meditation" by Thomas D'Urfey, unfolding from the perspective of a young woman preparing to leave her father's house and contemplating the mystery of married life that lies before her. It begins as follows:

> A Virgin's Life who would be leaving,
> Free from Care and fond Desire;
> Ne'er deceiv'd, nor e'er deceiving,
> Loving none, yet all inspire.
> We sit above and Knot the live-long Day,
> A thousand pretty harmless things we say;
> But not one Word of Wedlock's frightful Noose,
> For fear we chance to think what we must lose.

This concert-like opening was initially unsettling for Carlson:

> When we first approached it, I was very cynical because I didn't actually think that a song at the beginning of the play would be believed, but as we rehearsed it and performed it, I came around to quite liking it because it seemed to me that as well as making an effective bridge to our version of Christopher Sly, it also actively raised the question of perception. Tom Rooney as himself came out and made a little speech about this, so it was thematic and practical at the same time.
>
> I'll also confess that there's a little part of me that enjoys anything that's going to piss the purists off. Generally, it was a fairly traditional production. There wasn't a whole lot in it that you could say was taken out of context.

His director, Chris Abraham, was interested in the love story at the centre, recognizing that Shakespeare believed that Kate wins her self in the play: "Kate's true self is revealed to her, and I think that's a contentious position, given the mechanism through which she encounters herself, such as the violence and abuse." The play is chiefly remembered for the "taming" plot, Petruchio's boldly cynical courtship (where he is, in fact, a shrew in the word's original historical connotation of rascal or a railing, scold), and his "taming" of Kate. Carlson agrees: "It's clear to me that he is far more shrewish than she is."

Garber claims that Shakespeare's later bantering lovers (Beatrice and Benedick; Hotspur and Lady Percy) owe much to Petruchio and Kate. She goes even further, asserting that the "extended conversation, the first between this high-spirited pair, displays both their wittiness and their uncanny 'modernity'—which is to say, the heritage of wrangling courtship that would extend, through Shakespeare and Restoration comedy to the plays and films of the twentieth and twenty-first centuries" (Garber 62).

The role of Petruchio is full of twists and leaps, and that of Kate is also marked by surprising emotional transitions. An actor has to feel that the situations the pair are in have been developed in ways that make sense psychologically and emotionally. English actor Michael Siberry (who played Petruchio in Gale Edwards' production at the RSC in 1995) regards Petruchio as "someone who never explains himself: he may tell you what he is doing, but he won't explain why. There are few indications of motivation, little to tell you whether to play it this way or that. The irony is that, as Petruchio, you have an awful lot to say, but sometimes you feel you're not actually saying very much" (Smallwood *Players* 4, 45).

Carlson disagrees vehemently, pointing first to Petruchio's "Thus have I politicly begun my reign/And 'tis my hope to end successfully" (4.1.188-89). In this speech, the character declares very clearly what he intends to do, although Carlson admits that while Petruchio knows everything he is doing, he may not know why he's doing it. However, this anomaly does not raise a problem for motivation. Not everyone knows the precise reason for every action: "Nobody actually knows why they do everything that they do. You're responding to things as they happen, without necessarily knowing what is working on you. I think that Petruchio is a good example of that. He's just doing what he thinks is the best he can."

Although Petruchio starts off by performing actions for himself and his own gain, an actor who plays the role needs to show how the character discovers love. Carlson was very concerned that the interpretation not be about a man who beats up on his wife; his real-life wife, Deborah Hay, (Kate) was concerned that the play not be about a woman who was merely a shrew. Both performers were relieved to have a director who was really interested in psychology and exploring why people do what they do.

I ask Carlson when Petruchio first take Kate seriously. "I would say not until the very end," he suggests. "It's either there or, strangely enough, when it looks like she is capitulating in the 'sun' or 'moon' sections." His point is a good one, because by Act 4, Scene 5 Kate has figured out what Petruchio's mood is and how she will adapt and change to this mood. So, she "is willing to call the sun the moon, and the moon the sun, according to his whim. Direct contradiction, she sees, is not the way to deal with him: 'be it moon, or sun, or what you please,/And if you please to call it a rush-candle/Henceforth I vow it shall be so for me. (4.5.13-15)'" (Garber 64).

So, who really tames whom? In the same scene, as revealed in the filmed DVD version of the production (which Chris Abraham prefers to the stage version because he felt it was easier to zero in on a more nuanced relationship between Kate and Petruchio), Deborah Hay's Kate does many things with her face. She laughs in a half hysterical recognition of Petruchio's gratuitous will, while he comes to a serious recognition of a change in her, but he tests her again.

In the last act, she makes a lot of the scene where he bids her kiss him. She's not ashamed to kiss him, but she is embarrassed. Carlson reacts to her as if hurt by what she says, but then remembering the severe trial he put her through, he reverts to his authoritarian self. She finally yields but registers shyness rather than anger, compliance rather than defiance, and tenderness rather than toughness. Her face shows conflicting emotions and thoughts. And then Petruchio becomes surprisingly tender on "Come, my sweet Kate:/Better once than never, for never too late" (5.1.149-50).

Carlson's Petruchio is moved at the end when she offers her hand to him, daring him to accept her as an equal, before grabbing him for a kiss. This returns the discussion to identifying who really is the tamer and the tamed. Carlson sees the issue from a different angle:

> Do they tame each other to a point where they can live together and have a successful, happy union in this extraordinarily damaged world in which they live? Can they actually succeed as a couple? The indication is that they can. I get this from a play that is another

radical one by William Shakespeare. One of the problems of institutionalizing a man is that you forget that he's a radical. There's never a dull moment in his writing. You think of the late plays, when you think he has settled down. *The Winter's Tale*? That's a big, fat dramatic experiment. *The Tempest*, another huge dramatic experiment. *Cymbeline*. He was a maverick, and it's easy to forget that.[3]

Does Petruchio really mean it when he says to her: "'Tis the mind that makes the body rich" (4.3.172)? Carlson's reply is swift:

Absolutely, he means it. Why wouldn't he mean it? Like most characters (including Hamlet), he sees the world outside of himself but doesn't see himself. He needs guidance just as much as anybody. That's why he needs her—to complete each other, as so often is the case in Shakespearean comedy. I think it's always the case in Shakespearean comedy. One of his main themes is that man without woman is dangerous. The union is what keeps order and what civilizes us. It's not an accident that there are basically no women in *Timon of Athens*, that it is, basically, a completely male play. That world is very skewered because one half of the population doesn't exist in that world. I think you see that again and again in Shakespeare—that man needs woman to be civilized.

Responding to my question whether Kate is beaten into a *submission* or *recognition*, Carlson keeps an open mind: "Well, it's not for me to say because I never played the part. But my instinct is that she's not beaten into anything. She holds her own, and they wear each other down till they come to a mutual recognition or a mutual understanding. You could certainly interpret the play in a different way, but it would tell a very, very different story than one in which a happy marriage follows."

I maintain that many people who object to the "submission" scene do so because they have not entered Shakespeare's universe to begin with. "That's the first thing," Carlson agrees. "I also think that are some people who do not accurately live in this world of our own." He points to the wage discrepancy between men and women, and the suggestion from experts that in order for a solution to this problem of economic inequity, we may have to wait till the year 2045 or 2050—unless there's an actual revolution.

He adds: "The zeitgeist is here. Things are happening, but we don't live in a world where women are equal. I think people tell themselves that they are, but they are not. Women are not considered or treated as equals. And Shakespeare is examining a world in which women are not treated as equals, and he is asking the question: 'How does a strong-willed woman survive in such a world?'"

Carlson's point is sealed by the examples of Portia in *The Merchant of Venice*, who holds her own against any man (with or without her masculine disguise as a learned judge in the Trial scene), Rosalind in *As You Like It*, and Beatrice in *Much Ado About Nothing*. These female roles are fully dimensional, spirited, sexual, and written from somewhere inside the playwright, becoming worthy matches or even better for the male characters in their stories.

Carlson made a striking Benedick opposite Deborah Hay's Beatrice in Christopher Newton's version of the romantic comedy in the 2012 Stratford Festival season. "The least fantastical of all Shakespeare's comedies: no fairies, no forest, no separation of twins by tempest," points out Nicholas Hytner, who directed a London production starring Simon Russell Beale and Zoe Wanamaker as the warring pair at the heart of the romantic comedy:

> Beatrice and Benedick, like everyone in Shakespeare, are as much a revelation of their actors as they are of the playwright, who gives them far less to play with than you'd imagine after seeing a decent production. Benedick has 161 lines and Beatrice has 111. Hamlet has over 1,000, and that's still not enough for him to let us know all the stuff that an actor must decide for himself. The actors playing Beatrice and Benedick have to create a whole history for themselves, as the playwright says almost nothing about the origins of the palpable pain that they cause each other by being in each other's presence (Hytner 217).

Hytner declares that secret histories are "essential to actors' tools, never intended to be legible to an audience, but the foundations for suggestive, fully human performances" (218).

Being a married couple in real life helped Carlson and Hay, who enjoy a vibrant on-stage chemistry. Playing a professed cynic and misogynist, Carlson sketched a man who surprises himself by the passion beating secretly in his sceptical heart, while Hay's Beatrice revealed the hurt that has lain in her own heart of old. Hay was zany when it counted, sliding down a staircase when startled by gossip overheard about Benedick's ardour for her, but she revealed very effectively and touchingly Beatrice's "wild heart" after discovering his true feelings.

The similarities between Petruchio and Benedick were not lost on Carlson. For one thing, Benedick sees the world more clearly than he can see himself. As Carlson puts it to me: "He's certainly a person who does not understand the forces that are working on him, which all culminates, for me, in the moment when he actually tells her that he loves her, and never saw the consequence. That's just a brilliant piece of writing. Yes, he dated her years ago, but he can't stand her because he thinks she's an awful human being. He finds himself admitting to her and himself that he loves her more than anything in the world."

I point out that it's the same with her: She can't stand him yet finds herself in love with him. "Yes, and what's beautiful and moving about that story is that we know those people. We know who they are." Shakespeare sketches a man who is loyal to the army, his military comrades, and their particular male world, but he forces Benedick to choose between this world and one inhabited somewhat bitterly by Beatrice. So, it is a comedy that has light and dark areas, and there are two different romances and courtships: one between Hero and Claudio; the second involving apparent antagonists, whose names are ironic.

As Tina Packer points out, they mean "benediction" and "blessed." And as Packer explains, the first exchange between them, "witty though it is, allows the audience to know how powerful the attraction is between them, and leaves each lightly wounded" (Packer 147). But toward the end of the play, Benedick swears to Beatrice: "I will live in thy heart, die in thy lap, and be buried in thy eyes" (5.2.102-03). These are the words of a real lover, pulsating with eroticism, and seeming to predict a happy marriage because "both Beatrice and Benedick understand the ways of the world, and they put their love for each other into the enduring terrain of an ever-regenerative sexual/spiritual merging" (Packer 150).

"What is it like working with your own wife on stage?" I ask Carlson, who vouches for the experience:

> Luckily, we get along very well. What tends to happen is that we take the work home with us, and talk about it a lot—maybe sometimes to the point of its not being quite healthy. We do need to put the work away for a while, but mostly, I like working with her because she challenges me. If she doesn't agree with me, she'll let me know, and we can have a conversation about it. We can actually get quite heated, but it's not going to endanger either of our performances or our working relationship or the play. It's fluid. We are willing to challenge each other.

Does a similar dynamic of challenge and compromise function, as well, with a director whose concept he rejects? Carlson replies that it's a question of a "case-by-case scenario." He expands on the subject:

> Sometimes it's not so much fun being an actor. Sometimes you're put in a position where you're doing things that you don't agree with. Hopefully, you can try and make them your own, and if you have a corner to fight, you can fight it. I've been in both situations. I've absolutely stood my ground, and I've also been in a position where I've compromised. And compromise is important. There is a hierarchy in the theatre: It is not a democracy. However, nobody is making enough

money for it to be worthwhile to just capitulate to somebody who says: 'You just do what I say. Do it because I'm the boss.'

I can probably count the number of times on one hand where I've actually wanted to say to somebody: 'You know what, I don't think this is worth if for me anymore.' Only once have I actually done that, but it's bound to happen in any business where people come into conflict and explosions are going to happen. It comes with the territory.

Notes

[1] One of the stars of this production was a young tenor named Ben Heppner, who was already in the COC and who would become one of the great opera singers of his time.

[2] Sir John Gielgud played Hamlet on stage several times in the course of his long, distinguished career. His first attempt at the role was in 1930, followed by a second in 1934, then a New York version in 1936-37, a Lyceum run in 1939 (repeated in Kronberg Castle, Elsinore the same year), another version in 1944, and an ENSA tour to India and the Far East with the role in 1945. Multiple versions allowed him to keep refining or altering his interpretation, but, judging from the overall critical reception to his various Hamlets, it is fair to say that his 1930 Hamlet was compromised by his serving as his own director. Though the production ran for four and a half months and 155 performances—the longest run since Henry Irving's in 1874—and then toured for five weeks, some critics felt his performance to be "subdued," "cold," or tending towards an elocution that spoke the speeches "too trippingly." Other critics praised it for a "relentless insight and psycho-analytical profoundness," and for making Hamlet's thoughts seem new-minted. The Broadway Hamlet was adjudged to be lacking the demoniacal humour and thrilling theatricality that John Barrymore's had had, but at least one critic recognized that Gielgud's prince had "quite all the intellectuality of Forbes-Robertson's, and all the sardonic force and feeling that were Barrymore's" (Qtd. from *Gielgud (A Theatrical Life 1904-2000)* by Jonathan Croall.).

[3] English director Michael Bogdanov would concur with this view of Shakespeare as a maverick: "We easily forget that Shakespeare was writing in a very dangerous era. The two factions [Elizabethan and Jacobean] were ranged solidly against each other and he had to walk a very precarious tightrope to avoid being arrested or worse. People tend to forget that when they say he was some kind of Elizabethan propagandist. They don't look for the hidden insurrection in Shakespeare, which is there, undercover, all the time" (Qtd. in Cook 1989: 87-88).

Moya O'Connell as Lady Macbeth (Bard on the Beach, Vancouver, 2018)
(Photo: Tim Matheson. Courtesy of Bard on the Beach)

Moya O'Connell
Living the Human, Inside of It

She is married into a family of celebrated Canadian actors, musicians, and directors. Her husband, Torquil Campbell, is a popular musician, and a formidable actor (*True Crime*), whose mother, Moira Wylie, directed him as Malcolm and her as one of the Weird Sisters and Lady Macduff in *Macbeth* for Bard on the Beach in 2004. Her brother-in-law, Benedict Campbell (whose mother was Ann Casson), is one of the most brilliant Canadian stage actors, and her late father-in-law, Douglas Campbell (father to both Ben and Torquil),[1] was one of the pioneers of Canadian classical theatre, having been a major player at the Stratford Festival and the founder of the Canadian Players, a touring troupe that took the classics as far north as the Inuit community and as far south as the racist-contaminated Deep South in the U.S.

But Moya O'Connell is charting her own way in the profession. She is unique: an actress of stunning beauty and physical grace, who is emotionally open to acting risks, and often better than the productions she stars in, without ever being patronizing or vulgarly exhibitionistic. She is a marvellously instinctive actress who allows her emotions freedom to enlarge a text sensuously. She works on subtext, so when she appears in a scene, she is fully alive; she doesn't appear to be solving an acting problem or scoring points for the character she is embodying. She doesn't give the impression of calculating her effects, or egotistically distracting from the central focus of a scene.

I have admired her in everything I have seen her do—from Oscar Wilde, Anton Chekhov, and Tennessee Williams to Henrik Ibsen,

George Bernard Shaw, and Philip Barry. But until the summer of 2018, I had not had the good fortune of seeing her in Shakespeare. Then it happened: She played a stunning Lady Macbeth to Ben Carlson's Macbeth (under the probing direction of Chris Abraham for Bard on the Beach, Vancouver) in a pairing that was the best I had seen on stage for those roles. It was my good luck to witness just how far her talent could soar.

Our interview was conducted under a tent at Bard on the Beach on a hot June day, prior to a rehearsal for Meg Roe's gender-bending *Timon of Athens*.[2] O'Connell had just opened to an ecstatic standing ovation in Chris Abraham's *Macbeth*, but she wore her success lightly and lithely while we competed in our interview with a zestful Beatles soundtrack from the main tent where a tech rehearsal was in progress for *As You Like It*. She somehow managed to look cool under her broad-brimmed summer hat, her wide smile welcoming, her pale blue eyes looking translucent.

She is not the sort of stage beauty of whom it could fairly be said that her face is her only fortune. Her beauty is allied to amazingly acute instincts and a questioning intelligence, but she is no high-handed diva. In fact, she claims to recoil from being confrontational: "I try to be open because it is a collaboration. I try to have trust. Putting on plays is a tricky business, and I don't want to become a director-proof actor. Sometimes you can learn and be surprised by different peoples' processes, so I tend not to be very confrontational."

And she is full of praise for Chris Abraham, whom she calls "incredibly smart and rigorous. He asks for everything, for it all. He works from a place of psychology. His wife is an actress (Liisa Repo-Martell) and he does love the actor brain. He's hard on actors but never cruel. He's very kind but you work harder for Chris than you do for anyone else. Part of the reason I came out here was just so that we could work together on this play."

Bard is her artistic home in Vancouver, where she grew up, the fifth of three sons and three daughters. Given a collection of Shakespeare's plays by one brother on her 16th birthday, she read fervently and was willingly captive to the great playwright's genius. She later studied at University of British Columbia, where she performed her first Shakespeare, then began her professional career at Bard, playing small roles before winning larger ones because of her undeniable mettle. One thing she soon knew was that Shakespeare was not all poetry, although she admits to playing around with words and metre:

> I'm very aware of metre during early rehearsals, and then try not to ever think of it again. [Shakespeare] gives you so much in the metre that it would be foolish to do away with it for no reason. It is unlike Ibsen, unlike Chekhov, unlike Shaw, unlike other great writers in that the way it feels in your mouth, the way it sounds, and the way it comes out of your body are a full body experience. When things are going right, my body actually feels lit up. Body, nerves, and tendons are all aligned, and that's thrilling. That's what makes him the most fun to act.

Her words reveal just how sensuous and sensual she can be on stage. She responds to text and dramatic (or comic) situation as a whole thinking-feeling person, with, perhaps, the primacy being on the instinctive feeling part of herself. She becomes deeply embedded in a role: "I take it on fully. I want to create the human. I want to live the human, inside of it." This is essentially what acting should be: a response to life rather than a substitute for or mere mimicry of it.

Mimicry, of course, is important in acting, and actors (as O'Connell asserts) do mimic their roles offstage when they fail to observe the division between art and life. Anyone who knows anything about acting recognizes the extent to which O'Connell immerses herself in her roles, using subtext to deepen interpretation, prompting a viewer to feel how much acting costs her soul.

Realizing how intense and soul-shaking the role of Lady Macbeth can be for an actress, she elects the camaraderie of the dressing room where she and her fellow actresses can join together in entering the assaultive world of the play—especially in a production that accentuates the violence with full velocity.

In response to my question about how she prepares for a role, she says:

> Well, I read the text a great deal. I try to stay away from watching productions, although I have watched a lot of productions of *Macbeth* throughout my life because it's one of the plays that people want to keep doing. It's so filmic, and you can do so much that you can't do on stage. I've watched some of the seminal productions of it, and I have been in it twice before, so already know the play well. I watch a lot of other things that help me ignite. I look at pieces of art. I visited Haida Gwaii (formerly the Queen Charlotte Islands)[3] in winter because it felt sacred. The land had a magic that worked upon me gently but powerfully. I was potently aware, while visiting, that this was a place alive with spirits. The Haida people are very connected to their mythological belief system. Visiting there brought the idea of the supernatural and the invocation of spirits to my here and now.

How did she arrive at her overall concept of Lady Macbeth, and how much autonomy does an actress have in this regard? Because it is such a famous part—with everyone having an opinion about it—she talked to several others, but put her trust in discussions with Ben Carlson and Abraham:

> I thought the only thing to do was to just be open to Chris and Ben, and what Ben and I could create together, who we ended up being to each other. Chris felt very strongly that she should be a force that meets [Macbeth's] and that she dominates the first half, with [Macbeth] taking over and dominating the second. You do inevitably have a take on it, but it wasn't a take so much. Whenever I [attempt] a part, I find it often falls apart. I can have instincts about it. It's such a collective art form that you can have a take, but then you're just throwing it against a wall because it's never going to work. I just have to come in and meet [Ben] where he is.

Lady Macbeth is her most important Shakespearean role to date, and she gives a performance of inner thunder and moving vulnerability that eschews all the clichés of the role, aided, of course, by her director's psychological perspective on the play and characters, rooted in the effects of trauma—as Abraham revealed to me when asked what attracted him to the play:

> I think there are number of fronts that interested me when I looked at the play. The first that comes to mind is the lensing in on a portrait of a marriage, which is pretty unique in Shakespeare's canon and the way he grapples with it in this play. I was also interested in the way in which trauma conditions, shapes, and prepares individuals to be open to magical thinking. Both Lady Macbeth and Macbeth, having suffered the loss of a child, are perfectly prepared for a prophecy to provide meaning to a meaninglessness or a life where meaning is in crisis.

His production had a prologue in which an empty cradle rested downstage, Lady Macbeth showing visible anxiety beside it. When the cradle was abruptly snatched away, she emitted a blood-curdling scream of pain that melded with the scream of Witch 2, who was evidently suffering some sort of traumatic crisis herself. Abraham expounded: "I go back to a recent history of catastrophic loss of a child, and the husband's failure to grieve. This is a crisis in their coupledom, and for her, it is her enormous guilt for the loss of this child that requires a kind of punishment that her husband is unwilling to mete out. Something breaks down in her idea of his manhood, and something breaks down for him in his idea of his own manhood."

Accordingly, the couple enter into a bargain with a universe where you accept prophetic logic. A universe in which the witches were women who had been victimized themselves in one way or another, and who had their power removed, thereby compelling them to exercise power through other means. In other words, for Abraham, the witches are "a manifestation of nature's revenge" on a patriarchal system: "They're women who have unknowable, unknown personal histories that move them to take revenge on some guy. In all of Shakespeare there's either a rupture or return to balance between the divine feminine and masculine aspects of the natural world. In *Macbeth*, it begins with the selection of a male candidate as a target for the revenge of the divine feminine."

The witches are often blamed for prophesying Macbeth will be king, while Lady Macbeth, in turn, is burdened with the brunt of blame for goading her husband into killing King Duncan. However, feminist actresses and directors deliver new readings of the play, in which Lady Macbeth is no longer a starkly defined villainess or monster. As spelled out by her director, Trevor Nunn, Judi Dench incarnated a woman "who didn't disdain her husband, who didn't think he was somebody to be manipulated or baited. She adored him to the point of idolatry. This took her to the point where she could not bear that his career should lack fulfilment, and then lamented that this extraordinary man had too much generosity, sympathy, vulnerability. How could he be helped? She had, for however long it took, to transform herself to give him that push, so much did she love him" (Jacobs 89).

In another example, director Jules Wright challenges received perspectives of the play and of the central female character, and she has claimed that in the play "there is a complete denial of the feminine principle; all the women are wiped out" (Schafer 153). Wright contends that "if you track your way through *Macbeth*, there's a very, very clear and interesting journey for Lady Macbeth, and it's about denying all that is female for one reason, which is to ensure what *he* wants" (Schafer 155). Prior to Duncan's murder, she cites what she has done for Macbeth:

> She confronts him with 'I've given up all that is female within me, I've made myself a man, I've made myself stronger than you,' but she's essentially saying, 'I have denied myself for you; you will pull back now? I will

dash my child upon the ground; will you waver now, when I have done that?' You can play that scene as an urging scene or you can play it in a very confrontational way: '*This is* what I have done.' You have to look at the play as the journey of two people utterly engaged with each other, but she is the one who ultimately denies herself (Schafer 155).

Wright insists that if you portray a mutuality in the scene where Macbeth has to be convinced to go through with the murder, then you prevent the actor playing Macbeth from "withdrawing from the responsibilities of his actions. So often there's a 'she made me do it' element, but that's not in the text" (Schafer 157). Shakespeare does not map out every stage of Lady Macbeth's journey, but creates characters who often make choices in contradictory ways, thereby producing a complexity of human personality.

So, how and why does Lady Macbeth go from a position of psychological strength to a state of breakdown or deep psychosis? There is a void into which she seems to fall after the banquet scene goes awry. When a production challenges the conventional tracking of the two major roles, there is an increased emphasis of Macbeth's culpability. Chris Abraham sees Macbeth as someone who is unwilling to punish or blame his wife:

> Our vision of Macbeth at the beginning of the play is someone who throws himself into his work, into his identity as warrior, but there's a rupture between who he is as a husband or man and who he is at work. In the very instant she hears of the possibility of future happiness, Lady Macbeth makes a covenant with the universe. So, the way that we understand this is that her life, as it stands, her steady state of existence is empty. There's pain; therefore, the prophecy offers her the promise of feeling happiness again, and she leaps into it as one would, who has experienced trauma. The problem for her is her perception of her husband's morality as an obstacle to happiness. Fundamentally, I see her as having more power than her husband does, even before the action of the play.

O'Connell contributes her own perspective, hinging on the deep loss experienced by Lady Macbeth in a world brutalized by civil war and unspeakable violence: "When you start the play, they are a people for whom (and Macbeth in particular) chaos is just at bay. It's just beneath her, and she has the lines: 'Things without all remedy/Should be without regard' (3.2.11-12). In a way, that's her motto. I took it as meaning she had been able to deal with life by compartmentalizing it, and when you are swimming in deep grief, the appetite for happiness and hope causes her to seize on the prophecy readily, quickly, and immediately with her whole being."

Her reading of the marriage complements that of her director, for both of them disagree with an oft-repeated canard that this marriage is one of the happiest in all Shakespeare. However, where Abraham calls the marriage "miserable," O'Connell recognizes moments of mutual respect and shared glory, as when Lady Macbeth apostrophizes "Great Glamis! worthy Cawdor!/Greater than both, by the all-hail hereafter!" and Macbeth addresses her as "My dearest love" in 1.5.54-55, 59. O'Connell presses on:

> They have lost something—a child—and in our discussion about the play, we showed him receding and just becoming what couldn't be strong, [while] I had to close everything down. So, there's a lot of pain and resentment, but because of that grief and loss, they are deeply connected. I don't think it's a happy marriage in the domestic sense, but I think they're two people who need each other somehow on an emotional level. She has been closed and she re-opens after seizing on the prophecy, and it is her re-opening to him that makes him alive to the idea that he can pursue this. He needs somehow to show her that he can please her. He wants to do something for her.
>
> There's a *folie de deux*. He seizes on the prophecy and writes an oblique letter which she has to interpret because he's not explicit. It's as if he's channelling something that she takes up and runs with.

When I ask if the letter's contents are really new to Lady Macbeth, O'Connell responds:

No, I think she has an idea of his ambition but she says: 'What thou wouldst highly/That wouldst thou holily; wouldst not play false,/And yet wrongly win' (1.5.19-22). I love that phrase 'wrongly win.' Those two words put together are such a perfect example of what she feels about his character. But I think she misjudges him by saying he is 'too full o' th' milk of human kindness' (1.5.17). Yet, we hear about his savagery as soldier; he's split someone open from 'the nave to th' chops' (1.2.22). Later, she says to him: 'you shall put/This night's great business into my dispatch' and 'Leave all the rest to me' (1.5.67-8, 74). She really forces [the murder] to happen. Once it does, he goes off plan immediately by killing the two chamberlains—which is not what they discussed—and from that moment on, he is invigorated. The brutality of the man in war gets ignited, and she can't keep up. Then she recedes from the action of the play. She has awakened something in him that, perhaps, she didn't know existed.

What is the stronghold for them in the marital relationship? Is it sex? O'Connell doesn't think so:

One of the things Shakespeare is examining in the play is the patriarchy and a male universe. In order for her to help him commit the act, she has to unsex herself; she has to get rid of her milk. I do think Shakespeare is writing about violence committed in the absence of feminine energy, except that you have the Weird Sisters, who are fascinating. Who are they? That's always one of the big questions of the play. In our production, they become the Divine Feminine that has turned into a malignant force through their pain and the abuse of their bodies and psyches.

At what point does the marriage break apart? Would it be with her discovery that Macbeth has killed the two chamberlains or would it be during the banquet scene when he suffers a hysterical nervous breakdown? When Banquo's ghost appears, there is a significant, even astonishing exchange (asserts Jules Wright) between Lady Macbeth and Macbeth where "he completely cuts her. At the end of that scene that relationship is over and she knows that she has given utterly everything, and then she is rejected by him" (Schafer 156). Chris Abraham expands on

the same moment when the trajectories of the couple suddenly become unaligned:

> It's the moment when [Macbeth] enters and begins to lie. It's just after Duncan's murder, when he gives the 'violent love' speech in Act 2, Scene 3. I think it's his extraordinary sudden success at dissembling when he surpasses her in some way. He becomes the man she had wanted him to be. It is both an erotically charged moment for her, but also one in which she is overwhelmed. In [his] becoming a man, she loses her hold over him. That plays into the reasons why she faints. She's overwhelmed by what he has become not in an entirely positive way. That, to me, is the beginning of the end. That is his baptism into losing himself. There's almost no going back from that point.

O'Connell explains the significance of the "violent love" speech— the one when Lady Macbeth finds out about the murder of the chamberlains:

> It's a shock because he has completely gone off plan. Now, it might have been a clever plan or a terrible plan, but the fact is that he's acted alone without her aid. His action is the razor's edge of the beginning of the split. The next scene is the coronation, in which he calls to be alone. He says: 'Let every man be master of his time/Till seven at night. To make society/The sweeter welcome, we will keep ourself/Till supper-time alone' (3.1.40-43). She exits without a word. When she re-enters later, she says: 'Nought's had, all's spent,/Where our desire is got without content' (3.2.4-5).
>
> When Macbeth returns, she says: 'How now, my lord, why do you keep alone,/Our sorriest fancies your companions making,/Using those thoughts which should indeed have died/With them they think on?' (3.2.8-11). She recognizes there is a split: she needs him to need her but he is gone. He starts calling on the dark forces in the same way she did. 'Come, seeling night,/Scarf up the tender eye of pitiful day,/ And with thy bloody and invisible hand/Cancel and tear to pieces that great bond/Which keeps me pale' (3.2.46-50). That's when he makes plans to murder Banquo and Fleance, and she sees that she has helped to create a person who is spinning out of control. That scene is really the obvious point in the play where they are missing each other, and then in the banquet scene it intensifies.

O'Connell and her director did not lose the surprising combination of the funny and the frightening in the banquet scene. As Declan Donnellan has expressed: "Giving other people food is the essence of hospitality. Hospitality is a nexus in which power becomes very dangerous and very apparent. Macbeth is obsessed with dinner parties and gives two in the play. The great crime is not only regicide, but a crime against hospitality. The fact that it takes place in his own home makes it all the worse" (Berry 1989: 204).

Chris Abraham points out that the first banquet is his first public celebration: "It's one of the few opportunities that we get to see him attempting to enjoy the fruits of his murder, and it fails miserably. I find that scene quite funny." His point is borne out by the build-up of social expectation as Duncan calls Lady Macbeth "our honour'd hostess" and "fair and noble hostess" less than two dozen lines later (1.6.10, 22).

Her husband is noticeably absent, so her role of hostess becomes awkward. She apologizes and Duncan makes a joke of the breach in etiquette, but she knows that she has to cover for the failed protocol. Looking every inch the beautiful hostess, O'Connell achieves a masquerade through eloquence and ritual, aided by the king's courtly politeness.

Her way of handling the banquet in Act 3 is the stuff of social satire, quite independent of the sinister undercurrent in the scene, as she tries to maintain good cheer and decorum while things are falling apart for her husband. She reminds Macbeth:

> 'The feast is sold
> That is not often vouch'd, while 'tis a-making,
> 'Tis given with welcome. To feed were best at home;
> From thence, the sauce to meat is ceremony,
> Meeting were bare without it' (3.4.32-36).

In other words, unless the guests are reassured of their welcome, a banquet is not worth more than a meal one has paid for. And while retaining her cosmetic mask of glamorous composure, she urges her guests to keep dining and not pay any attention to her husband, even though she is at her wit's end trying to keep calm and preserve social etiquette. Abraham enjoys that the audience consistently laughs at her line (especially as delivered by Moya O'Connell with perfection of tone): "You have displac'd the mirth, broke the good meeting,/With most admir'd disorder" (3.4.109-110). "The understatement of the play," comments Abraham.

Perhaps the confluence of comic and dramatic tensions in this scene is easier to achieve than the horror of the witches. One of the toughest things for an audience to believe are the witches. How does O'Connell view Lady Macbeth's relationship to them? "Our production starts with the cry of the two of us (Lady Macbeth and Witch 2) that links us in an abstract way with the cry and pain of women."

Does she feel kin in some sense, or are they external to her? "I think they are fairly external. There is no indication other than when she reads the letter. She does believe in them, as when she refers to 'fate and metaphysical aid' (1.5.29), and she trusts the prophecy. On some level, she's deeply available to them or to the idea of them. I don't think she knows them."

Does she see a connection between Lady Macbeth's invocation "Come, you spirits/That tend on mortal thoughts, unsex me here,/And fill me from the crown to the toe topfull/Of direst cruelty" (1.5.40-43) and the Feminine Principle? O'Connell articulates her view: "My feeling about her is that she's impulsive and quite ferocious, but she's also quite feminine. She recognizes within herself that in order to be the spur to prick the sides of Macbeth's intent, she has to rid herself of her femininity. She has to fill herself with direst cruelty."

I remark on the interesting dynamic where she becomes masculine, as it were, while he becomes feminine in the sense that she has to virtually shame him into looking and acting like a man. O'Connell agrees: "Lady Macbeth says: 'What beast was't then/ That made you break this enterprise to me?/When you durst do it, then you were a man;/And to be more than what you were, you would/Be so much more the man' (1.7.47-51). She is appealing to his manhood, but she's trying different tactics in that scene. She sees him shutting down the idea, so she is trying whatever she can. In our production, it is an appeal to him sexually but she's also dressing down his manhood, in effect saying: 'Man up. Are you a coward?'"

How does she prepare herself in the role to call on the dark spirits? "I think I'm still answering that on a nightly basis." However, she does not think that there is much of a gap between these dark forces and our contemporary attachment to rituals and superstitions, such as teen Gothic cults or sports teams that believe certain habits or rituals (going to the bathroom before play or NHLers believing that touching a divisional championship cup before actually winning the Stanley Cup) could bring bad luck:

> People are very superstitious. People fundamentally know what the dark forces in the world are. I think what we really wanted to explore was what it felt like to murder someone. Chris was really interested in that—creating emotionally and physically a thriller-like horror. I feel in this play from the moment the murder happens, neither one sleeps again. Macbeth has terrible dreams or nightmares that prevent him from sleeping, and she sleepwalks. She doesn't really sleep after the banquet scene.
>
> 'I have seen her rise from her bed, throw her night-gown upon her, unlock her closet, take forth paper, fold it, write upon't, read it, afterwards seal it, and again return to bed; yet all this while in a most fast sleep,' says the Waiting Gentlewoman (5.1.4-8). Is she in between two worlds? She has light beside her continually. What is she writing on the paper? Is it a confession? I don't know.

O'Connell delivers a fascinating, vividly intense interpretation of the sleepwalking scene in Act 5, in which her Lady Macbeth transitions at times from calm to spastic kinesis, as when she wrings her hands and frantically attempts to remove all imagined bloodstains from them and other parts of her body. The actress had listened to a podcast where a summer camp counsellor witnessed a boy sleepwalking, lost track of him, but then came face to face with the boy in a corridor. Suddenly, the boy ran full tilt at him but rather than collide, raced past. This gave her the justification for her spasms or change of physical movement, and her director allowed her significant freedom. However, she keeps changing her movements from performance to performance.

> When I'm doing the kinetic movement, it is as if she does wake up for a moment and then lapses back. So, it is an act of consciousness sometimes. Sometimes I beat myself. That's a brand-new thing that I'm trying out. But I don't want to set it because there are all sorts of possibilities. To create a specific path might limit you, and what happens in a long run is you forget and go farther and farther [with acting choices]. I think it's a nice opportunity to show the breakdown of her mind and a real weakness in her where we've seen such strength earlier. So, I want the possibility of examining that.

Notes

[1]Douglas Campbell's first wife was actress Ann Casson, daughter of Dame Sybil Thorndike and Sir Lewis Casson. Ann and Douglas were parents of sons Benedict, Dirk, and Tom, and daughter Teresa. Douglas's second wife was actress-director Moira Wylie, and they had two children, Torquil and Beatrice.

[2]Our interview was conducted on June 19, 2018 at Bard on the Beach, Vancouver.

[3]A remote chain of islands on the edge of British Columbia, Haida Gwaii is a repository of unique indigenous culture. Hundreds of islands (including a temperate rainforest and thermal waters) form a dagger-shaped archipelago almost twice the size of Prince Edward Island. The area comprises about 10,000 square kilometres of mountain and forest, and has a population of around 4,300. Its economy, long based on forestry and

fishing, is now largely dominated by tourism because the natural scenery is beautiful, its numerous species of seabirds, whales, dolphins, and black bear hugely attractive to visitors. Its cultural heritage is 6,000-8,000 years old.

Tom McCamus as King John in King John *(Stratford Festival, 2014).*
(Photo: David Hou. Courtesy of the Stratford Festival)

Tom McCamus
"I Ended Up Loving Shakespeare"

"Actors are show-offs, bigheaded bastards, egomaniacs," claimed English actor Michael Gambon in an interview with Mel Gussow (Gussow 115). But while there is ample evidence to support this sweeping claim, Tom McCamus is an exception. One of his most remarkable qualities—apart from his vibrant acting, often at top speed—is his genuine modesty. Our interview in Mississauga (during a break from his preparation for a Robert Lepage production of *Coriolanus* at Stratford in the upcoming season)[1] is marked by his acknowledgement of theatre directors who have guided and influenced him, and by a startling revelation of his own insecurity as an actor.

It is startling because McCamus has been a leading player at the Stratford Festival and elsewhere for many years, having left his stamp on a number of significant principal roles, such as Arthur in *Camelot*, Valmont in *Dangerous Liaisons*, Vladimir in *Waiting for Godot*, Edmund in *Long Day's Journey into Night*, the ailing king in *The Madness of King George*, and two of Shakespeare's kings, Richard III and John, that have added weight and lustre to his other credits on film and television.

Winner of many awards for stage, television, and film work, he remains modest, just the way he and actress wife Chick Reid live with their four dogs on a 54-acre farm just outside of Warkworth, a designated arts community in the county of Northumberland. "We wanted to find a place that had nothing to do with where we worked," he explains, noting that they had lived in Toronto, moving there from London, where Tom had become part of William Hutt's Theatre London seasons.

In Toronto, he would find acting jobs, though not enough to make a living. His wife taught at local schools, everything from French and Drama to Shop. An actor's life in the usual sense of mobility, and uncertainty about future work or continuity. But, unlike many actors at Stratford and Shaw Festivals, McCamus is not one who suffers from a Staying On syndrome. He welcomes change or transition when it comes to plays and directors, because he is always willing to learn and deepen his craft.

Given his major credits in classical theatre, it is surprising to learn that McCamus was never initially interested in Shakespeare. Born in Winnipeg, he did his schooling in London, Ontario before moving to the University of Windsor, where he studied Drama and received a B.A. in Fine Arts in 1977. At Windsor, he had a number of American teachers who dealt with Arthur Miller, Eugene O'Neill, and Tennessee Williams. He did have limited exposure to Shakespeare, but the only striking thing about this early period was his falling in love with the role of Mercutio in Franco Zeffirelli's film version of *Romeo and Juliet*. He managed only a scene from the same play, opposite Jim Warren.

His first job out of theatre school was in Shakespeare, however, when William Hutt directed him as Andrew Aguecheek in *Twelfth Night* at the Grand Theatre in London. Hutt had offered to help him secure an audition at Stratford, but McCamus declined. He wanted to do only modern plays and new Canadian ones. However, he learned "an incredible amount" from just watching the great Hutt:

> I remember an early thing he taught me. He said to just take the script and copy all the lines down—forget that it's verse. Just write them down as if they were sentences. He taught me about breath, about taking my time—which I still haven't learned. I would speak it too

fast. I think part of the reason I thought I didn't like Shakespeare was because I felt it was too mannered and not naturalistic enough. He taught me an awful lot about acting, directing me in Arthur Kopit and Israel Horowitz. I always thought Bill was a classical actor, but it was totally surprising how great an actor he was across the board. He taught me that, maybe, there isn't that much of a difference between Shakespeare and what I thought was acting.

McCamus was able to add more Shakespeare to his resume when Eddie Gilbert lured him into playing Gobbo and the Prince of Aragon, under his direction, in *The Merchant of Venice* at Toronto Free Theatre in 1982, starring George Sperdakos as Shylock and Camille Mitchell as Portia. But his next big teacher was Christopher Newton, after William Webster recommended McCamus to Newton at the Shaw Festival, where he spent eight years, learning how to rehearse and improve his craft by taking his time to build layer by layer. "My process basically came from Chris Newton more than anyone else." Newton, having been an actor as well, allowed him the freedom to learn by osmosis.

But McCamus pays tribute to Neil Munro as the one who really influenced him the most about acting and Shakespeare in the bargain. The occasion was *Hamlet's Room* at Theatre Plus in 1991, a deconstructive, modernized adaptation by Munro of *Hamlet*, where the entire action of the play occurred in Hamlet's bedroom at Elsinore in a world replete with televisions and telephones, where nudity and cocaine were rampant, and where Rosencrantz and Guildenstern were Siamese twins. The cast had Brenda Robins as Ophelia, Benedict Campbell tripling as the Ghost, Claudius, and the Player King, Barbara Gordon as Gertrude, Al Kozlik as Polonius, Kate Trotter as the Player Queen, and McCamus as a cocaine-addicted Hamlet.

It was a trendy, high-tech production, never boring, but altogether bizarre—the sort of thing that a theatre rebel would relish, and McCamus was pleased to be part of Munro's experiment: "He would say great things. When we were doing the Gertrude/Hamlet scene, he would say: 'I just want to know there's some vague domestic argument going on. I don't want to hear the words.' He would go to the opposite of what I had been taught. What he taught me about Shakespeare is something I have carried with me the rest of my life."

McCamus was eventually brought into the fold at Stratford in 1994 by Richard Monette, a personal friend, with whom he had acted in Maxim Gorky's *Barbarians*, directed by Marti Maraden in an Equity Showcase production. With Monette's appointment as Artistic Director of the Stratford Festival, McCamus' nationalism kicked in because he believed that he should support a fellow-Canadian and friend at the head of our putative national theatre. Monette was an unpretentiously insightful director.

"In rehearsals, he didn't like to talk. He just liked to do things, but in a bar he liked to talk and he would give great notes. When I played Ford in *The Merry Wives of Windsor*,[2] I really didn't realize how good a part it was, till Richard said, 'You realize the only flaw in this man is his jealousy.'" It was as simple as when Brian Bedford directed him in *Godot*:[3] "I had all these ideas about how to play Vladimir, but Brian said: 'No, no. Basically, this man is always positive, so that when he finally says: "I can't go on," it pays off.'" In effect, each director made him simplify the complexities that McCamus was seeking to emphasize.

Actors can be great despite their directors; but some develop greatness because of their directors. McCamus is quick to give credit to the signal ones he has worked with: In addition to Hutt, Newton, Munro, and Monette, he adds Robin Phillips, Antoni Cimolino, and Tim Carroll. Ironically, he had never done Shakespeare with Phillips, and was mortally nervous about being directed by him in virtually anything.

"He'll probably say: 'You're a fraud!'" McCamus says, only half-jokingly. Phillips said no such thing, of course, when McCamus entered his orbit in the Soulpepper version of *The Mill on the Floss* (2000), not a glittering success by any past measure of Phillips. But McCamus loved the experience. "He was fantastic. How delicate he was! As long as you were open with him, he would take you anywhere. So, I regret not having done a Shakespeare with him. I've done a lot of Shakespeare with Antoni. I've actually acted Shakespeare with Antoni."

He is referring to the 1994 season when another close friend, Stephen Ouimette, essayed the role of Hamlet at Stratford, with Antoni Cimolino as Laertes and McCamus as Horatio. McCamus had known Cimolino from their University of Windsor days, and he noted his friend's progress as a director, beginning with the production of *Merry Wives*, when Cimolino was assistant director to Monette.

In this Shakespeare, McCamus found himself working closely with Cimolino on Ford's big speeches: "It was like two peers trying to figure out these speeches together. Over the years, we did a *Cymbeline*[4] and *The Merchant of Venice* together,[5] and because we have known each other for a long time, he just lets me go—which is not necessarily a good thing because sometimes he should direct me more."

The actor-director relationship changes from play to play, but a good director encourages the actor to give the best performance of which he is capable. Some directors are prepared to listen to an actor and use his ideas in a production. Other directors are less interested in collaborating with the actor on the internal life of a character, usually because they have already decided on a concept or because, not having been actors themselves, they do not understand an actor's process.

McCamus reserves some of his highest praise for Tim Carroll (Manchester-raised, Oxford educated director)[6], who directed him in *King John* at the Stratford Festival (2014), offering this perspective: "He's not an actor, and he says he's not an actor. He shakes things up so much, you have to be willing to give yourself over to him. And it took me awhile. I've done five or six shows with him, and I trust him totally. Wherever he wants me to go, I'll go there because I trust he's going to bring my performance to a finished place at the end. And I like his taste. That's important."

But playing Shakespeare can also be shaped by a particular stage architecture, size, and shape. The thrust stage (especially at the Festival Theatre) is demanding and exciting. Not especially large, it permits extraordinary intimacy between actor and audience. "Acting here has been driven by the architecture," explains Antoni Cimolino. "You don't have to hurl what you are doing across the void to the audience, so everything seems more natural and easy" (Fischlin & Nasby 49).

The late William Hutt once commented: "You cannot lie on that stage. On a proscenium stage [an actor] has the protection of scenery at his back. Here, if he is to be successful, he must be able to respond intuitively to the size and shape of the space which surrounds him" (Fischlin & Nasby 49-50). "The interaction among actors is different too," according to Pat Morden. "On a proscenium stage, they play to the audience and only pretend to play to one another. On the thrust, as Michael Langham put it, 'their bond of relationship is direct, true, and complete, and serves to pull the audience deeply into the experience of the play'" (Fischlin & Nasby 50). The thrust stage also requires directors to adjust to its configurations and challenges. Michael Langham resorted to circular or semi-circular choreographed movement; Robin Phillips went for diagonals. Both these directors discovered that once this stage is embraced, it becomes (in the words of Pat Morden) "a dynamic and exciting space with great flexibility and intimacy" (Fischlin & Nasby 51).

Having done Shakespeare at the Festival, Avon, and Patterson theatres in Stratford, McCamus is able to sum up the advantages and disadvantages of each stage and auditorium:

> The Festival is a beautiful stage. Because of my taste earlier on for naturalistic acting, I found it harder to do on that stage. I thought it required a presentational quality. I felt I was standing and delivering. The Festival is quite a small stage, so it's harder to get movement happening. Richard would direct us in diagonals, but I'd often find myself standing in line somehow.
>
> The worst [of the three stages] for me is the Avon. You don't want to do Shakespeare there. It's proscenium arch, and the problem is that the proscenium puts you back; you're not forward enough—particularly for the style of Shakespeare that we do now. If you're more stand and deliver, it's fine, but that's not what we do. So, it's really hard. We did *Richard III* there, and it was a hard go.
>
> The Patterson is more intimate, and I can do what I think I want to do with Shakespeare—make it more conversational or naturalistic. Another thing about the Patterson: it's such a long space, you can move and even run on there. It allows physicality to happen.

Our conversation moves to the subject of Shakespearean acting, and especially some of the leading roles McCamus has played. Some actors like to do a lot of research before tackling a role; some do not. What is his preferred approach?

> I do a certain amount of research. I've always thought that one of the things I had going for me at Stratford was that I didn't really know any of the plays. I ended up falling in love with the plays while I was doing them, discovering the characters while I was playing them. I remember seeing *Much Ado About Nothing* with Nicky Pennell playing Don John and he was fantastic. But when I played Don John, I could never get him out of my head, and I don't think I was very successful playing the role. So, in terms of research, I don't look at how others have done it.

Is it wrong to have a concept of a role before you rehearse? McCamus offers:

I don't think it's wrong. It depends on who you are, what kind of actor you are. I find that if I make too many decisions before hand, I'm in trouble primarily because I don't know what the director is thinking, who the other actors are. You understand who a character is by how you relate to the person you are acting with. And how would you know that until you've met that person? I also find that the problem is that if you're acting with someone who's already made those decisions about who their character is, then it doesn't give you any room to figure something out. I like to figure it out as slowly as I possibly can, and I like to do it in the rehearsal process, not beforehand.

McCamus' view is remarkably similar to that of Kevin Kline, who insists that an actor has a brain and his own resources to create a character, and Kline, therefore, disapproves of an actor's arriving at acting choices ahead of time. As Kline puts it: "Why bother? What's the adventure? Where's the discovery?" (Maher 4). Kline also proposes something else: "The author of the play is Shakespeare, but the actor has to own the character he is playing. Olivier aptly said you marry yourself to the character" (Maher 4). Sounds wonderfully impressive, but I ask McCamus how this "marriage" occurs, to which he responds:

That's the beautiful thing about Shakespeare. There isn't just one way to play the role. There's so much ambiguity and humanity that you can play it in an infinite amount of ways. Whatever and however it speaks to you, it's about how you find that thing in you that understands the character. That's why I ended up loving Shakespeare—because of the mystery. Even if you're playing a relatively small part like Hubert in *King John*, who spends a lot of time supporting John and saying very little, you can create a huge world by saying very little because what he says is so specific. That's because Shakespeare makes it that specific.

Kline also speaks of looking for the soul in a role. What would be the soul in *Richard III*, whom McCamus played at Stratford in 2002? "When I played Richard, Chick and I had just gotten dogs. So, I played him like a dog, and used a lot of canine physicality.

Part of it had to do with a dog that was beaten all the time. Richard lived in a world where no one took him seriously whatsoever. He knew how to use this. He got what he wanted by playing on everybody's sympathy. I also played him as someone with cerebral palsy. I would fall down a lot."

When I saw this performance, I felt it took away from the role because there was too much physically awkward comedy. McCamus counters: "He's a very funny man. The whole point is that when he trips, he gets sympathy from people. But, then, he trips when he doesn't want to trip—as in the Coronation scene. He gets angry at himself because of his own limitations. But that wasn't so much from the text, it was simply an idea I had. Then as you go through the text, you find lines you can play with."

One of his driving motivations is to surprise audiences with something they've never seen over and over again by making the role seem fresh and new. He cherishes Neil Munro's radical suggestion to do the opposite to whatever you have learned at theatre school. His Richard III owed virtually nothing to any other actor's interpretation, even Sir Laurence Olivier's great portrayal on stage and film. McCamus was intent on eliminating an audience's expectations based on old stage tradition. And his director, Martha Henry, liked his originality, especially when he invented a witty piece of business that he would repeat at strategic moments in the plot.

His Richard would keep a list of names on paper, and every time a specific name came up, he would cross it off the list. So, it was Gloucester's turn or Lady Anne's or Buckingham's, and so on. No other actor had done that before him. Henry would have allowed everyone else in the cast to go their own way but if they didn't, she didn't force them into a grid.

Perhaps, Martha Henry's flexibility stems from her being an actress before she turned to directing, and I have heard many Canadian actors praise her open-mindedness. "I love Martha," enthuses McCamus. "She's fantastic. She lets you go somewhere. She doesn't stop you. She'll let you go all the way because she knows that if you keep going with an idea, you have the potential of finding something quite extraordinary. If you stop, you may not find it. You may end up doing something that's way too much and too extreme, but you're actually searching for something that could be quite extraordinary. That's what you need to do in Shakespeare because he's been done so many times and in many different ways."

Henry does not insist that every cast member play in the same sandbox as the lead actor. But doesn't this create a problem of overall style? Who dictates the style of a production: director or actor? McCamus is unequivocal in his reply: "Ah, definitely the director. The director creates the atmosphere in the room, no matter what." McCamus likes a strong director who breaks the rules. "But that said, they must know what they are breaking in the first place."

One thing that this actor seems to have broken by his unique mode of vocal delivery is the familiar stand-and-deliver oratorical mode. In the Maher interview, Kevin Kline paraphrases famed Shakespearean director John Barton's view that "Shakespeare is not all poetry. He said to actors: 'Don't poeticize something that is in fact rather straightforward. Especially, don't intone in some elevated mode of speaking if the language is prose'" (Maher 15). I have never witnessed McCamus poeticizing. His strong, rapid delivery is supple and clear. He explains that he always tries to make a speech sound like real speech rather than what some in the profession refer to as "word-painting." He credits director Tim Carroll for teaching him a lot about verse:

> What I've always disliked is when it's sung. That's why I've always tried to make it as naturalistic sounding as possible. But Tim's taught me a beautiful one. He's adamant about stopping at the end of each verse line and not at the period. For example: 'To be or not to be, that

is the question.' You might say 'Yes?' mentally, taking a brief pause. 'Whether 'tis nobler in the mind to suffer' ['Yes?'] 'The slings and arrows of outrageous fortune' ['Yes?'] We don't speak in sentences. If you pause at the end of the natural heartbeat, the iambic, you can still do the poetry and it can have a naturalistic sound. You don't have to sing it. Tim plays with the text in so many different ways and that's how you become familiar with the words, and then, hopefully you can do whatever you want with them.

Carroll has long been an advocate for training in verse-speaking: "I start from the verse. I have them beating out the rhythm, I have them speaking it very rhythmically. I have them even dancing to the rhythm of the verse as they speak." Actors' unions do not permit him to insist that the actors be off book in the first week, so he gives them a lot of exercises which make them wish they had learned the text so that they can get on with it.

It's an interesting exercise in persuasion because you do have to say, 'This will feel strange. You will feel like robots. You will feel as though you sound way worse than you did when you were just saying it naturally, but you have to go through that to get to the other side where you will be able to say this naturally, and you will discover what's really in the language'... So, really, my big line to the actors is always 'Get good at the verse, and then if you still think it is a waste of time, drop it then.' I'm always safe saying that because anyone who gets good at verse, doesn't want to drop it. Once they've got good at it, they can see right down to their bones what it's doing for them.

I asked Carroll if he allowed for a first-rate actor's idiosyncrasies in speaking verse, to which he replied:

What verse covers, even in the hands of the most fascistic director imaginable, is relative stress of syllables. It says nothing about speed, it says nothing about changes of speed (*accelerando* and *ralentendo*), it says nothing about volume (*crescendo*, *decrescendo*), it says nothing about pitch of voice, it says nothing about attitude. So, given all of those things, I don't think there's any problem letting actors have their own idiosyncrasies.

Mark Rylance and Tom McCamus both speak beautifully, but you wouldn't mistake one for the other because they have different paces, they have different thoughts as they're going along. One of my friends is an opera singer and he has done a lot of work on verse with me because he was in a theatre company that I had, and he used to laugh when people said 'But isn't this reducing my individuality?' 'You have to be kidding. When I do an opera part, I have the pitch of every note organized for me. I'm not allowed to change it. I have the tempo organized. I'm not allowed to change it. I have the volume organized. I'm not allowed to change it. And I still believe I sound different from anyone else who sings that. I still think I'm going to be an individual with my individual flavour in that role.'

But what if an actor had the unique vocal style of an Olivier, for example. That great actor used rubato, a technique of stealing a beat from one line and transferring it to another, or to put it the way of the Oxford Living Dictionaries definition: "the temporary disregarding of strict tempo to allow an expressive quickening or slackening, usually without altering the overall pace." Carroll offers his perspective:

What I would do with anyone who is really pulling *against* the verse, I would pull the way *towards* the verse and let that be the tension. Because you're not going to win with an actor like Olivier. He's still going to go out and do what he wants, so you might as well just say cheerfully: 'I'm going to *tell* you when you do that.' I would say to Mark Rylance if he took a great big pause in the middle of a line: 'I'm going to push you not to take that pause. I know I won't always win, but I'm going to be a little bit of pressure on you so that you feel the pressure to finish the verse line.' He agreed with the principle; it's just sometimes he was struck too strongly by the need to stop. He knew that the verse line has its integrity and needs to be complete, but he developed a brilliant way of somehow being able to pause the line in such a way you never felt he'd stopped.

I suggest that Brian Bedford, too, had his own idiosyncratic way with pauses and verse-speaking, eliciting Carroll's agreement. "Bedford and Rylance can do completely regular verse in such a way that you'd say: 'Wow, that's fantastic!' And then they will start to stretch it and pull it a bit, but they can always come back to that because they're building on that. They're not walking on wreckage. But anyone who just thinks 'Oh, I need to have my own individuality,' they're just walking on wreckage. So, they end up not meaning much, and that's when all the shouting and forced vehemence starts."

McCamus has absorbed Carroll's instruction well, in addition to having learned from an older generation of Canadian actors. He points to William Hutt and Martha Henry's expertise with iambics. "When we did *Coriolanus*, Martha played Volumnia.[7] I looked at her script, and everything was marked stressed and unstressed—everything. She's a fantastic speaker of Shakespeare. She has her own kind of music but it's not sung."

Henry once explained how she examines iambic pentameter in dialogue to use its structural information to make decisions about how to speak it: "I meter out the lines. I've done a lot of it by now, so it comes easily. Yet there are places where I say, 'Why am I having a problem with that?' I'll look at it, ferret it out and bang it around, and then realize I have been mispronouncing something or putting the accent on the wrong syllable. Or the beat is not where I think it is—it's over *there* instead—and often the whole thing falls into place" (Maher 2009: 178).

Singing the verse is an old-fashioned habit that can be a convenient fall-back device for those who are uncomfortable with a modern naturalistic vein. McCamus has learned not to be afraid of the verse. "I was afraid because I thought the verse led you to that singing. I found that that's not necessarily the case. So, now, I'm all about the verse. I'm all about finding where the stress is." He demonstrates with an example from *Measure for Measure*, when Angelo has a soliloquy after Isabella has pleaded with him to spare her brother's life, to condemn his sin but not the man himself. Her supplication appears to have affected cold-hearted Angelo who reveals his secret lust for her in an astonishing debate with himself. McCamus demonstrates, quoting from this soliloquy:

> Shall we desire to raze the sanctuary
> And pitch our evils there? O fie, fie, fie!
> What dost thou? or what art thou, Angelo?
> Dost thou desire her foully for those things
> That make her good? O, let her brother live!' (2.2.170-75).
>
> If you go to the end of the verse line, the pause in the moment after 'things,' shows the brain is thinking really fast, so you make the decision in the middle of the line, not at the end of the line.

For McCamus, such an example also shows that there is a subtext in Shakespeare. "I've done a lot of Shakespeare where I'm saying one thing and thinking another. *Richard III* is full of it. Richard is always trying to get somebody to do something and he's doing it by subterfuge. The evil characters are great that way. If you say 'I am angry' and you smile, that has more import."

The first thing McCamus does in preparation for a new Shakespearean role is scholarly work:

> I go through all the words to know what every word means. Even if I think I know the words, I find out what they mean in context. I use the lexicons to find out how all the words work. Usually, that's the work you do beforehand, so when you're in rehearsal, you have that material ready to use if you need to. Then, you have to throw it away, but you know it's stored in the back of your brain. What's important is how do I communicate what I'm trying to say to you.

Such communication is vitally important in Shakespeare because "there's so much talking to the audience. With Tim Carroll it's totally about that. Everything is about connecting to the audience all the way through."

Did he have sympathy for the evil characters he has played, such as Iachimo, Richard III, or King John? To which he answers:

I've loved all the characters I've played. I don't judge. I love the foibles of humanity, when people do stupid things they don't intend to do. That's what we all are. Now, the villains take it to an extreme. I don't love what they do necessarily. When I'm acting a role, I have to figure out who the character is because it could never be me. It's got to be somebody else. That's where I start, and that's why it takes me a long time. Basically, I take all the input from directors, designers, and other actors and put them all together and then decide. Okay, out of all this raw material, what can we create? What kind of person can we create?

I marvel at what McCamus did with *King John* in the 2014 season at the Tom Patterson.

The play is better known to scholars than to modern theatre audiences. Based on a morality play by John Bale, dating from the time of Henry VIII, it eschews an allegorical treatment of English history. The play is packed with anachronisms and its relationship to historical fact is about as probable as a Hollywood film biography's. But this is nothing unusual in Shakespeare's English or Roman histories.

Shakespeare does not concern himself with John's large, violent family or with his signing the Magna Carta or with his fluctuations between great energy and total vacillation. In fact, Shakespeare does not concern himself with anything other than this king's being an energetic vehicle for dramatic action. As Harold C. Goddard sees it, King John is an adult-child, uncertain about what constitutes normal behaviour, because he is "about the unkingliest king [*sic*] Shakespeare ever created. The fact is, John has never grown up. He is mentally dominated by his ambitious mother" (Goddard Vol. 1 140).

To compound matters, he is not as articulate as other Shakespearean kings. Nicholas Woodeson, who played him in Deborah Warner's production at The Other Place in 1988, addresses this in an essay in *Players of Shakespeare 3*: "John seemed opaque, silent in situations which cried out for vengeance, a crude villain with an inconvenient guilty conscience, a sort of second-rate Macbeth or Richard III. He seemed to lack self-promotion, the textual resources to reveal himself to the audience. Most damagingly, he had no soliloquies" (Jackson and Smallwood 3: 89). John himself seems to be aware of his own limitations as a dramatic personage when he sums up: "I am a scribbled form, drawn with a pen/Upon parchment" (5.7.32-33).

McCamus didn't want to play John at first because he had a generic idea of a boy-man and a fundamentally boring king, but then real-life events changed his mind. Colonel Russell Williams, decorated air force pilot and Commander of the Canadian Forces Base (CFB), Trenton, was accused of bizarre sex crimes and murders of women. By pleading guilty to 88 crimes, he was branded a sex offender and sentenced to two terms of life imprisonment with no chance of parole for at least 25 years.

Williams actually lived fairly close to McCamus' farm, and when the actor studied the videotape of the murderer's police interview and confession, he was struck by the total lack of drama and the undeniable sign of a sociopathic personality. This criminal became the seed out of which grew the sociopathic identity of McCamus' startling King John. Tim Carroll was totally taken with this concept, and advised him to be utterly cool in the scene where the king instructs Hubert to kill Arthur. He also suggested that McCamus act coldly throughout the play, and the actor realized that the character was immature in various ways and, worse, "a man who doesn't see why anything would be wrong."

McCamus also saw that Shakespeare's John was "not kingly the way some people would think is kingly," but he was one who knew how to wield power. "He's smart in that way. He knows how to exist in the world of kings, queens, princes, and dukes. And because he's the king, he knows his authority. Sometimes, he's petulant. He's a mommy's boy." In fact, the actor recalls chuckling the first time he realized that King John had a son. "How could this guy have a son?" But he saw that the king's immaturity propelled him to trust and regard the Bastard as a sort of surrogate son.

McCamus captured John's various anomalies in his stunning portrayal, becoming physically sloppy, shoulders hunched as if expecting attack, his hands waving mockingly or dismissively at opponents, or, at other times, playing with his armour or tracing idle patterns with a leg. He made a threatening run at Chatillon but, then, came to a dead stop. Brusque and arrogant at times, he showed impudent boredom with the papal legate before snatching the cardinal's biretta and planting it over his own royal crown, only to fling it to the ground a moment later. He gratuitously knighted Philip (The Bastard), and later acted scornfully derisive when asked by the French if he would lay down his arms and yield the throne.

In the second-half of the play, when Peter of Pomfret, a prophet, asked if he would give up his crown, he broke into a wild, hoarse laugh, and was as likely to dance with glee as to flash fire in speech. He was vulnerable one moment, then suddenly became as dangerous as a cornered animal. The actor's swift tropes of thought and feeling constructed an interpretation that may have been the wittiest King John ever seen. Fast, mercurial, unpredictable, it was also eminently vivid, colourful, and intimate. Indeed, it seemed to substantiate a perspective of the play as an Elizabethan black comedy or tragic farce—a sort of Elizabethan Ubu Roi, as promulgated by director Deborah Warner in England.[8]

His bold, thrilling performance seemed to contradict his own off-stage modesty. As an actor, he must have ego, but what does this actually mean to him? "It's more about confidence in performance," he responds: "Everybody has an ego, but it is what ego does to you and how you control it. I tend to think I'm not very good and that I don't know what I'm doing. So, if anybody has a solution [to how to play a role], I will go with his, as opposed to going with my idea. I tend to think that my idea is the worst and theirs is the best." Does this mean that he trusts every director? He replies that he does for the most part. "I find it easier to defer to the director. It's a great protection because, especially in Shakespeare, there are so many ways that you could go. So, if you can narrow the choices down, that is a good thing. If you try and encompass the whole, it is impossible. The ego part of me says that I can find something from the choices left over, unless they're extreme."

Has it ever come to the point where he has given up a role because of a director? "Very rarely," he says, indicating a problem he once had playing Antonio in Antoni Cimolino's Stratford production of *The Merchant of Venice* in 2013, opposite Tyrell Crews' Bassanio and Scott Wentworth's Shylock. Antoni wanted him to play Antonio as gay (as contemporary actors often have interpreted the part), but McCamus thought: "It doesn't really matter if he's gay or not. He's a man who prefers the company of men, and there's a difference between that label and the quality of who the person really is. To me, it's not about his sexuality. It's about why he cares for Bassanio so much and the way he sees the world. This makes him a richer character. We never had an argument or battle about it. It was more a question of semantics than anything else."

McCamus did clash fulsomely with a designer, though, whose costume for a Shakespearean role seemed created to be exhibitionistic rather than pragmatic. "I was wearing something quite nice, and he said: 'Just show it off. Show off the vest. Do a couple of twirls.' So, I did it as a joke backstage, and he said: 'Could you do that more on stage?' And I said: 'No!' I probably should clash more often because sometimes costumes have not helped me at all."

He appreciates the late William Hutt's concern that a costume should never declare more than an actor could possibly play as a character. McCamus also voices a concern between the comfort of rehearsal clothes and the sudden change to full costume that can throw off an interpretation. "On the other hand," he says, "sometimes you put on a costume and there's your character. All those things I was acting, I don't have to act anymore."

My interview takes up a final issue: acting philosophy. I recall William Hutt's extensive reflection on the subject: "I would dispute the theory that actors are themselves on stage. They are themselves in a different set of circumstances. I cannot pretend that I am not Bill Hutt onstage, but so long as I wrap myself in the experience and illuminate the audience that it is a different set of circumstances, to *them* I become a different person. You cannot perform Lear, Timon of Athens, Hamlet. All you can do is e*xperience* those roles" (Garebian 1988: 269). McCamus agrees, but adds a specific qualifier:

> Depends on how you go at it. Bill was a pretty dynamic human being, and he believed he could just be Bill on the stage. He would get angry at me because I was so doubting all the time. In order for me to be on the stage, I have to pretend I'm somebody else. As soon as I'm me, it just doesn't work. I think what the audience sees is exactly what Bill's talking about: how you convince yourself that you belong on that stage. If I'm just Tom on that stage, I don't belong on that stage, but if I'm somebody else—Richard III or whomever I have discovered—I belong. Then, I can do *anything* because I don't get in my own way. That's why I can play all those evil guys because I'm not evil. If I convince myself I am that evil guy, then I can do all sorts of things that Tom couldn't ever dream of doing.

Notes

[1] Our interview started at Lale Bakery, Mississauga, on December 1, 2017 before being moved to the small condo library in my Mississauga apartment building the same afternoon.
[2] In 1995, a production in which William Hutt played Sir John Falstaff, William Needles Justice Shallow, Dixie Seatle Mistress Ford, and McCamus's wife Chick Reid as Mistress Page.

[3]Brian Bedford directed this production at the Tom Patterson Theatre in 1996, with Stephen Ouimette as Estragon, James Blendick as Pozzo, and Tim MacDonald as Lucky.

[4]In 2012 at the Tom Patterson Theatre. McCamus played Iachimo, Cara Ricketts Imogen, and Geraint Wyn Davies Cymbeline.

[5]In 2013 at the Festival Theatre, with Scott Wentworth as Shylock and McCamus as Antonio.

[6]Tim Carroll, former Associate Director of Shakespeare's Globe Theatre (London) and former Artistic Director of Kent Opera, was appointed Artistic Director of the Shaw Festival, Niagara-on-the-Lake, Ontario in 2018.

[7]In 1997, directed by Richard Rose.

[8]"If I was pushed, I would be tempted to say it was an Elizabethan black comedy about politics, perhaps an Ubi Roi [sic] … it is a black political comedy in which there are terrible casualties, the main ones being Arthur and Constance." (Qtd. in Cook 1989:104)

Juan Chioran as Don Adriano de Armado in Love's Labour's Lost *(Stratford Festival, 2015).*
(Photo: David Hou. Courtesy of the Stratford Festival)

Juan Chioran
Making a World We all Understand

Born in Alberti in the Pampas region of Argentina, Juan Chioran came to Canada at the age of twelve in 1975 during the Dirty War (*Guerra Sucia*), a period of state terrorism (1974-83) conducted by a military junta or civic-military dictatorship.[1] He spoke no English when he arrived, but soon made the language his own. Both his parents were from Italy—father (Bruno) from Padua, and mother (Alba) from Venice. His parents had immigrated to Argentina to make enough money to send back to relatives in Italy. Bruno was an auto mechanic with a Grade 6 education, and one of his sons is a carpenter, so Juan grew up surrounded by machinery.

Chioran is not the slightest bit interested in hiding this humble blue-collar background. In fact, he often helps his father in Stratford prepare home-made sausages and charcuterie. Yet, on the stage, things change somewhat for to see this tall, slim, tanned actor with a striking profile is to recognize a Latin temperament that is well-suited to larger-than-life exotic or eccentric roles, such as Don Quixote, Don Armado, Frank'n'Furter, or Juan Peron. In the 2018 Stratford season, he was transcendental to the nth degree by playing the role of God the Father in a fascinatingly cryptic manner in Erin Shields' *Paradise Lost*.

Some wits might well be tempted to crack that to have moved on from Shakespeare to God is an organic progression for it is simply to pass from one God to another. But it may not be simply a cursory witticism. After all, his interest in the arts began with his singing in a *church* choir. "I felt better singing in the choir than sitting in the congregation," he explains. He also did folk dancing: "As a kid, I was always involved in some performing arts." In high school in midtown Toronto, he felt very comfortable in front of a group.

His introduction to Shakespeare was a sorry experience: Without any real knowledge of English literature, he and his peers in Grade 11 were practically tortured by a teacher, whose method of covering a Shakespearean play was to plunk on a recording of a bad Old Vic production "from God knows when." It was so tortuous that when the Polonius was stabbed in the plot, the students all cheered. "That was my introduction to Shakespeare. I had no connection, no kinship to it at all," he confesses.

But when he and classmates were taken to the Stratford Festival to see Brian Bedford and Maggie Smith in Robin Phillips' exquisite version of *Much Ado About Nothing* in 1980, he was stunned to discover that he understood the language. Instead of sounding like aliens speaking an impossibly inaccessible language in a pompous tone, the actors seemed to be just speaking naturally. He was hooked, and his delight was compounded by the fact that he recognized Bedford as an actor he had seen in his first movie back home: *Grand Prix*.

His delight deepened after he joined the Stratford acting company in 1988 and got to work with Bedford two years later. "I adored him dearly, and we became good friends. I would tease him mercilessly: 'Brian, I saw you on the screen when I was 9!' And he would protest: 'Oh, stop it. I'm not that old.'"

But before this professional and personal friendship developed, Chioran had to complete his university education. Initially, he thought he might become an architect or engineer, but soon gravitated towards singing and theatre at York University before realizing that York was not a good fit for him and consequently moving to the University of Alberta, where in 1987 he completed his BFA in Theatre. Shortly after graduation, he was cast as Frank'n'Furter in *The Rocky Horror Picture Show* at Stage West, Calgary, subsequently playing the role in Fort McMurray, Edmonton, and Toronto.

When he first entered the Stratford acting company, he played small roles and understudied principal roles. He left when an offer didn't appeal to him, and spent a year and a half performing with Opera Lyra in Ottawa, Opera in Concert in Toronto, and, most modestly of all, Opera Mississauga. Then Harold Prince happened. After Chioran auditioned unsuccessfully for the original musical version of Manuel Puig's novel, *Kiss of the Spider Woman*, Prince offered him a six-month contract as Standby for Jeff Hyslop who was playing the key role of Molina, the homosexual window-dresser imprisoned for corrupting a minor.

He did go on for fifty performances when Hyslop's back problem was aggravated, and got to star opposite Broadway legend Chita Rivera in her last performance and then Vanessa Williams in some of her early performances. Rivera taught him some of the biggest lessons he carries to this day: "She taught me how to be the leader of a company, how to do it by example, not by behaving like a diva. She was the hardest worker, always on time, always generous both on stage and off. She was young at heart. And she was a life lesson, as well as a career lesson." Prince was another career lesson: "The man is so intuitive. He knows his art. He can crystallize it in a few words because he is succinct and precise. He is incredibly visionary, and gets to the heart of the matter quickly, without being fussy."

Chioran won raves for his performance from the *Los Angeles Times* and *Variety*, with the *Times* asserting that he was "the show's heart" and *Variety* reporting that he was "effectively fey, flitting about the cell with gentle flourishes to his movements, girlishly crossing his legs or playing with a scarf or, more important, initiating Aurora's actions as Rivera brings to life the movies in Molina's mind." The actor triumphed in another flamboyant gay role in 2003—that of Roger de Bris, the impossibly camp director in Mel Brooks' *The Producers*, who enters wearing a dress and winds up as a singing Hitler.

But Chioran could not be pegged. He was an imposingly masculine Peron in *Evita*, a sinister Rochefort in *The Three Musketeers*, the terrifyingly seductive Count Dracula, the androgynous emcee in *Cabaret*, and the severe director Zach in *A Chorus Line*, in which his performance had more credibility than Michael Douglas' in the film version. And then there are his major Shakespearean performances: Parolles (*All's Well That Ends Well*), Don Armado (*Love's Labour's Lost*), and the Player King (*Hamlet*).

Consequently, he sees himself justifiably as "an actor who can do pretty much any genre or era. I've loved the experience of doing just about anything over the years and of feeling comfortable no matter where you put me." His versatility has even taken the form of a triptych in a single play—the roles of Ghost, the First Player, and the Gravedigger in *Hamlet*. Does he have a preference, however, for a specific genre? "I naturally love laughter. I love the sound of it because it is antithetical to the horridness that is our world today. So, I would much rather have people laugh than sob, but there's nothing quite like what you get in tragedy, where you affect people on a deep level. My acting career has been like a smorgasbord where you sample a little of everything all the time."

In the 2018 season he is appearing in *The Comedy of Errors*, a play he is doing for the third time. It was, in fact, his first Shakespeare at theatre school, as well as part of his first Stratford season in 1988. Is comedy technically more challenging than tragedy? "Yes," he responds, "and more difficult. Comedy is offbeat. So much has to be about things turning about unexpectedly. The style with which Brian Bedford directed comedy was a master class. But it is through discipline and rigour that you acquire those tools. He also had a natural gift for timing that was second to none. You can help make someone funny if they understand the way with which certain things ought to be done." His focus quickly hinges on the issue of style:

> Each period has its own style. You would play Wilde and Coward very differently than you would do a comedy by Mamet. It's understanding the world you're in, as if you lived in that time. There's an elegance, a finesse. There's a craft to all this style which is not being learned anymore. Perhaps no one is interested anymore. It's the times: aesthetics change, demographics. The company here is very different from the one back when I started. The audience is very different. I am heartened that the audiences are younger, in general. That's great because we also have to be audience builders in the theatre.

He agrees with me that a lot of modern Shakespeare is coarsened by a lack of craft: "You're caught in the position of having to sell tickets because you don't have the subsidies that you once used to have. So, you have to make it somewhat populist. How far do you go artistically in order to push the envelope so that you don't alienate everybody? It's hard but sometimes we need to risk being edgy. You have to explore it all. The pendulum swing is such an interesting thing to see onstage."

Given the rather excessive anxiety over making Shakespeare relevant to contemporary audiences, how are we to stage such things as the fairy world of *A Midsummer Night's Dream*, for instance? Chioran once played Oberon at Stratford (directed by Richard Monette in 1999), and, therefore, is able to offer his perspective: "So much has to be done by your designer and director. When you're talking about this play, you are thinking about the elemental. All my guy fairies[2] were the biggest guys in the company—like 6'2", 190 pounds, not fleet of foot. It was hard."

At least, his Puck, Jordan Pettle, was smaller and athletic, so Chioran was able to mount him on his back and go into a bit of a Cirque du Soleil world, while letting "old Will do the rest. I thought that if I ever direct *A Midsummer Night's Dream*, I would find an Oberon about 4' tall and would get Robert Persichini [a bulky tall actor] to play Puck. He would be a chain-smoker who would bumble as he utters 'I go, I go.' What is the fairy world? I would shake it on its ears, and make it absurdist. Do you get into *Lord of the Rings* territory?"

It is an open question. Peter Brook's brilliant 1970 production for the Royal Shakespeare Company subverted the fay of Victorian tradition, but would muscular fairies with rippling biceps and heavy feet be a spurious eclecticism? Perhaps, but the play itself manifests eclecticism, a point that Chioran hints at when he alludes to Oberon's interaction with Titania as being a case of Edward Albee's dark revenge drama.

Moreover, as shrewd readers of the play know, each world of this play has its own rhythms of language and facets of identity. The world of the court is quite different from the fairy world's, just as the fairy world is quite different from the vulgar world of the "mechanicals." And within each of these worlds there are distinctions of language and rhythm. Hermia and Demetrius use rhyming exchanges that have zest and a colour all their own. Oberon and Titania both ripple with sexual undercurrents and power struggles in their dialogue. Puck speaks differently from his supporting sprites. A physically large Puck (that Chioran proposes for an imagined production) could have an awesome sound and presence. However, we have to bear in mind that whatever works today may become irrelevant or old-fashioned tomorrow. Everything in the theatre, as in life, is relative. There are no absolutes.

I turn the discussion to a difficulty with some of Shakespeare's comic characters and ask if one of the problems is the language itself, as in the cases of Lavache or Touchstone, for instance. He advises: "You've got to put terrific actors in those parts. You need actors who can be inventive, not only by making the language understandable (because a lot of those jokes don't ring today) but being clever in accompanying that with something else. A director can help. I remember Richard Monette crafting comic performances out of people who didn't have a funny bone in their bodies. He knew what worked. You can't turn somebody into a comedian just like that. You can choreograph moments. You can help."

When the conversation turns specifically to acting, I ask how important it is to find a character's "wound." "It's not something that I seek out to do, but looking back at how I build characters, I have done that subconsciously," he admits. "You can't play an entire evening saying to yourself 'I'm winning, I'm winning, I'm winning.' That's so dull." He located a comic "wound" for the fantastical (and penurious) Don Armado, borrowing from his own autobiographical experience: "Spanish is my first language. *Love's Labour's Lost* is a play very much about language, so I asked myself how I could turn these facts to my advantage. I bend the Shakespearean text in many ridiculous ways, with some degree of style, I hope, that you don't find it coarse. People laugh at the murder of the language, the affectation—all of that. Speaking Spanish really helps."

A case in point is the passage where Don Armado utters the following when speaking of the King: "I must tell thee it will please his Grace (by the world) sometime to lean you upon my poor shoulder, and with his royal finger, thus, dally with my excrement, my mustachio" (5.1.101-104). The audience thinks he is speaking pure filth but he is merely referring to the hair of his spectacularly flared moustache, that Chioran accompanied by the gesture of twirling it fancifully.

Maggie Smith used to remark that if you didn't laugh in comedy, you would cry. Her claim was repeated by Nicholas Pennell, with his own annotation: "Comedy, she said, arises from the need to disguise the pain. It comes from the place that is informed by the unbearable pain of living and of relationships. It's skating along on top of the thinnest possible ice, so that at any moment it can tip into a tragic dimension, but it never does" (Maher 144).

Don Armado's pain (expressed by his extravagant melancholy or silhouette as a Quixote figure) is (as Chioran says) "that he cannot help himself but be in love. The seat of his melancholy lies in his loss of power—his inability to say [to his rival in love], 'No, I will fight you' but then just completely giving in. Deep down inside, he doesn't tell himself he is too old or not the right match for Jaquenetta [a dairy maid]."

Chioran is well aware of Don Armado's resemblance to Don Quixote, a character that he played in *Man of La Mancha*. Both characters are defined by a madness: Armado's being a love sickness expressed by an extreme affectation of language and manner; Quixote's by his delusion of chivalry as he tilts at windmills that he imagines are giant monsters. "If the play was set in modern times," Chioran suggests, "Armado could look like Dali. He has a sense of self-creation and makes absolutely no apology. He just shows up and says 'This is who I am.'"

The actor appears to specialize in rather crazed characters such as Parolles, Armado, and Quixote, but along with the madness there is often a deep vein of melancholy. "These melancholy characters are more difficult for me than the ones that aren't melancholy because I'm not a melancholy person myself," remarks Chioran. "You can't play melancholy any more than you can play general emotion. You can only play intention. You figure out what the DNA or makeup of that character is, and if you need to enter in a state of being, so be it. By finding the anchors of characters, you find out a fair bit."

His entry into a role starts with understanding every single word of the text. He undertakes what he calls "detective work" with lexicons. He doesn't pay much attention to literary critics because "with all due respect, [what they write] is unactable. It is interesting as a dissertation but I cannot act any of that." In this regard he is rather like the late Nicholas Pennell (a model Shakespearean actor) who found every clue from the text and not from literary criticism. Pennell once recalled how he made the error of reading Ernest Jones' *Hamlet and Oedipus*, swallowing it whole, and only managed to escape its negative effect on his acting the role of Hamlet two weeks before the opening: "I swore that I would never read anything again to do with the play. The moment you do, you start taking on other people's baggage. It's fatal in creative work" (Maher 131).

Chioran shares other details of his own preparation: "I tend to learn lines very quickly—especially Shakespeare. So, I don't generally come in with my lines memorized because I don't want to lock into a rote. If you do a certain speech the same way, believe it or not, muscle memory will stay, so to try and break that might get a little hard. I break the scene down the way we learned in theatre school: What is my objective? What do I want, and how am I going to get it?" He examines the *verbs* of the scene and tries to understand who's driving the scene. Then there's specific character work:

> What does my character say about other characters? What do other characters say about me? What do I say about myself? And what does the playwright say about me? Those are important clues. I look at the first line and final line just for a lark. When I was playing Jaques in *As You Like It* [directed by Jeannette Lambermont at the Avon], I noted that he was in seven scenes. The Seven Ages of Man! If you apply the essence of the child, the schoolboy, the soldier, et cetera to each scene, it's all there. Investigating that is like a little Sherlock Holmes. I like to do the work in the room, in the rehearsal hall, and explore, even if it means falling on your ass.

There are so many ways you could launch into the Seven Ages of Man speech, but what I found with Jaques is that the other scenes are very difficult because there's very little interconnective tissue from one scene to the next. That's what made me look at each scene to see if they matched the Seven Ages speech. You get a beautiful aria and a lot of difficult *recit* throughout.

Is Jaques a cynic or realist? Chioran provides a temperate answer: "He is definitely cynical. He is, perhaps, all about seeking the truth, but the truth is unfortunately tainted by his view of humanity. He is more elemental, tonality wise. Above all, he has to be real, he has to bring, not a pall but a change in the temperature of a scene."

One of the distinguishing features of Chioran as actor is his voice in the tenor range. Michael Langham once advised him to develop the bottom of his vocal compass. "I listened to the teachers," Chioran explains of learning how to place his voice during his early years at Stratford:

The voice works in an interesting way. You have a chest voice, a head voice, and resonating chambers. You need to know where the main resonating is happening. You'd like to have them all going all at once for richness, but it depends on the character you are playing. It's hard to explain voice because it's not like ballet, where you can say, 'Oh, that's the right place' or 'That's the wrong place.' Voice is internal, so you rely on sensations a lot more. I don't know if the sound is resonating in a certain chamber but I can feel or sense that it is there.

How does he prepare his voice for performance?

I do a singing vocal warmup for about 10-12 minutes when I'm showering or shaving. If I'm doing a musical or if I have a cold or allergy or if the voice is not working well, then it's a little bit longer. I have a physical warmup. I'm in athlete mode when I'm performing. I come in two hours before the show, do an hour of yoga or some weight-lifting. I thoroughly believe that these are athletic spaces that we have to play in and it's a long season. I hydrate and try to eat well—all the boring things. I try to eat probably around 5:30 pm or 6. I sometimes bring a second dinner or snack and have it at intermission. I metabolize very quickly and need the caloric intake.

I was a trumpet player in high school, so breath has never been a problem. I can deliver half a page at just natural speed in one breath. Normal speed is more difficult than fast because at fast speed you get a lot of words out with not much breath. I trained operatically, so I have a lot of tools at my disposal. I've been working for 35 years on this, so I am able to have an intimate conversation and be heard in a 2,000-seat theatre. We don't train actors to project nowadays, so we mike them. That's ridiculous.

Chioran's ability to sing is an asset because it has helped him refine his vocal technique. Good speech in Shakespearean acting entails knowing where to find parenthetical phrases and knowing how to raise the voice on the end of these and allowing the voice to come down to close a sentence at the end of an independent clause. Scansion is another technical thing that is helped by musical knowledge because singing helps a performer discover the beats and extra beats. Chioran elaborates:

When I look at a piece of Shakespeare, it's like looking at a piece of music, where there's fortissimo, pianissimo, accelerando, ritardando, staccato, etc. It's all there, just without those markings. I can see it in his language. I can see the rhetorical devices. I can see the antitheses, the lists, and the ladders. They will help me unearth phrasing, if nothing else.

I am put in mind of Nicholas Pennell's comparing Shakespearean text to a musical score, an idea inherited from Michael Langham: "I realized what Michael Langham meant when he talked about a good classical text being like a score. You must look at the way that it's put together and how tempo and legato and other musical ideas creep into discussions about text. I'm not talking about 'singing' the text, because that's not an accepted way of performing, of course" (Maher 138). So, is what the Player King recites (whom Chioran played so vividly in Antoni Cimolino's version of *Hamlet* in 2015) an example of a musical score? Chioran agrees, with important qualifications:

> Yes, and a very different musical score from the rest of the play. If you look at the line structure, that in itself is almost Jacobean. There's a clue. Stylistically, the man is acting. What is that about? I start out with way too much and then refine and refine. I will continue to play the role till the end of the season, which is a real luxury. I'm not interested in going out every night and doing a carbon copy of what I did the night before. I'm always looking for some kind of real communication.
>
> I'm going to give away a state secret with the Player King. The problem when you do a show where there's a play-within-a-play, where the actors become the audience as well, is that after about two months, the cast gets tired of your doing your thing. So, you've got to keep their attention somehow. I would therefore introduce something called the disease of the night. On a given night, I would indicate a small symptom—under the radar, subtle—of whatever that illness was, and the cast would have to guess what the illness was.

Chioran's acting has been accused of being large at times, but he counters by explaining that he is Latin: "I live in a somewhat more demonstrative way than an Anglo. I express myself very differently. Maybe that's why I have been given all these roles of size: Player King and Armado. You can't just show up and be casual." He also asserts that there are no strict rules for speaking Shakespeare: "Whenever a guru shows up and says: 'This is how it is done. This is how it was done,' I really bristle at that. There are many ways to do it, each valuable. My approach is to have borrowed whatever I could from various methods to create my own way. And I think it has served me well. I don't believe in adhering to something so religiously that it becomes metronomic." In his earlier days at Stratford his models were Brian Bedford, Nicholas Pennell, and Colm Feore: "I listened to *them* the most because I was a young actor when they were playing leads here, so they were my points of reference."

He also learned from some of the best directors. David William was one such teacher:

> He was *incredibly* smart. He was really all about the texts. Certainly, he was one of my mentors here when I was a young actor. He would have 1-on-1's with the whole cast, and you'd go through your whole role, with him reading the other parts. Just the rigour with the language was just incredible. He would help actors change the angle a little bit when they were stuck. He'd say, 'Put that in your think tank.'
>
> I don't know that he always necessarily understood masculine/feminine dynamics in love stories. Sometimes he could be sort of 'headmasterish,' but that whole generation was. That's how I came up the ranks, and I was immune to that. I didn't get beat on very much. I didn't like seeing others being beat up, but it made you pick up your heels and run a little bit faster and come in a little better the next time. There's something to be said about that.

He did not get to be directed by Robin Phillips and has yet to be directed by Chris Abraham, but he has worked with Joseph Ziegler, Marti Maraden, John Caird, John Doyle, William Gaskill, and Richard Monette. He articulates what he expects from a director:

> What I expect is someone who is prepared, who has done his work, who has thought a great deal about the play, who knows the play really well, and who can create a world that we can all inhabit. It doesn't matter how normal it seems or how strange it is, but if they get that right, then we [the actors] can take care of the rest. Preparation is my big bugaboo right now. I don't find a lot of directors are terribly well prepared. They go for concepts rather than the nitty gritty of staging it, such as the stagecraft required to move people in, out, have them be heard, seen, and have some elegance to it.

When should a director release a production to the actors? Should it be on opening night? "Theoretically. A lot of directors do keep coming back to give notes." He'd like to say to them: "'You've had your three months, go away.' When we open, then it's ours—the actors. That's my feeling." Who establishes the style of a production? He believes the director should but "quite often it's established by the actors by default because the director has not established one." He expands:

> Some kind of a galvanizing hybrid gets formed by the acting company, and that's the style. It's harder to get everyone to play on the same field when you don't know where that field is. It's quite easy to make a grand proposal or have a cultural thesis, but it's another thing to actually put on a play with the stagecraft that a Michael Langham or a Robin Phillips had. You don't see that anymore. We're in a post-colonial world that is poo-pooed. I'm very lucky to have hitched my wagon to the tail-end of that era when I started.

What would he do if he disagreed with a director's concept?

> That's a hard one because you signed your contract to tell their story. That's the story we have to tell. It's a collaborative effort. You have conversations. You try to meet halfway. Most directors are not tyrants. Those days are gone. It's about creating something together. Set the story on Neptune in the year 3419. I don't care, but make it a world that we all understand. Make it truthful and make it relate to what is here. It's when concept fights the play, that I don't much care for it.

I pose three more questions. Does he have a favourite role? Benedick in *Much Ado About Nothing*, he reveals, before adding: "I never got to play any of the *big* tragic parts here. I would love to do the whole canon, quite frankly. I've done about 75% of it. I don't care what role but I've got to stop doing two or three of the same ones because I'll never get through it at this rate." One of his acting models, Nicholas Pennell, believed that acting was a form of memoir-creation: "Every time you hear a poet or a novelist, you hear about their memoirs. What are memoirs? They are autobiographical, but they are not actually autobiography. I think acting is a memoir. It's a series of reflections on your life and on what happens to you" (Qtd. in Maher 145).

So, does Chioran think of an actor as a memoirist? "Yes, I study humanity and behaviour 24/7. We have to. We are the caretakers of the story in some sense. But the problem with that is that acting is not written anywhere. Once you commit it to the elements, especially in live theatre, it's gone, unless you're lucky enough to record. But, then, I can't watch them. There's no bigger hell than to watch myself on the screen doing a theatre performance." My final question concerns what he thinks of contemporary trends towards gender-bending and colour-blind casting? He offers an expansive response:

> I'm presently in a show, *The Comedy of Errors*, where both are very much the focus. I'm all for it. I'm playing the Duke of Ephesus dressed as a woman. I'm just playing a man who identifies as a woman. A feminine self-identifier. There are others, so it is very normal in our world that we've created. I'm letting the costume do a lot of the talking. I don't have to do anything in *that* regard. I don't change my voice. I may move in a slightly more feminine manner. I'm in a skirt and long boots. Beyond that, I'm just playing the words. I don't care if you use a 350-pound green elephant so long as it can play the part, so long as it has the goods as an actor. I don't want political and social justice (both necessary) to debase the standard of acting needed. You've got to have the ability. Period. That is my only criterion.

Notes

[1] Our interview was conducted in a room in the Stratford Normal School building, May 16, 2018.
[2] Milton Barnes, Thom Marriott, David Snelgrove, Vito Tassielli, and Andy Velasquez.

Chick Reid
(Photo: Helen Tansey)

Chick Reid
Gladly Does She Learn and Gladly Teach

Petite and slim, Chick Reid was born to Scottish parents in Canada. Her father had all of $40 at the time of emigration from Scotland, but he had a job—as a motor mechanic in a large British-owned company in Scarborough. Although her father played the bagpipes on the side, her parents were not keen on her turning to the arts as a profession. Indeed, her parents' generation treated formal education as a waste of time: "They were of the age where you left school at 14 and went to work. I was the first one of the family to go to university. They were thrilled with my going to university but they just didn't understand why I didn't put it to good use." And they understood even less when she decided to take dance lessons and become an actress.

However, she did not allow their bias to interfere with her own ambitions. She attended Queen's University, Kingston, where she earned a B.A. in Drama and French in 1974. Her classmates in Drama included Nancy Palk, Wendy Crewson, and Judith Thompson, all of whom would go on to distinguished careers in the profession. However, the undergraduate courses in Drama did not provide essential grounding in the promotional side of show business: "You left Queen's with a really solid background in and knowledge of theatre: how to read a play and analyze it; and act it well. But you didn't come out a hotshot, you didn't come out with your 8"x 10"; you didn't come out with your resume. So, I had no show biz skills."

Nevertheless, by combining academics and a teaching diploma, she was able to have a double profession: teaching and acting. And when she was able to save up enough money from her acting to undertake a trip to Scotland to visit her grandparents, aunts, and uncles, things got sorted out about the worth of higher education and the acting profession.

Reid did not glamorize her status in the theatre. Although she never achieved her dream of being a ballet dancer, she was good enough at tap to perform with the National Tap Dance Company of Canada. She met her husband-to-be, Tom McCamus, in 1980 when they were collaborating at Theatre Passe Muraille in Toronto on a collective piece, *From Saigon to Sudbury*, about the trauma of refugees, and they married in 1984. The pair have worked either separately or together across the country, from Sudbury and Manitoba to various alternative theatres in Toronto, before making it to the Shaw Festival in Niagara-on-the-Lake for four seasons (1985-88), where she appeared in *The Women, War and Peace, Peter Pan, Marathon 33,* and *Cavalcade*.

Reid did not get to Stratford to indulge her love for Shakespeare until Richard Monette invited her in 1995, after they had worked together in Toronto at Theatre Plus on *Saint Joan*. She and her husband wanted to support Monette Canadianize Stratford and Shakespeare more than they had ever been. They felt that the festival was overdue to have a Canadian artistic director, fewer foreign leads, and more Canadian plays and actors. In her first Stratford season, she played Mistress Page in *The Merry Wives of Windsor* (in which McCamus was Ford and William Hutt Falstaff) and Mrs. Squeamish in *The Country Wife* (in which McCamus was horny Horner).

It was a most congenial situation, for Reid had been making trips to the festival ever since childhood, and recalls the thrill of her first visit to the Festival Theatre: "I thought my heart was going to stop when I walked into that theatre." The first Shakespearean play she ever saw there was John Hirsch's 1968 production of *A*

Midsummer Night's Dream, in which Martha Henry was a stunningly sexy Titania and Barbara Bryne was Puck. Seeing a female Puck led Reid to wonder later why males customarily played the role. As it transpired, she became the first actress since Bryne to play the same role in Chris Abraham's vigorously amusing 2014 version that was framed by a gay wedding and in which Jonathan Goad and Evan Buliung alternated the role of Titania.

At the time of our interview,[1] gender-bending or cross-gender casting had become embedded in the festival season: a transvestite Duke of Ephesus (Juan Chioran), and a female Dromio and Antipholus in Keira Loughran's version of *The Comedy of Errors*; Michelle Giroux as Mark Antony, Irene Poole as Cassius, and Seana McKenna as Caesar in Scott Wentworth's *Julius Caesar*; and a headline-grabbing Martha Henry as Prospero for Antoni Cimolino's *The Tempest*.

Reid's views on the subject are tempered by common sense: "There are probably roles that lend themselves to it. I don't go down the rabbit hole of historical authenticity, such as would there have been a Duchess of Milan at that time? I don't know. I don't care. That doesn't bother me. Would I feel the same if a man wanted to play Beatrice? I'd say: 'Fuck off! You've got your own parts.' There's precious few for the women to do, particularly if the actresses are of a certain age." Does an actress cast a different light on a male role? Can a female Brutus, for example, show what a male actor could not? Reid replies:

> Maybe. I guess you don't know till you see it or until you're in it. If you're talking about Brutus, there's something in the philosophic side of his being that can be identified as female, with an instinct for peace-keeping. There are certain emotions that have been traditionally identified as male reactions, so it's not surprising, for instance, to see Lear get vengeful against his daughters. Revenge is typically a male thing. It's very jarring. You accept that, but when you see a woman playing Lear, that raises questions because you don't really see a woman take

that kind of mother to daughter revenge. The same with Prospero: he's all about revenge. He makes it all happen just to get those people on his island so he can have his revenge. But to see a woman plot and be responsible for that, it's a different sensibility but it's not confusing at all because the story's the same. Doesn't matter if it's Duchess or Duke—Prospero simply is a parent, acting for his or her child.

Reid's generalizations about male emotions or passions seem questionable, because (to offer only a few examples) Medea, Electra, Lady Macbeth, Goneril, and Regan were certainly not inhibited in their malevolence or violence. However, I agree that in *The Tempest*, for instance, it doesn't matter if Prospero is a Duke or Duchess. In fact, a female Prospero would sharpen the character's motive for revenge because it would be a woman who was ousted from her rightful dukedom and she would be isolated, as a woman displaced without her counterpart on an island.

Reid agrees: "Typically, it's the mother who would do anything for her child. She would kill, if she needed to. We are going to see more and more of this gender bending. The key question is 'Does the play work or does it change the play?'" Therefore, I suggest, the central issue is not really about optical illusion or a convincing imitation of a male. It's about what light you can cast on a male role. Reid concurs with my opinion:

I think so. I haven't seen enough of the gender-bending to have a super-formed opinion or judgement of it. I think the director has got to have a reason to do it. *The Midsummer Night's Dream* of 2014 was our world. Chris did it for a reason—not to give a girl a chance to play a good boy's part but to be inclusive. His production was all about love—all kinds of love. There was an all-female *Measure for Measure* in Toronto.[2] I didn't see it and I don't know what the reason is. Was that a way to get 14 women in a room, which is reason enough, or was it saying something that *all* the parts were played by women.[3]

All I'm saying is that however it's done, it shouldn't be confusing for us. Doesn't mean it shouldn't raise questions, but I don't want to spend my time going 'I don't understand this. I don't get the play.'

I don't want to feel stupid. There's a big difference between being asked to ask yourself a question by watching a piece of theatre and being confused by it.

Reid was understudying Martha Henry's Prospero. "Why not?" she asks rhetorically. "I get a chance to watch her steer that big ship, Prospero." She admires Martha Henry because she is "an amazing person," whom it is a pleasure to understudy because the legendary actress doesn't adopt the status of a remote untouchable with acting colleagues. "We talk to one another about difficult passages. Whatever she decides about that whacked syntax, that's what I decide it is too."

This is not the first time she has understudied Henry. She went on three times for her on Broadway in Monette's version of *Much Ado About Nothing*, with Henry as Beatrice to Brian Bedford's Benedick. The first occasion, she was notified at 6:30 pm that she would be doing the show that evening, and she was donning her makeup in Henry's dressing room adjoining Bedford's when Bedford poked his head around the door and said: "Oh, hello, Chick. [surprised pause] Chick?" "Yeah, Martha's off tonight."

Bedford took this in stride, saying casually: "Oh, all right, see you out there." His casual manner relaxed her, though she did appeal to him to run lines with her for the first scene. The reason was not to test her memory but so she could hear his acting voice and how the lines would sound when he spoke them: "For comfort. Everyone is in a state of alert. So, you have to get rid of their worry. You need to go on as if to say: 'You don't need to be alarmed. It's just going to be me, not her. You have to get all the worry for everybody else off the table."

But her remarks show me that she is no Eve Harrington (from the classic 1950 film, *All About Eve*), who has sinister designs on usurping the star's status. "That's a young actor's dream—to actually go on for a big part. It's absolutely terrifying to me. Adrenalin will take you so far, and you've got your company members around you, but it's not yours. It will never be yours."

This leads to a discussion of the essential function of an understudy. Her answer is surprisingly revelatory: An understudy is required to be almost a photo-copy, as if were, of the actress she is replacing in terms of delivery of lines and patterns of blocking. Reid started memorizing Prospero's lines when Henry did, was completely off book by April 1, and then watched Henry attentively: "My function is to be Martha. It's not my job to give my interpretation of Prospero. I won't imitate her vocal style but there's a big difference in our speaking rhythms, so I try to match Martha's. My rhythm is like Speedy Gonzalez."

She explains that what would throw other actors off as much as her not knowing the text properly is her own distinctive rhythm. "They will literally not be ready to speak. That's not to say that actors do the same thing every single night, but there is a general rhythm that you develop as a character. It's going to be different in a sense, anyway, because it's a different human being, but it's not my version of Prospero. This is Martha's view of Prospero that is in my brain and body."

The two actresses appear to have a strange but complementary twinning, that showed itself in rehearsals: "Instant by instant, where I stumbled, Martha stumbled, and where Martha stumbled, I stumbled. That's interesting because she's pretty smart just in terms of making sense of something. Why? The syntax of this play is unlike any other I've learned." As an understudy, she is directed by the stage manager rather than the director, and, unlike the regular cast she gets only one shot at it with lights, sound, costumes, and the whole *understudy* company.[4]

Some members of the acting company might come in to help with scene changes and transitions, and the director will check once to see if everything is safe. "I'm on my own," she claims. However, she pays Antoni Cimolino, her director, a compliment: "I like him very much. He really adheres to the text, and gives it its due by paying attention to it and using the text to help search for answers."

What if she disagrees radically with a director's interpretation of a role or play? She recalls what Peter Hinton (who has the reputation of being an unpredictably exciting director) once said to her and fellow cast-members in a rehearsal: "Don't be in the show that you *think* you should be in. Don't be in the show that you *want* to be in. Be in the show you *are* in."

Reid took this advice to heart, realizing that you still need to make the same investment as an actor, whatever the play or production, and to just see what happens in the process. "It is tough to do," she acknowledges, "but you have to, or otherwise that energy brings you to a negative place. To carry that into a rehearsal room or an auditorium doesn't serve the play. Audiences don't pay money to be sent a negative message. They pay money to be sent a positive message. Your job is to serve the play and what the director wants to bring to that play. Being negative doesn't keep you open to discovering something good. It closes you." Fortunately, she has never been treated tyrannically by a director:

> I don't know if I've been in the situation where what I've been asked to do as an actor goes completely contrary to what I believe. There are always going to be directors who are more open to discussion than others, but I haven't ever been totally shut down by anybody. There are directors, as there are actors, who have a propensity to dig their size 6's in. So, I say, 'You're the director, and I'll do what you want. I'll never agree with it, but I'm not going to not care. If that's what you want, I will give it to you. I will find a way to marry my choice with yours.'

It is always difficult to explain the nature of acting, but it has been often said that acting is a series of memoirs or pieces of yourself. Does she agree? "Oh, absolutely! Even if the character has nothing to do with my life experience, it's still me that's doing it, so it does have to do with me. It's still your voice, heart, body. You can't change them. You can't change who you are. However, I don't like playing people that are close to me. I like to play people who are very different from me. When people say: 'Oh, just be yourself in that scene,' I ask: 'Why?'"

How does she interpret herself as an actress? "I see myself as versatile. I'm game for anything. I embrace all forms of what we do. I love doing farce, straight comedy, drama, tragedy. I like the art of storytelling, and I love that there's such a craft to what we do and to learn about it. And the great thing is you're never ever finished. That's what makes it so special. I like to keep going. If there's nothing more to learn, then just quit."

But because she has played more comic roles than dramatic ones at Stratford, I ask if she favours playing that genre. "I think people consider me more of a comedic actress than the other, but that's being pegged—as one always is. But I've done big dramatic roles and I've liked them, but I do love a good comedy."

She speaks with awe and love for Brian Bedford and his direction of *Noises Off* by Michael Frayn: "I have no desire to ever see the play again. I have no desire to *be* in it again. He was such a good comic himself. He paid attention to the craft. He gave it as much weight as he would give a *King Lear* in terms of what you need to do as an actor to make it *perfect*—to tell that story with the same honesty and truth as you would do with any other story, with the same attention to the text."

Having heard of complaints from other actors about Bedford's insistence on table readings, I ask how Bedford had worked on *Noises Off*. "We did a couple of good table reads to decipher the stage directions (i.e. the stage directions of the impossibly complex Act Two) before we got on our feet." In the rehearsal hall, the cast worked with an exact mock-up of the set used at the Avon Theatre, but rehearsals were exhausting. Bedford spent two full weeks blocking the second act alone, and he was hands-on but would not give line-readings or get up and demonstrate.

He had a very good eye, and there was no room for laziness: "You took his notes to the bank, in a sense. He liked what it is we do as actors because it was what he did. He was happy in the room but he was a taskmaster and we got away with nothing. But we had a production of *Noises Off* of a quality that's never been seen since, I guarantee you. It was one of a kind."

Reid needs a director's hand right till the opening night, though she feels that sometimes there's a point in rehearsal where she appreciates having the freedom to let her go her own way for a day or two so she can find her way through a role. Some directors like to micro-manage a little more than others, but she prefers a director letting her know what he or she sees in rehearsal because after the opening, the show is handed over to the stage manager who has to keep a sharp eye on interpretation. "Some let the show veer more than others," she reports. "Some keep the show right on track."

Turning to the nature of comedy and comic acting, I wonder if comedy is a question of attitude. She answers:

> To act a comedy, you have to be in the world of it. The funniest thing is when the audience and another character know something but you, as a character, don't. That to me is scream-worthy. It's the situation that makes for great comedy. It's not playing at it; it's knowing the world you're in, knowing what your function is [in that world]. I'm really big on that. I really like to know who my character is and what her function is. Knowing your function tells you when you've got to *take* a scene or when you've got to *feed* that scene.

Some actors advise others to find the happy in the sad and vice versa. "That makes perfect sense, doesn't it?" she says. "Because no one is only happy or only sad. Otherwise, you wouldn't be human. We can be open to everything. What Shakespeare understood so much was the human psyche. He *got* it, just *got* it!" As Dominic Dromgoole writes in *Will & Me* (one of the very best records of a lifelong obsession) that Shakespeare "wrote with the freedom, the speed and the automatic, unconscious fertility of genius" and his special gift (apart from language) was "that, however preposterous the situation, he makes you care for every one of his characters" (Dromgoole 29, 32).

But to understand character, one needs to know the context, and so Reid emphasizes the central importance of context. Accordingly, she is not one who would accuse Shakespeare of being a misogynist or anti-feminist, for instance, in *The Taming of the Shrew*, where Kate is subjected to a succession of indignities and cruelties until she finally submits to Petruchio's command:

> It's the world, and I believe there is a great big hunk of love that rules everything in his plays. Even the struggles between men and women are from love because if there were no love there, they wouldn't be bothered. They'd walk away. I'm one of those people who believe that when Kate sees Petruchio, it's love at first sight, but they know it can't happen because she's got baggage and he's got his, so they spend the time fighting it till they can fight no longer and then they come together. I believe that speech [of submission] comes from a place of love and truth because in those times, men did do all those things for women. What she's talking about in that speech is absolute truth. I don't think she ever says she's going to roll over. I think she's throwing down the gauntlet. I think it's a two-way speech.

In the Acting Shakespeare 1 (DRAM 331) course she teaches at Queen's University (the only such course at any Canadian university), some of her students (20- and 21-year-olds) select the submission speech, but change their minds in a week because they find it runs counter to their idea of themselves as young feminists. Under Reid's astute leadership and guidance, they eventually learn how to read, interpret, and deliver Shakespeare, after allowing their naïve preconceptions and false perspectives to fall away.

It is clear from our interview that Reid loves her course and her students. She relates how the course came about, and with it, her continuing tenure at the university. She and Tom McCamus had known Craig Walker as an actor in Toronto and at the Shaw and Stratford festivals before he became Director of the Dan School of Drama and Music at Queen's. Walker enticed her to teach a seminar as Guest Lecturer at the university, allowing her to select a focal topic.

She suggested Shakespeare, and her stint was so successful, that she was hired to develop and teach acting for the camera for stage and screen for three years and to lead what are now two courses on Acting Shakespeare [DRAM 331 and 431], with the first for third-year students and the second for fourth-year students focussed on Research, Rehearsal, and Presentation of a Role for Performance.

The first Shakespeare course (120 hours) is described as follows: "An introduction to playing Shakespeare. Ways of breathing life into the text thereby communicating a character's thoughts, wants and emotional state to an audience will be explored." The course objectives are listed as well:

>—through play reading, exercises, monologue and scene study, the students will:
>—demonstrate that they have an understanding of verse and prose
>—develop listening skills
>—develop movement skills to connect mind and body through speech
>—use the text to define character
>—use the text to define emotional state of character
>—use the text to define objectives
>—use the text to define situation
>—choose, examine, explore and learn one monologue for presentation
>—examine, explore and present one assigned scene study.

There are academic pre-requisites but no auditions are required and she does not select the students. The first course is capped at 20 entrants, while the advanced course is topped at 10. In the first course, Reid teaches them to walk, "not like kings and queens, nor quite as themselves. They learn to take the casualness out of their own 2018 bodies and be neutral," preparing them to have an ease of style in performance. She encourages the girls to wear long skirts, corsets, and comfortable shoes for rehearsal, and the boys to wear jackets. The purpose is pragmatic: to teach correct posture and silhouette but primarily to introduce them to a different world. Fourth-year students get to use the wardrobe and props for scene work.

"I *adore* my students!" she exclaims with genuine feeling, but she is rigorous in her instruction. She realizes that students tend to over-emote in monologues by forcing their own emotion into a scene rather than allowing the text do its work. She cites, for example, Juliet's lines in a letter scene from *The Two Gentlemen of Verona*: "O hateful hands, to tear such loving words!/Injurious wasps, to feed on such sweet honey,/And kill the bees that yield it with your stings!" (1.2.102-104).

After one of the girls (evidently drawing a blank about context) stresses all the adjectives as if they are apocalyptic horrors, Reid takes over: "Okay, those hands didn't strangle your mother. They just ripped up a letter from your boyfriend down the road. And the girl goes: 'Oh!' Yes, she does hate her hands at that moment but not because they killed anybody. It's the situation. That to me is what makes great comedy. It's knowing the world you're in … I've developed what my students affectionately call a Chick List (really a Check List), basically a list of 20 questions, such as: 'In your speech is there any indication of the age of the character, a stage direction, time of day, etc.?' The whole reason is to get away from generalities and to get into specifics."

She illustrates her teaching method with lines from *Romeo and Juliet*: "Now is the sun upon the highmost hill/Of this day's journey, and from nine till twelve/Is [three] long hours, yet she is not come" (2.5.9-11). She delves into the text for the student actress:

Why does it tell you it's noon? Because, perhaps, she's been pacing. It tells you about how you are feeling, how long you have been waiting for the Nurse to come back. So, you don't make your choices based on what you'd like to smack on top of that. Your choices come out through the text. And then all the poetic devices: alliteration, assonance, consonance, et cetera. The guy was such a genius. If he uses the same word five times in one speech, you need to ask why. He could have used twenty other words. It's all leading to specifics. That's how my students start their work and how I start my work.

Word meanings are also on her list. She makes students check the words to understand their meaning in context because "if you don't or can't commit to the word, you can't commit to the thought or anything else."

It is eminently clear that she loves teaching, and she gets emotional when talking about it. "I am so much better an actress now since I started teaching. I'm not saying I was a bad actress thirteen years ago. I don't think I was. I think I was pretty damned good. But having to impart to kids what I believe myself has kept me present in the process. It has kept me from taking my knowledge for granted. That's why it's made me a better actress. It's kept me honest."

She tears up at this point in the interview and is embarrassed: "What a baby I am!" Actually, whether she realizes it or not, she reminds me of Chaucer's Clerk from Oxford who would gladly learn and gladly teach. And she does admit: "I'm not just learning more about Shakespeare year after year, as I'm not just learning about teaching year after year. I'm learning to be part of a bigger world."

After her wide experience as actress and teacher, what has she learned about Shakespeare that she didn't know earlier? She hardly pauses before explaining:

Oh, gee, everything. Everything. It's always made sense to me as a watcher, even before I started to speak it. Seeing it here, I understood that stage. It made total sense to me the first time I walked onto that stage. I don't know why. It just did. And I think it's because the people

I was watching as a kid were liking it as much as I was. So, that feeds it, doesn't it? I love it for the language and what he does and gives you: all that word sleuthing, how rich his characters are. I love a good problem-solver and his stuff is full of problem-solvers. I love the humanity of his work. Now I know why I love it.

Notes

[1] Our interview was conducted in the Playwrights Circle Lounge, Festival Theatre, Stratford on May 16, 2018.

[2] In 2016, Thought for Food Productions assembled an all-female cast in order to give women access to a great text that is typically dominated by male casting.

[3] The director, Tyler Seguin, explained: "What is illuminated by this casting is the role of women in this narrative and in this society—even Isabella is only a tool of her brother, and then the Duke; Mariana pines for a man who wronged her; Juliet is asked to repent her sin. The only woman who profits is the brothel-owner, Mistress Overdone, but her livelihood is built on the exploitation of women! The Duke says to Mariana near the end, 'Why, you are nothing then. Neither maid, widow, nor wife' and then Lucio suggests that she could be a 'punk' and that pretty much sums up what a woman could be at that time. It's horrifying but there's something delightful hearing that line when the stage is full of women being so much more than those prescribed roles." ("Measure for Measure Gets a Feminist Twist/Shakespeare in Toronto" by Tori Carlisle, *theshakespearestandard.com*, Nov. 22, 2016.)

[4] She reports that at the Shaw Festival in Niagara-on-the-Lake, she would have had two understudy runs.

Tom Rooney as Malvolio in Twelfth Night *(Stratford Festival, 2011)*.
(Photo: Cylla von Tiedemann. Courtesy of the Stratford Festival)

Tom Rooney
The Riddle of It Is Never-Ending

He's one of the most versatile actors I know.
   —Antoni Cimolino, Artistic Director, Stratford Festival
He's a real chameleon as a performer.
   —Chris Abraham, Artistic Director, Crow's Theatre
"He's one of the most inventive and original actors I know.
   —Marti Maraden, former Artistic Director, National Arts Centre

His gifts are numerous, but perhaps the largest of which is his ability to be fully present in every moment of a play, whether it is by Shakespeare, Chekhov, Molière, Michel Marc Bouchard, or Kristen Thomsen.[1] So, how did this actor turn into one of the major Shakespearean actors in Canada after distinguishing himself as Hamlet in 2004 at the National Arts Centre, Ottawa rather than at the Stratford Festival?

He was almost 40—hardly the age to be discovered by the nation's most prestigious cultural institution and hardly the age to essay his first Hamlet. He was in choice company: His fellow actors included Douglas Campbell, Victor Ertmanis, Fiona Reid, David Schurman, Ben Carlson, and Michelle Monteith. But he delivered an outstanding performance characterized by intelligence, sensuousness, and vibrancy. His director, Marti Maraden, took a chance on him because she thought his range as an actor encompassed all the major qualities of the Prince enumerated by Ophelia: "The courtier's, soldier's, scholar's eye, tongue, sword,/Th'expectation and rose of the fair state,/The glass of fashion and the mould of form,/

Th'observ'd of all observers" (3.1.151-54). Above all, Maraden knew he had great heart.

Born in Prince Albert in 1964 and raised in Saskatoon, Saskatchewan as the youngest of seven children and the only son, Tom Rooney could easily have been a prairie flower born to blush unseen. His father worked in a federal penitentiary, and his mother was a singer. In fact, everybody sang in his immediate family. As a schoolboy, his first experience with Shakespeare was having to study *Twelfth Night*: "I was told it was a comedy but wondered: 'What's funny about this?' I suppose Toby Belch is a funny name, but I didn't get it. I didn't really care for it. I wasn't interested."

Things changed for him slowly at the University of Saskatchewan when, after trying computer science and economics for two years, he switched to music, earning a B.A. in Music in Performance. However, as his voice changed in time, he felt he needed other tools to help him adjust to this reality, so he cultivated an ever-deepening interest in theatre. In his third year, he was cast as Benedick in *Much Ado About Nothing*. "I thought: 'Oh, my god, I don't know how to do this! Is this a comedy? I don't get it.'"

But he plugged away, and then at a dress rehearsal in an auditorium filled with people, he heard enthusiastic laughter. They loved his Benedick, though he was rather non-plussed:

> I'm not doing anything, except saying the lines! There must be something about the lines. It was a great moment of discovery. 'Oh, my god, Shakespeare is an amazing writer.' I had had no idea. It was a real revelation—he makes it easy if you work at it. I remember playing Feste in a production of *Twelfth Night* at the Globe Theatre [Regina] and thinking: 'I don't understand the humour. How do you play this? I'm not smart enough.' But I discovered if you worked hard, Shakespeare would take care of you. The text is so alive and so smart. Audiences are smarter than I am, they get it before I get it. I have to put in hours of work, before it goes from my brain into my heart, body, and nervous system.

I'm not one of those guys who had the opportunity to work with Robin Phillips or William Hutt or Michael Langham. I saw some of their work, and I was fortunate enough to work with certain directors and actors that were wonderful. It was a real smorgasbord of experiences and teachers. Because I grew up in Saskatoon, where the community was quite small, I was given the opportunity to do a lot of different things and a great variety of roles in musicals and Shakespeare. For ten years every summer, I was part of a company who performed Shakespeare in a tent. I wasn't very good at it but I was interested in the challenge, and I was able to practise speaking the language for two months every summer.

I still find it challenging. As I get older, I realize how little I know. There's so much more there that I'm not seeing. The riddle of it is never-ending.

Two of his inspiring mentors were Henry Woolf (a British-born actor, director, and teacher of theatre, who had been a long-time friend and collaborator of Harold Pinter) and Jane Casson (also British and from a famous theatre family, who had come to Canada in 1965, going on to act at the Crest in Toronto, the Charlottetown Festival, the Vancouver Playhouse, and the Stratford Festival). He got to work with Tibor Fereghazi, Tom Bentley-Fisher, and Marti Maraden, and later with Robert Lepage on a curiously conceived bilingual version of *Romeo and Juliet*. He did many productions for Persephone Theatre, and stayed in Saskatchewan until the mid-90s before trekking to various other Canadian cities and eventually being discovered by Maraden for his life-and-career changing Hamlet.

This is an Everest of a role that requires an actor to have a huge "imaginative and empathetic capacity to track a psychologically and emotionally plausible path through the play" (Hytner 206). Academic criticism doesn't help much if it thrashes about with theories that could hardly ever be translated into performance. The text is full of anomalies, deliberately so, for Shakespeare seems intent on making Hamlet's mutability one of his signal qualities.

Every leading actor has his own version of Hamlet, and the Prince can be played with any of the four Renaissance psychological dispositions dominating his temperament: the melancholic, sanguine, phlegmatic, or choleric. The character's wild mood swings (a function of his distemper) fascinate academics who often attempt a diagnosis: Is he bipolar or clinically depressed?

How did Rooney play him? "I started reading books on manic depression. Hamlet declares: 'The play's the thing/Wherein I'll catch the conscience of the King' (2.2.604-05). He's got the plan, he's ready to take action, but the very next time you see him, he's contemplating suicide with the 'To be or not to be.' I was fascinated by the extremity of Hamlet's character and behaviour—one moment ready to act, to soar, and then suddenly crippled by doubt and depression." Complicating matters for an actor are Hamlet's bursts of inspiration, energy, and clarity. He always seems to be walking a fine line between reason and madness. When Laurence Olivier declares in his film version that it is the story of a man who couldn't make up his mind, he is partly right. Hamlet knows what he wants, but he also wants to ensure that he has the right moment to exact his revenge against Claudius. This comes to the fore in the scene when the Prince finds Claudius at prayer and silently debates within himself if he should dispatch him then and there:

> Now might I do it [pat], now 'a is a-praying;
> And now I'll do't—and so 'a goes to heaven,
> And so am I [reveng'd]. That would be scann'd:
> A villain kills my father, and for that
> I, his sole son, do this same villain send
> To heaven.
> Why, this is [hire and salary], not revenge (3.3. 73-79).

So, what, I ask, is Hamlet's strategy throughout the play? Rooney responds:

I think, perhaps, he's trying to figure out who he is, what he is. What does it mean to be a man, what does it mean to be human. He's searching for meaning in the chaos of his life. The people in his life either disappoint or betray him. He's not inspired by any of them. None of them, in his opinion, are very noble examples of what it is to be human, but what's worse is that he doesn't know who he is. He doesn't know his own 'stops.' At the very last moment he learns something. Perhaps. He learns that the truth is in the silence somewhere.

However, I point out the irony of dying Hamlet's words to Horatio: "in this harsh world draw thy breath in pain/To tell my story" (5.2.348-49). If Horatio does act on this appeal, there is no real silence. Rooney laughs as he concedes the point.

Is it possible that we are over-intellectualizing Shakespeare, in general, and this tragedy, in particular? As Nicholas Hytner asserts, Shakespeare's "intuitive openness to interpretation is sometimes mistaken for unfathomable complexity. His relish for ambiguity is taken as a challenge to those who would pin him down" (Hytner 174).

Rooney's own point of view (delivered with a streak of dry satiric wit) cuts through all the (academic) chaff. When he assumed the role, he felt as if he were going to a big box-store, with rooms, rows, aisles, and shelves crowded with an extravagant surplus of material (films, articles, scripts, books) about everyone who's ever said anything about Hamlet:

All these books. It's wonderful, and you can read and watch and listen to other people do it. And at the very back [of the store] there's a play called *Hamlet*. Eventually, you just have to pick that up and go away with that. All the other stuff is very interesting and useful, to greater or lesser degrees. But, ultimately, you learn the lines and you figure out to the best of your ability what's happening in each scene, and how it's affecting you. Of any of the parts, Hamlet is the most personal. I loved playing Hamlet. I think every actor should have the opportunity to play Hamlet because it's a great workout on every level: physically, intellectually, vocally. It's a great three-hour workout which ends with a huge swordfight. Every night you think, 'Well, that wasn't it. That was nowhere near it, but I get to do it again tomorrow.'

Self-discovery is a theme and process that Rooney finds continually in Shakespeare, especially in the roles he has played at Stratford. His Richard II in *Breath of Kings*, Graham Abbey's condensed version of four histories (*Richard II, Henry IV, Parts 1 and 2* and *Henry V*), was, as with Hamlet, a case of an actor playing a figure continually acting. *Hamlet*, as Anne Righter asserts, "is a tragedy dominated by the idea of the play" (Righter 142). Righter points to the play metaphor that appears in a number of forms (the dissembler, the Player King, "the theatrical nature of certain moments of time," and, most importantly, the Prince's refuge in "an illusion of his own devising" (Righter 144).

Richard II is essentially an actor, as well, because (as Judith Cook explains) he is "conscious at least some of the time of role-playing, and he is certainly considered to be doing so in the Deposition scene" (Cook 1983:46). Rooney agrees, adding: "That's why Shakespeare is so amazing. Humans get trapped in and by their own stories. We are storytellers. The human animal needs to tell stories."

Rooney maintains that although it is a tricky thing to practise the actor's "double consciousness" (i.e. living a role while judging his effects in relation to fellow actors and the audience), everything, fundamentally, comes down to telling the story clearly and understanding what the story is from moment to moment to moment: "If you can hold on to that and simply tell the story, everything else follows. However, if you start the other way—coming in with the emotion first, for example—then it's more difficult. The story needs to be in the forefront, and everything else follows or has to support the story. As long as the story is being communicated, you are doing your job. I don't think people come to the theatre to see emotion. They come to see a story. If emotion is involved in that story, so be it. Ultimately, we want story."

When he essayed the role of Richard II, he was struck by how much this is the story of a man-boy's journey:

He is playing a part he was born into: he's expected to play the part of the King. He doesn't really discover who he is until the last five minutes of his life, when he becomes a man. He's such a fascinating character to play, but I find talking about this really difficult because it's so elusive. It is also difficult for me to articulate my ideas clearly because they're always changing, and because I sometimes understand what was happening only after the fact.

As with all the Shakespearean characters I have played, it's a journey of self-discovery. You can go in with as many ideas and strategies as you like, but eventually within two weeks you find out that they're not serving you. And then Shakespeare starts talking to you. Shakespeare starts bringing things up in you that you didn't see or realize. It's a constant learning process. It's wonderful and at the same time frustrating and extremely challenging. It's always new. Every single character is new, every single play is new, and you're always beginning again.

Like many great roles, Richard II permits a range of interpretations, as can be seen in the very different performances of it by Gielgud, Redgrave, Hutt, Bedford, Pennell, Mark Rylance, Richard Pasco, *et al.* Besides creating an impression of "shyness, petty vanity, and callous indifference" (as Gielgud iterated), the actor also has to encompass such things as the king's well-bred sensitivity, loneliness, headstrong frivolousness, and lack of sympathy with "older men who try so vainly to advise him and control his whims" (Cook 1983: 49).

Yet, an effective stage Richard II has to be able to win sympathy as he becomes more understandable and pitiable. Richard can be played elegiacally, very much as a Christ figure who really believes devoutly in the Divine Right of Kings, or, more psychologically, as a man trying to find his identity, and not finding very much. The latter interpretation gets to the heart of the tragedy for, as Rooney asserts: "Richard is tragic because he's born into a prison (royalty) and trapped in it. He doesn't get out till he's in a real prison [at Pomfret Castle]. I'm talking about the fact that he's born into a role and told he has Divine Right."

Rooney quickly draws a comparison with Malvolio in *Twelfth Night*, a role he has also played to acclaim in Des McAnuff's 2011 Stratford production:

> Malvolio's also trapped in his own story. He's trapped in his own belief of what and who he is, something that others don't see in him. He's absurdly tragic. That's what I was interested in. I always get a little bit uncomfortable talking about an approach to a character because it's always very elusive. You always discover more as you do it. It's never set. What I enjoy about Malvolio is that he is a man who believes he is the best man in Olivia's household, the best man at court, and obviously the best man for her. He believes he's the most masculine, the most intelligent, and the obvious choice as Olivia's lover. So, he's already halfway down that path before he gets the letter. That's all Shakespeare, that's all there. I tried to make him a very manly man, a man's man.

Rooney's officious, tightly buttoned-up steward had a cultivated dour masculinity that sorted well with Donald Sinden's earlier conception of the role in Britain. Sinden saw Malvolio as "always the odd man out, the loner. Nobody likes him, nobody ever has" because "he's *always* right. Nobody has ever been as right as he is. He has absolutely no doubts, and every step he takes throughout the play is the *right* one. He has no sense of humour at all, not a shred. He's the completely petty bureaucrat" (Cook 1983: 152).

Rooney also sees the character as essentially humourless, with the actor crystallizing this in a gloriously funny bit of business in the cross-garter scene in Act 3, Scene 4 where Malvolio attempts to smile, as instructed by the letter he mistakenly believes is from Olivia. Rooney's face was superbly illustrative as the actor forced his mouth to shape, at first, the merest hint of a smile that could crack his stern façade, and then very, very slowly broadening from a smirk to a grin into a beaming smile to cap his triumph.

This was Rooney's own invention: "Malvolio gets an order from Olivia to smile, and he doesn't quite know how to do it. He's never even thought about how one smiles." Rooney created his own challenge: Could he make himself smile while maintaining the character's stern, rigid personality? "That was the exercise in some way. Could I entertain *myself* in that moment—*me, Tom the actor*—giving myself a moment of joy? How long would it take me? How long could I draw this business out? It was, one might say, a little perverse"—but no more so, perhaps, than Olivier's lisp for the same role or Bedford's hugging a teddy-bear in one scene in Robin Phillips' Stratford production.

Rooney did not neglect Malvolio's suffering. The steward suffers a deep blow to his ego in the letter scene, but this is exceeded by his humiliation in the dungeon scene where he is deemed a lunatic and cowers in the dark while calling pitiably to Sir Topas the curate (Feste in disguise) for rescue:

> *Mal.* Sir Topas, never was man thus wrong'd.
> Good Sir Topas, do not think I am mad; they have laid
> me here in hideous darkness.
> *Clo.* Fie, thou dishonest Sathan! I call thee by the
> most modest terms, for I am one of those gentle ones
> that will use the devil himself with courtesy. Say'st thou
> that house is dark?
> *Mal.* As hell, Sir Topas.
> *Clo.* Why, it hath bay windows transparent as
> barricadoes, and the [clerestories] toward the south
> north are as lustrous as ebony; and yet complainest
> thou of obstruction?
> *Mal.* I am not mad, Sir Topas. I say to you this
> house is dark.
> *Clo.* Madman, thou errest. I say there is no darkness
> but ignorance, in which thou art more puzzled than
> the Egyptians in their fog.
> *Mal.* I say this house is as dark as ignorance, though
> ignorance were as dark as hell; and I say there was
> never a man thus abus'd. (4.2. 28-47)

Rooney sees parallels between Malvolio and Richard II in terms of each man's vulnerability:

> I suppose what they have in common is that they are two men out of place. I think Richard feels out of place, feels that he's always acting, feels he's always having to be something that doesn't come to him easily or that he doesn't understand or that he doubts. And Malvolio is similar in that he believes he should be someone else and recognized by others as such, a man of power and authority. Richard doesn't know what he should be or who he is. Malvolio is trying to achieve something he sees in himself but others don't. They both end up in a dungeon and in darkness. Richard discovers himself, his true self, in that darkness; Malvolio doesn't. Malvolio's bad experience makes him more of who he is, makes him hold on to his belief of personal greatness and worth, even more. He moves forward with the idea and intent of revenge, which he'll never achieve. In some ways, Richard achieves clarity but Malvolio becomes even more insane.

I point out that Shakespeare gives Richard a mirror, but I ask Rooney whether the king sees himself or an actor in that mirror. Malvolio doesn't have a literal mirror; his mirror would be others who see a different reflection of him. Rooney responds: "I think the mirror for Richard is the beginning of the realization. Once in the dungeon, that realization is complete. He sees a truth that I don't think he's been able to clearly see: the realization of what it is to be simply human."

The remark confirms my conviction that Shakespeare always considers how we *become* human or how we *discover* our humanity—even in *The Tempest* that is often commonly and inaccurately read simply as his farewell to his art and to the theatre. It took William Hutt's supreme performance as Prospero for Richard Monette in 2005 to bring that point startlingly to life in Act 5, when Ariel points out that his special mission (decreed by Prospero) to make prisoners of Alonso and his followers has been completed. The scene, however, is not merely explicatory in a literal sense; it opens out into a higher wisdom for Prospero and for all those who fail to recognize the "rarer action":

Ari. Your charm so strongly works 'em
That if you now beheld them, your affections
Would become tender.
Pros.   Dost thou think so, spirit?
Ari. Mine would, sir, were I human.
Pros.   And mine shall.
Hast thou, which art but air, a touch, a feeling
Of their afflictions, and shall not myself,
One of their kind, that relish all as sharply
Passion as they, be kindlier mov'd than thou art?
Though with their high wrongs I am strook to th'
quick,
Yet, with my nobler reason, 'gainst my fury
Do I take part. The rarer action is
In virtue than in vengeance (5.1. 17-28).

Rooney summarizes his own insight into the over-arching Shakespearean pattern, particularly for the roles of Richard II, Malvolio, and Angelo that he has played to acclaim. "All [Shakespeare's] characters are put into a crucible." I concur, but sometimes they are agents of their own destruction. Richard has a lot of himself to blame—Malvolio does too—but when we come to Angelo, it's a fascinating question. Is he really a puritan or is he denying what he already knows about himself? "That's a great question," agrees Rooney, but he reveals his own particular stamp as an actor by admitting to incertitude:

> I don't know. I never really discovered that, I don't think. I suspect it is the latter—that he's denying something. It's been held in check for so long with such determination that there is only one direction it can go. Eventually, it must reveal itself. His denial and fear of that part of his humanity is what takes him down eventually. In all those characters, there's so much fear. They're afraid of not fulfilling their story—the story that they believe and with which they identify. In the course of their plays, they discover who they truly are.

Rooney's comments speak to a goal in first-rate acting: to avoid being locked into an interpretation without being open to important new discoveries. There are actors who work out every single gesture, inflection, or business for a role, and seek never to divert from their master plan. But there are others who prefer not to seal their interpretations (even when well developed in rehearsal for the crucial opening night) but to continue refining and sharpening their interpretations in actual performance. Rooney is evidently of the second type. Just as an ideal actor must act as though he is not sure what is to come in the advancing plot from scene to scene, so should he be totally engaged with his fellow actors, allowing them and the audience access to his thoughts and feelings in a role.

As Nicholas Hytner observes: "It is never true of a play that all the answers are available in the text. It isn't how plays work. Novels can give you everything you need to know, but plays are only dimly detectable until they are performed. It is primarily through the imagination, craft, and personality of the actor that you encounter Hamlet, Gertrude or the gravedigger. Even Shakespeare's great parts ask more questions than they answer and require an actor to fill in fascinating gaps left quite deliberately" (Hytner 169). Rooney is quite certain that he doesn't have all the answers, and he, therefore, strives to fill in the "fascinating gaps" from performance to performance. This modesty, this dynamic mutability is what makes him eminently watchable on stage in any role.

One of his beliefs about Shakespeare surprises me: "I'm not sure if there is subtext in Shakespeare. I think if you say what you mean and you mean what you say, everything else is taken care of. I think audiences are smart enough to hear subtext." But what if the text is difficult to speak—as in the case of Angelo, for instance? Rooney sees the difficulty being in finding the mind of the character and knowing how he thinks. "That's always the challenge, and that's always what's you're looking for in the *music* of the text and in a character's word choice. It's always the oddness of the verse or the things that are difficult or less clear—that's perhaps where the truth of the character lies. That's the ongoing riddle which, again, is so rewarding yet incredibly frustrating because it never ends."

How does he suppress parts of himself in order to assume the qualities of the character he is playing? Not every Shakespearean role demands of an actor the same degree or depth of self-revelation as the role of Hamlet does. It is often the combination of the personal and the character that makes the text come alive. Rooney explains that he used to try to suppress parts of himself to find the character, but now his thinking has changed: "I'm more interested in finding myself in the character. I try to find my truth in the character, not my words or my opinions or ideas."

An example is Polonius. He played the role opposite Jonathan Goad's Prince in Antoni Cimolino's 2015 production. Cimolino and Rooney both considered the possible consequences if Polonius really knew that Claudius had murdered Hamlet's father. It was not a new notion: The Polonius of tradition is a man puffed up with self-regard and public lies. Perhaps he did help Claudius assassinate the old king. But when Rooney started with that proposition in his head during rehearsals, it wasn't really working either for him or his director:

> It felt as though I was having to twist something or bend it out of its natural shape to make it work. What I started to hear in the text was the word 'love.' I was struck by how often he used the word. That's what I kept hearing, so I began to think, maybe he actually loves his family. Maybe he actually loves his daughter, his son, his country. Maybe he actually loves his king. Maybe he actually believes—not that he would phrase it this way—that love can solve the world's problems. And I found that easier to play.

So, I ask, when Polonius counselled Laertes before the son's departure for France, if he really believed what he was saying, especially his own conclusion: "This above all: to thine own self be true,/And it must follow, as the night the day,/Thou canst not then be false to any man" (1.3. 78-80). Rooney maintains: "Yes, that was an act of love. He's not a perfect parent by a long shot, but his advice to his son comes from a place of love."

When it comes to the question of direction, Rooney prefers a director who takes charge. "There has to be somebody driving the bus, and if that person is driving clearly and with intelligence, then I'll get on that bus and go along." But this is not to say that he is sympathetic to a director who elects concept over context. He dislikes a director's imposition because "in my opinion it rarely works. It gets in the way unless it is directly tied to and in support of story. Everybody comes up with ideas. Some work, some don't. Some serve and some don't. Every production is an experiment." Does he prefer somebody who is more "hands-on" or somebody who gives him liberty to try and fail or fail better? "A little of both," he declares, adding:

> Marti [Maraden] was great at that. She let me play but she was also very much aware of and concerned with story. Chris Abraham, too, is all about story. He's searching for the story, the most interesting story, so he'll send you in different directions. It can be a little disconcerting—a lot of ground is covered but he's an intelligent guy and a very good director so, ultimately, it's all useful. I've enjoyed Antoni's [Cimolino's] flexibility. He's willing to talk and try things. I like that. Robert Lepage has an incredible ability to tell story. Even when there is a great deal of technology being used, I always feel that it's there to tell and support the story. Used in that way, in service of the story, I have found it makes my job easier.

Does it help if a director had been an actor earlier in his career—as in the cases of Gascon, Phillips, Neville, William, Monette, or Cimolino? Rooney's answer is candid: "Not necessarily. Sometimes it does. Directing is incredibly difficult. A lot of it has to do with communication skills. It's not for me. I did it once and never want to do it again because I realize that's not for me. My brain doesn't work that way. I'm not a great communicator. I know how I would act it, but, as a director, that's not my job. I remember getting to previews and thinking I want to be up there [on stage], not here."

Does he like a director who gets onto the stage and illustrates for an actor? Not necessarily illustrate, he responds, but someone who can entertain a discussion about choices and a path: "One of the great things about Chris Abraham is that I can have an unending dialogue with him. He'll say something to me, and I can say to him: 'I don't understand that. I need you to say that to me in a different way.' And he'll sit there and find a way to say it in a way that makes sense to me, in a way that I can understand. Then I have it and can take it with me. I appreciate directors who can get everybody into the same story, the same world."

Not for Rooney (I sense) the extravagant inventiveness of a Thomas Ostermeier, whose 2008 *Hamlet*, for instance, included a fat-suited, clowning, ad-libbing prince, an audience sing-along, rapping, and a shrunken cast of six, with Gertrude and Ophelia doubled up so as to erase the distinction between Hamlet's mother and his lover. Rooney acknowledges the inventiveness as well as the volume of entertainment, but knows that everyone has ideas, but if you are doing Shakespeare, the point is to tell the story as clearly as possible after you have decided whether the story reflects the play's world, your own world, or whether it is a theatrical distortion of the play and your world.

A vivid case in point is the 2018 season's *Coriolanus*, which Robert Lepage (certainly the most exciting, controversial Canadian director) stages in modern dress and with up-to-date technology, ranging from iPhones, recording booth, television studio, *trompe l'oeil* video projections, and sliding boxes and panels of differing shapes and sizes to suggest a film camera's repertoire of close-ups, tracking shots, pans, irises, and letterbox effects. The technology, however, never obscures the central story, and Rooney (who plays the people's tribune Sicinius) expertly combines the suave with the pugnacious, the polished demagogue with the master manipulator of social media, thereby realizing Lepage's idea of the extent to which mass and social media affect politics and public opinion.

Rooney and other seasoned peers (Tom McCamus, Stephen Ouimette, Graham Abbey, and Lucy Peacock, in particular) transcend the filmic elements, technology, and vivid stage environments to command the stage with flesh-and-blood characterizations. It shouldn't come as a surprise, of course, when human characters triumph over stage technology and design. Shakespeare's language, stories, and characters allow for surprises.

Which returns me to what Rooney felt about Shakespeare earlier in his career when he thought that the text was insurmountable. Launching into Shakespeare as one whose notions about the plays were free of decoration and corrosion of previous ideas, he was able to see things for the first time, without indulging in clichés. He continues to act in the belief that he knows very little and that he is open to discoveries because the text is vividly alive. When asked what he now knows about Shakespeare that he didn't know when he began acting the plays, he sums up succinctly: "I know now what I know now is how much I don't know."

Notes

[1] Our interview was conducted in the Playwrights Circle Lounge, Festival Theatre, Stratford on June 2, 2018.

Graham Abbey as Philip, the Bastard in King John *(Stratford Festival, 2014).*
(Photo: David Hou. Courtesy of the Stratford Festival)

Graham Abbey
Seeking the Middle Ground

Born in Toronto, then moved to St. Catharines, Graham Abbey saw his parents divorce when he was 4. His father, Robert, was a judge; his mother, Sharon, a professor at Brock University,[1] but after the divorce, Graham and his sister moved with their mom to Stratford because she was offered a job there. In Stratford, he was able to sing in the Boy Choir. At the same time, John Hirsch was looking for young boys who could sing to play fairies in *The Merry Wives of Windsor* (1982) and young Graham Abbey auditioned successfully. Hirsch cast him again when he was 11 in *As You Like It* the following year, feeding porridge to Mervyn "Butch" Blake as old Adam.

As was his wont because of his tortured experience with the Holocaust, Hirsch created a bitter opening, with young Abbey being required to walk barefoot onstage and buy a potato from a vendor. "Stop!" the director screamed at a rehearsal, feeling that the boy looked happy rather than desperately impoverished. "I want you to go to the centre pillar on stage and bang your head against it 50 times and say 'Shit' each time." Abbey thought he was joking, but Hirsch actually kept count of the head banging, and at the end, the boy looked embarrassingly distraught. "You, see, that's what we want. Now we go on."

Another significant lesson in the craft of acting came when young Abbey watched and listened to Nicholas Pennell reciting the Seven Ages of Man speech as Jaques: "His use of the language, the poetry, and the music was just mesmerizing. I memorized every intonation of that speech. I still remember the pauses and the inflections."

However, Abbey never went to theatre school. He did perform in musical sketches and improvs with the Queen's Players on the side and on his own free time while at Queen's University, Kingston, but at that time the university had no Dan School of Music and Drama and certainly no Chick Reid offering courses in Acting Shakespeare. Abbey studied politics and law with a view to becoming a politician, but his ambition changed after he interned at the Ontario Legislature and hit the 1995 election campaign trail.

Theatre became his chosen profession. At the age of 26, Abbey was accepted into the John Sullivan Hayes Training Program (a precursor to the Young Company and the Birmingham Conservatory). He recalls Douglas Campbell's asking quite pointedly: "Why would you want to be a politician when you can equally affect the world as an actor and still be respected in the morning?"

The Hayes Training Program was his first real formal training. Michael Mawson and Susie Turnbull were leading teachers, but Abbey believes that a lot of his theatre training came through osmosis, by listening to actors such as Pennell and William Hutt. In fact, when Abbey was cast as Ferdinand in Richard Monette's version of *The Tempest* (1999), he would run to the hole backstage every performance and watch Hutt delivering Prospero's "Ye elves of hills, brooks, standing lakes, and groves" (5.1.33 ff.).

A propos his training, he remarks: "I came at it by being immersed. A lot of it came by doing, as an artisan, or as somebody who was falling on my face but learning and listening." His singing voice helped, because there can be a real link between a musical sensibility and Shakespearean poetry, as in the cases of Juan Chioran, Colm Feore, Geraint Wyn Davies, Albert Schultz, Brent Carver, *et al.*, to whom poetry seems to come naturally.

Is his own ear particularly attuned to the music emerging from the mouth of an actor? "Yes, yes, 100%!" he says emphatically. "I'm a stickler for rhythm and verse. There are others who are more hard-core on that than me, but we need to be on the heartbeat of the play. Then it's about listening—the most simple and difficult thing in acting. And it's about objectives, such as what you are fighting for in a scene, which is so easy to lose track of."

I express how, for me, it has always been the language of the plays that was stimulating to hear. My idol (since my teenage years) was Laurence Olivier, who made it absolutely thrilling to hear Shakespeare performed. "You mean the sound of it?" Abbey asks. "Yes, absolutely," I say, but clarify this by explaining that I am not referring to "singing" the poetry. John Gielgud used to do that habitually—dive back into the honey of his voice. But Olivier's delivery was passionate, with his expressing the passion through the line, not *under* the line or *above* the line. That was sheer skill because it cannot be done spontaneously without craft.

Olivier used to be criticized mightily by English critics at the outset of his Shakespearean career because of his unconventional vocal style that often entailed the use of rubato or placing the emphasis on a most unexpected word. In other words, for not following the "rules" or received practices of speaking Shakespeare. But when he played Henry V on stage, the audience knew what he was achieving with his unique style of delivery: "They weren't listening to someone singing an aria; they were hearing a man's thoughts set before them as clearly as I could" (Olivier 1986, 43).

Abbey also appreciates the way passion funnels into poetry. He worked quite a bit with Richard Monette, who was instrumental in bringing him back to Stratford. Abbey claims that Monette was "a heart-first guy. He had a zest for life. He was very good to me as a young actor. He insisted that I do a Shakespeare every year to hone my craft, to hone the skill of it. I remember Richard coming to me when I did Henry V in 2001 and saying: 'You have that heart. It comes through.' I learned that most from Richard. And you need poetry in the end. We analyze and get all heavy with it, but you have to balance that quite equally with the heart and the song."

This seems simple to utter but it is really difficult to achieve, complicated further by what Kevin Kline calls "the double consciousness that operates in an actor during performance. There is a kind of split in an actor's mind, where one part of him is monitoring and watching and even being a sort of director. The paradox is that the actor tries to use and yet subdue that consciousness" (Maher 11). In simpler terms, it is an actor's way of looking at his own performance from inside himself. An actor can sense he has done the wrong thing or feel that a performance "sucked." It is the tricky aspect about acting. "Yes," agrees Abbey. "It's live theatre, isn't it? It's the joy of live theatre too. It happens and it changes every night, but it's only in relation to your fellow actors and the energy of the audience who are witnessing it. It's alive each time."

Abbey rose quickly through the Stratford ranks, and has played such major roles as Macbeth, Jaques, Bolingbroke, Henry V, Romeo, Petruchio, Iago, Henry VIII, Philip the Bastard (*King John*), and Aufidius, while also adding the roles of Laertes and Jaques to his memorable gallery of performances. When preparing for a major role, his research depends on the role:

> I was fortunate enough to do Prince Hal and Henry V[2] in the same season. I took a trip over to England and France and traced the journey of Henry's army from Harfleur to Agincourt. I woke up in the middle of the night and went out to the centre of the field at Agincourt to watch the sun come up and to see the image the king witnessed before he does the Crispin speech. I took some dirt from the battlefield. I still have it. I gave some to the cast for *Breath of Kings*.[3] So, I've done that for a role.
>
> If it's a historical piece, I do as much work as I can on the period. When I did Iago in Othello, I got immersed in psychology about the ways sociopaths and psychopaths think. I went down the rabbit hole with him. So, it really depends on the role. But because I come from an academic strain, I tend to do academic research.

His academic research puts him outside the general practice of the likes of Tom McCamus, Joseph Ziegler, Tom Rooney, Juan Chioran, Lucy Peacock, or Nancy Palk, but Abbey never forsakes the text. A curious thing about the trajectory of his acting career is the number of notable villains he has essayed—going back from his Antonio in *The Tempest* and Tullus Aufidius in *Coriolanus* in the 2018 season to his Philip the Bastard in 2014 and his Iago in 2013.

What does he like about the villains? "I've grown to love them," he explains. "In my youth, I was doing the ingenues. I loved the big picture at the heart of the ingenues. I guess that translates into villains in my middle years because it is a big picture for those guys too. It's life or death." The fact of a "big picture" tempted him to overdo simple lines, but Joseph Ziegler (who directed him as Laertes opposite Paul Gross' Hamlet in 2000) taught him an important lesson. It came in Act 4 of the play when Claudius asks: "What would you undertake/To show yourself indeed your father's son/More than in words?" Laertes replies: "To cut his throat i' th' church" (4.7.124-127).

As Abbey kept giving the response too much weight, grit, and strength, Ziegler advised: "Just say it. As simply as possible because the weight is in the language. Just see what happens." When Abbey simplified his tone, you could hear a ripple pass through the audience. "And you get that a lot with the villains," the actor expands. "When Antonio is accused of supplanting Prospero, he replies: 'True./And look how well my garments sit upon me,/Much feater than before' (2.1.272-274). The villains get these great lines that cut through and are chilling at times."

Olivier mentioned an important lesson he was taught by Tyrone Guthrie about having to love his characters, even the nitwits. When Olivier sulked about having to play Sergius in Shaw's *Arms and the Man*, Guthrie asked: "Don't you love Sergius?" This shocked Olivier: "Love that stooge? That inconsiderable ... God, Tony, if you weren't so tall, I'd hit you, if I could reach you." But

Guthrie stuck to his guns: "Well, of course, if you can't love him, you'll never be any good in him, will you?"

These words changed the course of Olivier's thinking for the rest of his life as he learned to love even the absurd dolts he was sometimes compelled to play (Olivier 1982, 110). Repeating this anecdote to Abbey, I ask what he loves about Iago, a role he played at Stratford in 2013? "I love his brain," comes the swift reply, with Abbey's going on to draw a parallel between Iago and Antonio (Prospero's treacherous brother):

> Antonio tries to convince someone or lead someone down a path of danger, murder, and self-destruction. They're both incredibly smart. They know how to manipulate, and they think in simple ways. In the 50s they used to have a series of questions in a test to see if you were a psychopath. One of them is as follows: A man is attending his mother's funeral and another man shows up in a black coat and black hat. The son goes home and kills his father. Why? You can go through a number of complicated answers. People will say, 'Well, it's now an affair.' The sociopath's answer is that the son liked the man in the black coat and hat, and figured that if he killed his father, the man would show up at that funeral as well, dressed the same way.
>
> It's a very black and white way of thinking. If I like your shirt, I kill you so I can have your shirt. Iago thinks that he has been wronged, so he will exact his revenge without emotion. Antonio is the same. When he sees Alonso, Gonzalo, Adrian, and Francisco sleeping, he thinks there's not much difference between sleep and death. 'Say this were death/That now hath seiz'd them, why, they were no worse/Than now they are' (2.1.260-262). He suggests that with three inches of steel he could just lay Alonso to bed forever. It's a chilling thought but that's the brain of these guys. It's very simple but savvy. They're exciting to play because to drop into that brain is fascinating.

American Method acting incorporates training for identifying the "spine" of a character. Perhaps, it is more fruitful to find the "wound," some point of pain or vulnerability. So, is Iago's "wound" his humiliation at having been passed over by Othello for a promotion? Abbey elucidates:

That's one thing. The other thing is what he mentions: 'Thus do I ever make my fool my purse' (1.3.383). There's a rumour Othello's had a dalliance with Iago's wife. He stops the play for a second to say this: 'I hate the Moor,/And it is thought abroad that 'twixt my sheets/ [H'as] done my office' (1.3.386-388). It's like a private chat with the audience who somehow gets sucked into the plot. Iago and Antonio are mirrors. Prospero talks about Antonio convincing himself he was, indeed, the rightful Duke of Milan. So, Shakespeare, through another character, describes someone actually being able to convince himself of a wrong. That's Iago to a tee. When he talks to the audience and says what he is about to do is completely within reason, you don't have the ability as an audience member to speak back to him.

But it is also possible that Iago has sexual designs on Othello. Olivier indicated as much when playing the role opposite a non-plussed Ralph Richardson who was attempting the Moor.

Abbey is inclined to agree, immediately pointing to *Coriolanus*, where there is an extraordinary relationship between the title character and Aufidius that contains sexual innuendos in the language. "Those things can be played overtly but it's more interesting sometimes when they're just under the surface," Abbey suggests. "Iago never comes out and says that. I think it's love between him and Othello, a deep love or hero-worship—of a man he feels he should be *beside* as the ensign."

Isn't the actor intimating subtext? "The answer is always in Shakespeare's text," Abbey insists. "It's always there in the play. There are moments in *Othello* where that is a reasonable conclusion. If I had the script in front of me, I could find five or six instances where we could say: 'That's love.' Love is way more interesting answer than hate. You could play Iago as someone who hates Othello, and Aufidius as someone who hates Coriolanus, but they love the other, and that is why the intensity is so much and the pain so great."

Anthony Quayle, who played Iago twice, would have agreed, for he has been quoted as saying:

When you come on to play him, and play the scenes with Othello, you realize there is a tremendous bond between the two men. They are linked with a kind of knowledge. Iago, in particular, has a kind of awareness which is very akin to loving, which might be a peculiar thing to say but it's true. Hatred is very akin to love and I couldn't play it another way. If an animal trainer wants to train a wild leopard he finds it the most difficult thing, it's worse than a tiger, you can hardly do it. He knows it will turn and kill him just like that so if he goes into the cage with a chair or a stick and provokes it, which is what Iago does, then he knows the thing has only to turn around and attack him and snap his back. Iago knows Othello could kill him at any moment, yet he goes on, goes on, goes on—almost like hurting yourself (Cook 1983: 130).

The imbalance of passions in Iago is very dangerous, especially as it is hidden within a body and beneath an exterior of seeming candour. He is called "honest" many times in the play, so his feverish passion is almost schizophrenia, which some may think of as a "fantastic courage"—as when he drops dangerous hints about Desdemona's infidelity into Othello's ear. W.H. Auden claimed that Iago is a singular villain who is completely triumphant: "Everything Iago sets out to do he accomplishes (among his own goals, I include his self-destruction). Even Cassio, who survives, is maimed for life" (Qtd. in Cook 1983: 131). The fall of Othello is "the work of another human being." Yet, is it as simple as that?

When Chris Abraham directed the play at Stratford, he talked to his cast about how it is *love* in the end that saves the day. Abbey paraphrases Abraham's comments: "Emilia's love for Desdemona breaks the spell. Iago has a very powerful spell and it will work as long as everyone plays what they are supposed to play. And everyone does up to the point when Emilia breaks out and says 'No, no, no.' She accuses him and he tries to stifle her. His is a courageous, ridiculous plan but because of his power everyone plays their part up to the point of absolute tragedy."

I counter that even at the end, however, Iago has power because, in facing punishment for his villainous crimes, he refuses to speak anymore:

> *Oth.* Will you, I pray, demand that demi-devil
> Why he hath thus ensnar'd my soul and body?
> *Iago.* Demand me nothing, what you know, you know.
> From this time forth I never will speak word (5.2.301-304).

My view is reflected in W.H. Auden's analysis of this chilling moment, though Auden interprets Iago as a "Practical Joker of a peculiarly appalling kind" (Qtd. in Tynan 1966: 99). This sort of joker shows contempt for others, but behind this "lies something else, a feeling of self-insufficiency, of a self lacking in authentic feelings and desires of its own." Auden continues:

> He manipulates others, but when he finally reveals his identity, his victims learn nothing about his nature, only something about their own: They know how it was possible to for them to be deceived, but not why he chose to deceive them. The only answer that any practical joker can give to the question—'Why did you do this?'—is Iago's 'Demand me nothing. What you know, you know' (Tyan 1966: 100).

Abbey believes that Shakespeare is playing with archetypes: "You look at *Cymbeline*. Iachimo is more or less forgiven by Posthumus. Those things happen in Shakespeare's plays, but very often they don't. The resolution in *The Winter's Tale* is very difficult. It's written as if everyone goes off, hand in hand, but it's hard for us to fathom there is a cost to that. A boy [Mamillius] died. So, Shakespeare quite often won't resolve the music—like life, I guess."

I concur because I believe that Shakespeare is interested in showing how characters discover their humanity—as Harold Bloom shows in his magisterial *Shakespeare: The Invention of the Human* (1998), in which the critic demonstrates (by leading us through a comprehensive reading of the plays) each breakthrough in human characterisation, and culminates with his assertion that "Shakespeare invented us (whoever we are) rather more than we have invented Shakespeare" (Bloom 725). Perhaps too perversely sweeping but with more than just a kernel of truth.

Abbey delights in memories of having had "the privilege of chatting about Shakespeare with Robin Phillips in his living room a few times. I wish I had had a recorder then, but I do remember Robin saying that at their heart, the plays are domestic stories. They're about human volition, understanding, and discovery. You can see this all the way down to *The Tempest*, as magical and epical as it is."

We next explore the "wound" in Philip the Bastard in *King John*, with Abbey asserting: "He's denied land because of his birth. He's a bastard, so his wound is bastardy or the lack of rightful legitimacy. He's outside the norm; therefore, he's going to try to figure out this game he needs to play to get inside. He makes the beautiful speech about Commodity (2.1.573-598). He's an observer who thinks: 'Okay, if this is the way it works, I'm going to watch and learn how to move up in the world by smarts and by my wits.' What he learns is that there's no purity to it."

Abbey shares the inner workings of the Bastard's mind: "Everything we've gained in our battle, he (the King) just gave away by a backroom negotiation. So, on his journey, he's thwarted by it, and he follows a king he's believed in and that king turns out not to be as pure as he had thought. It's an extraordinary trajectory of learning."

I recall a nobility in his portrayal of the Bastard, but press him to articulate it for others—which he does: "When he finds out that there's royal blood in him, it is an extraordinary change of events. How that would affect your brain! The boy who his entire life thought he was just some vagrant but had thoughts and ambitions suddenly finds out he has blood in him that connects him to this power, this monarchy. His nobility is *discovered*. It's innate in him but he wants to try to do the right thing. He wants to learn about sacrifice and honour. He learns the hard way and he goes a bit awry."

When I watched his performance, I noticed Philip's wit and charm with Elinor, and his excitement over learning that his father was Richard Coeur de Lion. I also remembered his interaction with Hubert. Abbey seizes on Philip's speech in that scene (4.3.118 ff.):

> It's one of the most beautiful speeches in the canon. I think that's at the core of him. He's born with a sense of right and wrong, and has a sense of what is absolutely deplorable—the blinding of young Arthur and his death. He says to Hubert if you have done this, the world is not big enough to hold what you've done. He just knows innately that no matter what the political trajectory is, there are things you just can't do. You talk about the wit, as a lot of the Shakespearean bastards do, they are able to speak to the audience because they have two sides. Kings don't normally. Kings stay in their own thoughts but the Bastard has the ability, as a commoner, to pierce that fourth wall.

Just as in *Henry V*, when the king can share his most private, personal thoughts only when in disguise in the company of three soldiers in Act 4. "Yes," agrees Abbey. "He can't shake off that mantle. The one moment you get something close to piercing the fourth wall is the prayer before the battle. It's the first time he's alone with his thoughts. It's an extraordinary point in that play."

The reference is to Henry's speech, whose first four lines run as follows:

> O God of battles, steel my soldiers' hearts,
> Possess them not with fear! Take from them now
> The sense of reck'ning, [if] th'opposed numbers
> Pluck their hearts from them (4.1.289-292).

The king is wracked with historic guilt because of his own father's deposition of Richard II, and beseeches God: "Not to-day, O Lord,/O, not to-day, think not upon the fault/My father made in compassing the crown!" (4.1.292-294). Director Tim Carroll calls this speech and the earlier "Upon the King!" soliloquy (4.1.230-284) *illusions* that we have glimpsed something behind Henry's public mask: "They're two speeches but they add up to one became they come in the same sequence and make you feel privileged."

Abbey has the distinction of having played both Henry V and that man's father, Bolingbroke, before he became Henry IV by usurpation. There are contrary interpretations of Henry V, ranging from Olivier's apotheosis as the "star of England" to contemporary perspectives on a grittier war criminal or, a paradoxical hero-cum-criminal. But what about Bolingbroke? Is he a villain through and through? "Oh, sure, sure. It depends how you turn that," offers Abbey thoughtfully, adding:

> I think certainly the treatment of Richard could be put in the realm of villainy. I don't think it behooves any actor to think of anyone—including the worst of them—the Iagos and Richard IIIs—as villains. Bolingbroke doesn't fall as far down the spectrum as the real bad guys, but even in his case, in the deposition scene, it was my job to convince the audience that Bolingbroke is doing something good for his country. This man [Richard] is unfit to rule. We will fall into a mess, and the country does. There's a trajectory with him that starts with an affront made to him and his family. If you go back to the decision Richard made to banish him, there's a root that was wrong. That started the ball rolling, and so he's just coming back for what is his. He happens to be coming back with a very large army but his motives are simple.

Abbey has made a feast of playing villains, but if it is true that an actor has to own the character he is playing, how does Abbey "marry" himself to a role without becoming a marriage counsellor? Laughing in response to the conceit, he cracks an ironic comment: "If I had the answer to that, I could put it in a book." But he adds:

I immerse myself in it. Once I understand the thoughts and I've done the work and am on my feet with it, I engage with the energies of the other actors—which is important because they endow you with that role. Then it comes alive. My brain has an ability to switch in. Sometimes it's hard to leave that role behind. I've had that issue here at Stratford, especially playing the Scottish king or Iago, the darker guys. It's hard to leave that in the theatre. When we took the bows after the first preview for *Othello*, I started to lose my breath. I came offstage and burst into convulsive tears. I'd never had this in my life. I think it was sitting the first time in the energy of that man, with an audience witnessing it. Douglas Campbell used to talk about an ectoplasm that passes between actors and audience. And that ectoplasm was so *intense* that when the show ended, it just gushed out. As the shows go on, you learn how to handle that but it was a powerful energy. It's just the nature of live theatre.

Abbey is one of a handful of top rank Canadian actors who has also directed Shakespeare. A graduate of the Michael Langham workshop for classical direction at the Stratford Festival, he has served as an assistant director to Tim Carroll, Antoni Cimolino, and Martha Henry. He has also been the Artistic Director of Festival Players of Prince Edward County, and, most significantly, a founder and Artistic Director of the pocket-sized The Groundling Theatre Company in Toronto, which launched its inaugural production of *The Winter's Tale* in 2016 to sold-out houses. When I say "pocket-sized," I am referring merely to the performing space, not necessarily to the calibre or scale of achievement.

At Groundling, he can exercise his love for Shakespeare, drawing on some of the very best actors he has known and worked with at Stratford: Tom McCamus, Brent Carver, Seana McKenna, Lucy Peacock, et cetera. His latest ground-breaking production was a chamber-size *King Lear* with a female Lear. This play is decidedly a domestic tragedy, with a single parent—not unlike the pattern in other Shakespearean plays, such as *Hamlet*, *Coriolanus*, and *The Tempest*. Usually, the single parent is a father, with Volumnia's being an exception to the pattern. Was it because of the restrictions of the Elizabethan stage, where boys played female roles? "Yes, I guess that's the practical answer," Abbey says, before opening up the subject:

One likes to think Shakespeare had a dramatic answer to it as well. I think there's much food for thought for actors, directors, and artists on this topic. Those missing units [parents] in the plays create great back stories that are backed by text about what the reasons could be. Even so far as we start to switch the genders in these plays—as we did with Lear this winter, with Seana McKenna—what came out of that play was extraordinary, with a mother cursing her daughters' wombs. When you take the framework of his plays and just change the lens, all this comes out.

But what is the rationale for a female Lear? The simple rationale is that we have a collection of plays that are male-dominated in terms of roles, and in 2018 we need parity in terms of a pool of actors. I have to say that when we did *Lear*, one of the best actors to take on that role was Seana McKenna. I didn't have an answer or a clever answer when I was asked why I had a woman. I should have had an answer, but I didn't, so we just dove in, and it changed minds, including that of Martha Henry, who said in the *Globe and Mail* that it changed her mind about women playing these roles. What happens is that you put a different lens on that play—a maternal lens—and, all of a sudden, what comes out of the other side is extraordinary. For instance, the cursing of the daughters' wombs becomes much more powerful and rooted through the voice of a woman. When Lear says, 'I gave you all,' she did. She birthed her. The mother is the centre of the Great Wheel of Life, and that relationship becomes incredibly profound with a female Lear.

I would argue that you gain as much as you possibly lose, perhaps more. We certainly did in *Lear* where the madness of Lear and the sexual undercurrents (which I've seen played by men numerable times in ways ranging from very good to very bad), they're always in the vein of a sexuality that only a man can have. Some of them have been twists on female sexuality so they come off as mockeries. In Seana's case, heart and mind and mouth were a woman's who had, her entire life, subverted her sexuality because she was a royal head. We didn't change anything but suddenly it cast a whole new light on it.

The alignment of a male and female perspective between Seana and myself became very interesting, as we both learned. For instance, with Lear's rage at the beginning ('Come not between the dragon and his wrath'), I was picturing in my head Plummer, Hutt, and Bedford throwing tables around, but Seana was finding her own way through that scene, that was equally effective.

When we got to the back end in the madness scenes, Seana was discovering all sorts of things that I could feed on. At one point, she came very close to a birthing image just before she says, 'Let me wipe [my hand] first, it smells of mortality' (4.6.133). The two of us just spun on this moment and the idea of the great cycle of life.

When I raise the concern that we lose a lot of power when it is a female Lear, Abbey retorts that I am on the same learning curve as his: "There are different angles on power. We have a sense of what we think it is or what it's known to be. That's only because we've often associated power with men. It's interesting how women come at power. I cycle through all the plays, even the histories, and I think about what they could be when inhabited by women. I would suggest that while we may lose something that is, perhaps, familiar to us, we gain a whole new understanding of what those plays could do."

I concede that he has a point, if approaching the subject as psychology, but I am talking about text. If something is written expressly as an aria for a male voice, I can't imagine most women having the sort of vocal power to render this effectively. Abbey agrees in general but claims that in terms of the tenor of a voice, Seana McKenna and Martha Henry have power and tenor in their voices. He illustrates with an example from his own acting experience:

> When I first came to Stratford, I did *Death of a Salesman* with Martha, and I would phone my mother at night, very upset and say, 'Mom, Martha Henry hates me. She absolutely hates me.' 'Why?' "Because of the way she talks to me and the sound of her voice.' 'When? What are you talking about?' 'In the play.' Then I realized that Martha's such a good actress and she was hitting me personally, actually piercing my character, [as required by her role as a mother protecting her husband]. So, if I had a choice between Bill Hutt or Martha Henry yelling at me, I don't know which one I'd rather have, because they both hold power.

For Abbey, it has been particularly stirring to witness Martha Henry tackling the role of Prospero in the current Stratford season:

> It is exciting to see a mother's journey through that play. I told Martha, 'I can hear Bill [Hutt],' because you just do. Those ghosts stay with you. Martha is certainly capable of finding all of the fire and fury that Bill or any other man finds in that role but her interpretation has a flavour of maternal protection. Here's another example: when you change that role to a female, you get the mirror of Sycorax and Caliban. You have a mother and a child who came to that island first, and then you have the mirror of a mother and Miranda. Your brain becomes aware of a cycle and a connection to mothers coming to that island and nurturing children or not nurturing—in Caliban's case.
>
> I don't think we're putting anything on this playwright that he didn't battle for in smaller aspects of his plays. But I think we are giving our great actresses a chance to play those great roles, which is exciting in itself.

Listening to his repeated insistence that he does not like to impose his own views on or dictate to actors or actresses, I ask how he worked on *King Lear*. His answer is informed by a theatrical pragmatism:

> I'm not a big believer in long opening day speeches. I'm more interested in the *broader* questions of the play and what the actors bring into the space. This doesn't negate careful detail in the work, but that detail is often found while the actors are on their feet in rehearsals. I don't believe in imposing something on a play. You can talk about the macro questions of the play, and you certainly have to put the actors in a world. So, we decide, for instance, that we're not in a world where recorders or cell phones exist. We're in a world where letters have to be passed, or where you can wear a sword on the hip.
>
> Once those parameters have been put in place—once you've told the actors the general shape of the sandbox, then you can get into the sandbox and start playing. I like to work in a very collaborative room. I like a lot of voices, and I like tough questions and challenges. You should be able to answer everything and keep feeding the centre of the play.

And what has he learned himself from some of the best Shakespearean directors?

The first name that would come to mind would be Brian Bedford, whom I was fortunate to work with as an actor and director. Brian was an extraordinary stickler for detail and precision with the language. He would often refer to Gielgud who taught him and who would sing the text, finding variety in language. When I was a young actor in *The Winter's Tale*, I thought I would really impress Brian Bedford in one of the early rehearsals in the scene where Florizel fights for his love (Perdita) and for his life. He decides he is not going to listen to his father (Polixenes) but will run away. I decided to just go for broke, emoting and weeping. I ended the scene on the floor, pounding it in tears. There was a dead silence, and after about 30 seconds of silence, from behind a table came Brian's voice: 'It's all right but we simply can't charge people money for this.'

When Abbey got to direct the same play years later for Groundling in Toronto, he recalled something Bedford had said when he directed *The Winter's Tale*: "At the end of that play, we see a statue coming to life and we know it's an actress unfreezing. But what if, in fact, we were witnessing a real miracle?" This has prompted Abbey to wonder: "What if all of us—actors and audiences—are witnessing something that is transcendental? That's the thrill of acting. I once read a quotation: 'Great art should disturb reality.' If you could disturb reality, you're doing something effective."

I voice a criticism I have heard from some actors that Bedford spent too much time on table readings.

Yes, I know, but you'd also find actors saying he didn't spend enough time. I love table work because we can sit and analyze every little bit, and we could go on for hours about a single word. Robin Phillips was a stickler for that. It's never time wasted around the table. Yes, some actors would feel panic and complain, but it gives you a brilliant foundation so that when you get to your feet, you've got clarity. You must have that. I've been in productions where we don't spend enough time with the text, and we get all the way to opening night on energy and adrenalin but by the time August rolls around, you're lost. You don't know what any of [the text] means.

If an actor was having trouble with a specific passage, would Bedford demonstrate how to do that passage or would he let the actor go home and figure it out himself?

He would never do a line reading but he would get pretty darn close, if after several times you were unable to find the lift or energy in something. Then he would be on you. Once, while doing Molière comedies with him in Chicago, I spent five hours one morning just doing my entrance, not even speaking a word. There was beautiful music, I had to come through a door, and look up. It was the introduction of the ingenue. Brian spent an entire morning just rehearsing me in breathing the air and smiling. He was that precise about how that character should enter the play.

We have to be that careful and precise in carving Shakespeare's language, and not revert to the point that it becomes a museum piece. But we also have to be careful about the clarity of it. He was a big mentor that way.

I was directed by Martha Henry in *Richard III*, and assisted her last season on *Twelfth Night*. She worked a lot with Robin. She's very careful with the text, but very helpful to actors in terms of allowing a freedom to discover things. She's very much about discovery, and even if something feels odd, will allow an actor to dive into that and figure out what that could be.

Another one in my later years would be Chris Abraham. I did *Othello* with him and then *Tartuffe* last year. I really enjoy Chris's brain. He's a director with a really thoughtful approach to the play, but he isn't averse to actors asking questions. He will always get into a debate with you, but he's somebody who is concerned with detail. *Tartuffe* could have just been a frothy piece that we crank out because it's funny and in rhyme, but Chris had a real desire to ground it in something relevant to an audience today.

I object that Shakespeare is always relevant. I was born in an Asian country where the national language is not English but I was able to read and be thrilled by his plays. That my own mother tongue was English certainly helped, but the Elizabethan Age was quite different from my post-colonial era. Yet, I could relate to Shakespeare's characters, themes, and language. When I immigrated to Canada and went to university, I wondered why everyone was so worried about relevance. Why was there such a mania? Stories about families, parents, children, heroes, heroines, villains, and victims share universal traits of humanity, no matter their period or country. Robin Phillips was certainly able to express this truth for Canadians when he set Shakespeare near a Mennonite community or in a Victorian or Edwardian period with which Canadian society had a relatively recent affinity.

"You're preaching to the converted here," Abbey offers, "because this circles back to my idea about a universality that speaks. However, I think it behooves actors and director in a room to talk about why this play and why now." He elaborates: "I think the actors need to discuss the echoes that are going to be heard in the audience when you drop a play like Lear into the modern age. What is going to echo out there? When those words come through you, an ectoplasm is sent out, but what's going to be received? What message are we sending without warping the plays? Again, I return to Robin saying that they're domestic stories. They've survived all these years because they are stories about your life—whatever that means to you."

There is no actor who has not, at some time or another, disagreed fundamentally with a director. How does Abbey cope in such a situation? He acknowledges that all the directors he liked especially were ones that he disagreed with occasionally vehemently, but all of them found what he calls "a middle ground" by which to settle their differences. "If the rehearsal hall isn't a place of hard work and occasional adversity—in the best of ways (with nothing to do with ego or abuse), fighting for the worth of a production, then you do a disservice—especially to Shakespeare's plays," he contends fervently. "They should be fought for. I've never taken offence to an actor or director being adamant about something because it means you're passionate. But you have to find a middle ground, and eventually you do."

I pose one of my favourite questions: Who dictates style in a production? To which he replies:

> It depends on the actors and director. I keep taking the middle ground on these questions, but I think any director worth his salt casts his show already with a sense of the style based on how he's casting. The voices you're placing in those characters will create your chorus that will impose style on the play. I think that can change throughout rehearsals. But a good director should create the parameters which are fairly wide and then allow play within those parameters. If they're narrow, there's not much room for actor volition, and I believe in the energy of actors.
>
> But style can be imposed by a designer, as well. I've had times at Stratford when things designed for me in the off-season don't fit at all with what I had in mind to play. And those are sometimes difficult negotiations. When I played Jaques in *As You Like It* (2005), it was set in the 1960s, so already you've got a period that has a fairly specific parameter. Antoni had thought ahead of time that Jaques would be a burnt-out rock star who had left the world and gone to the woods, so Santo Loquasto created beautiful snake-skin boots with big platform heels. When I saw these, they didn't seem to jell with the research I had been doing.
>
> I had been watching *The Deer Hunter* and focussing on Vietnam. That was my entry point into someone who was outside the norm in the 1960s. I wanted Jaques to be a photographer who had witnessed things in Vietnam as an observer but not as a soldier. I picked a photographer because he was able to take pictures of children and lovers and soldiers. He is always the outsider who can comment. I made him an observer or watcher—somebody who doesn't engage but who comments. He's a realist infused with a ton of cynicism, so that when he talks about the Seven Ages of Man, it's a story he's retelling. It's an observation about man, about the cycle of life. To his credit, Antoni said: 'Okay, let's re-shape this.' And we found a mix: costumes that took away the rock 'n' roll but kept elements of the bohemian guy [headband, long hair, and beads], while adding some of the Vietnam dog-tags and stuff. So, we found a fusion, and that is the perfect scenario when you have a director and designer who are willing to listen to an actor, because at the end the actor has to wear the skin.

I engage Abbey on the question if there are rules in Shakespearean acting, admitting that I hate the word "rules," even as I utter it.

He claims that if he was to talk about rules, he would be de-valuing what he has learned:

> I can list lessons I have learned from Brian and Bill and Martha—lessons they didn't necessarily pass on to me directly. I just observed. There are things we pass down. I tell young actors about what Brian had told me, which is what Gielgud had told him, and which is what an older actor [Beerbohm Tree or Granville Barker] had told Gielgud about singing the language or finding variety. Those things are valu-able, and they're about the tradition of a place like this. I like rules as lessons we pass down because they work. Those were not for naught.
>
> I think as the generations go by, we also do a disservice to Shake-speare if we don't open it up to different voices and people coming in. I'm not a big guy for tearing it apart or conceptualising things but I think inhabiting it from the inside-out is exciting. But it's harder than you think.

Notes

[1] Scott Wentworth directed both parts of He*nry IV*, while Jeannette Lambermont directed *Henry V* in the 2001 season.

[2] Abbey's two-part adaptation of four of Shakespeare's history plays: *Richard II*, *Henry IV Parts One and Two*, and *Henry V*. Performed at the Stratford Festival in 2016.

Lucy Peacock as Volumnia in Coriolanus *(Stratford Festival, 2018).*
(Photo: David Hou. Courtesy of the Stratford Festival)

Lucy Peacock
Language Through the Chaos of the Heart

"Lucy Peacock emerged, almost from nowhere, as a high comedienne, expert in asperity and how to melt it," enthused Robert Cushman of her Mrs. Sullen in *The Beaux's Stratagem* (1985) (Cushman 149). Two years later, Cushman applauded her Nora Helmer in an adaptation of *A Doll's House*, pointing out that the Stratford production seemed "most significant for marking the decisive emergence of Lucy Peacock as Stratford's new leading actress: the most durable, or so it was to prove, since Martha Henry," (Cushman 163) though Seana McKenna might have something to say on the issue, especially as McKenna's credits are no less massive than Peacock's and the two actresses once made a fine pair of humorously volatile bosom-friends and rivals in Coward's *Fallen Angels* (2005), with their bibulousness becoming a hilarious case of glamorously sheathed ladies turned into neurotic, rival Amazons of lust.

Nevertheless, Peacock deserves the highest praise for her versatility. She was a slinky, sexy Titania in 1989 and a "witty and unshakeably confident Rosalind" in 1990 (Cushman 181), and, to take examples from her more recent successes, I found her Mrs. Hardcastle in *She Stoops to Conquer* (2015) to be a delectable mixture of unconvincing sophistication, silly vanity, and heightened fluster. Deliciously funny when protesting "I shall be too young for the fashion" when speaking of London high society, she was the image of hysterical indignation at being called a "hag" at another moment.

The next season her Kate Keller in *All My Sons* (2016) was a superb study in cunning self-protection that carried emotional and mental freight bordering on the tragic. She became the strongest bond with the primitive, the raw, and the deranged when she played mad Agave in *Bakkhai* (2017), totally and tragically oblivious to the fact that the severed head she carried around like a trophy was that of her own slaughtered son.

Given her extraordinary versatility in everything from the ancient Greeks to Arthur Miller, Shakespeare to Chekhov and Ibsen, Restoration comedy to Coward, it could certainly be said with eminent justification that she is a leading lady, rampant with feeling and acute intuition, as subtle as the sliest smile or as tempestuous as an ecstasy of hurricanes. Shakespeare cannot be too heavy for her, nor Coward too light. Comedy is mother's milk to her, and drama or tragedy a jagged summit she scales with staggering force and courage.

Perhaps there's a lot to be said about genetic genius for, certainly in her case, there are deep connections to British theatrical history. Born in England, she's a fifth-generation actress on her mother's side. Her mother, Georgia Thorndike, was a cousin of Ann Casson and, thereby, niece of Dame Sybil, widely celebrated as a stage force never to be trifled with. Ann married Scots actor Douglas Campbell and was mother to Benedict Campbell, actor and half-brother of singer/songwriter/actor Torquil Campbell; Dame Sybil and her husband, Lewis Casson, worked with Laurence Olivier and John Gielgud, the two greatest English stage actors of their day.

Lucy's father was David Peacock, who stage managed at the Royal Opera House before immigrating to Canada with his wife and growing family, at Michel St. Denis' invitation to teach at the National Theatre School (founded by St. Denis, who also founded Juilliard in New York). David eventually became General Director of the National Theatre School in Montreal, before taking over the arts division of the Canada Council.[1] He returned to England as cultural attaché and retired there. In this knotted history, England and Canada are intricately connected, as is quite befitting any discussion of Shakespeare in Canada or, more pointedly, Canadian actors playing Shakespeare.

At Massey Vanier High School in Cowansville, Lucy's Drama teacher, Eugene Jousse, encouraged her to study *Othello*. She undertook her first close reading of Shakespeare with this play, but when she got to the end, she began laughing out loud. When her parents asked what she found so amusing, she replied: "Well, okay. How many *bodies* are there on the stage?" But she returned to the text and on reading it more closely, she was hooked. "I understood it. I loved the story. I had a vivid imagination as a child, and still do. I believe the imagination is a muscle that an actor must keep strong and invigorated."

A year after her training at the National Theatre School, she joined the Stratford Festival company, where her mentors were (she remarks with blissful enthusiasm) "*everybody*. I would listen, I would ask questions, and make myself useful. My mentor was the language. It taught me so much, as did listening to how Martha Henry, Brian Bedford, and William Hutt dealt with it." She wanted to know how the language worked and why Shakespeare used certain words the way he did. Her "theory" at the time was to make herself the text's instrument that could bring that language to life. "That was my craft-building goal: to create a vessel that would be able to channel the living energy of the language and story," she says, adding: "Of course, it took many years, and I still have a lot to learn."

The Canadian side of her biography and experience has, of course, been deepened and extended. Her husband, Christopher Thomas, used to be an actor who did regional theatre, film, and television. The couple first met when she was 17 and studying at CEGEP while he was attending Bishop's University in Lennoxville. They have two sons: Harrison has graduated from the NTS as a director; and Benjamin, who studied Drama at Queen's University, has won a full scholarship to do his M.A. at the University of Ottawa. He also would like to be a director—especially of great classical texts.

Peacock manages to cope with marriage, parenting, and her career without ever losing her zest for acting or for Shakespeare. She recalls very clearly that when she played Rosalind for Richard Monette in 1990, it "was like a dream come true. That was exactly where I was supposed to be. I felt that everything—being born in England, moving here and to the country, listening as a teen to recordings of Edith Evans and Gielgud in *The Importance of Being Earnest*, getting interested in Shakespeare—meant that the theatre stars lined up. I was ready; Richard found me; and Shakespeare said: 'This is for you.' I was put there to play that part."

She was in seventh heaven, especially as she enjoyed the role more than Dame Peggy Ashcroft apparently had, even though Ashcroft had played it at numerous times in her long career, even in middle age, successfully playing the *idea* of feminine youthfulness. Invited to tea by Ashcroft in her Chelsea home, she was quite surprised when Dame Peggy brought up the role: "I hear you're playing Rosalind next year at Stratford. Oh, wonderful. [pause] She talks too much."

Peacock triumphed in the role, as she did in other Shakespearean leading and supporting roles. What was especially significant about this triumph is that it came in Richard Monette's production that was Canadian through and through, with aboriginals, *coureurs de bois*, birchbark canoe, trappers, peasants, and gentry in a setting representing the environs of Quebec City and L'île d'Orléans in the late fall of 1758, not long before the battle on the Plains of Abraham when the English defeated the French. The opening number was a Quebecois folk song ("Un Canadien errant") that culminated in a step dance to the music of fiddle and spoons.

But the setting was merely locale colour. What was more important was the fact that the performers were acting with their Canadian temperaments and sensibilities. Perhaps it is time not to belabour the point about nationalizing Shakespeare. Would Christopher Plummer be considered less Canadian for working in London, New York, or Hollywood? Would he be Canadian only because he can act in both English and French or because he occasionally graces the Stratford Festival with performances or because he accepts roles in Canadian films?

Although acting is not something that can be discussed in isolation from the society surrounding it, the best acting is something that connects directly with the world at large. Shakespeare's plays are not mainly celebrated for this nationalism but for their universalism in terms of what they show about our humanity.

Accordingly, it behooves professional actors to not stand still as human beings but to indulge in work aimed at professional growth. Lucy Peacock is joyfully earnest about the exercise of her talent. She is not the type to accommodate great roles to the limitations of her own temperament. Instead, she extends her personality and skills to match the characters she plays on stage. When asked what sort of preparation she does to play the major ones, she indicates that her main research is the text itself:

> Of course, I'll do my readings of secondary sources, but I don't do a ton of it. I'm not an academic. I only graduated from high school. I never finished CEGEP. I did go to the National Theatre School, but I feel I have a real practical education in Shakespeare. What I do is get five different versions of the text: Arden, Penguin, Oxford, all those, and the variorums (which are very helpful but I don't think they make them anymore). The Arden is absolutely in my back pocket. I start putting it in my body. I read it and immediately my body reacts. The detective work has to do with the language, and just slowly building my familiarity with it. Also, especially as I get older and understand more about what I am doing, it is important not to assume that I know what the choices might be. I do an

architectural dig my own way. Everybody does it a little bit differently but with the same end in sight. I look for the character being
revealed through the text.

She is not a purist about metre, but finds it helpful to distinguish
among metres when she feels stuck. She is practical because, for
her, the words themselves are what matter and the language has
to be visceral. She knows instinctively where the pressure is in a
particular passage and how high the stakes are: "It's doing it over
and over and not assuming, but changing, feeling, and tasting it.
The challenge is also the finesse of it, and the subtleties that can
be found, for example, in four lines of text. Shakespeare speaks to
me: 'Yeah, Lucy, that's good, but why don't you look at this?' I was
brought up in this company with more old school British teachers
and mentors, such as Nicholas Pennell, Brian Bedford, and John
Neville. They were considered the greatest speakers of that text at
the time, so listening to them was very important to me."

She would consult Pennell for help in understanding and being
inspired by the text, and his instructions were invaluable: Don't hit
the personal pronoun, and if you do, know that it's a choice for the
sense. Always lift the end of the line, and if you do choose not to
or if you can't find a way to do that, know that you can't find a way.
Always shine a light on the verb as it is the propeller and will help
clarify the forward momentum and sense of thought. Shakespeare
is likely sending an encrypted message to you through the inconsistencies regarding the emotional or the character or the story.

She also likes to study pictures and paintings: "One of the
muscles is the imagination in order to be able to pretend to be
someone. I look at portraits and photographs of women's frocks
or hands—especially if it's a historical period. You try and imagine
the life inside the image." In this regard, she could be echoing a
method of Laurence Olivier, who, in describing how he arrived
at his audacious interpretation of Othello, wrote: "To visualize a

character, I first visualize a painting; the manner, movement, gestures, walk, all follow. It began to come. Pictures and sounds began to form in my mind, subconsciously at first, but slowly working their way to the surface" (Olivier 1986: 105).

But it is the language itself that is the prime mover. When teaching a class on Shakespeare, she will pick up the play and declare: "This is living energy. It's an explosion, a pressure of real energy. It was meant to be spoken. There are genius and inspiration there that maybe even Shakespeare didn't realize were there. Richard Monette told me a story once about a very famous French actor who said: 'I love to do Shakespeare because he makes me look like a genius.' It's kind of true. If you have the tools and the technique, he'll do the work with you and can make you look fabulous!!"

She waxes warmly about Shakespeare's generosity: "He's so full of heart. I tell actors I am teaching or mentoring that he is one of the most generous playwrights ever. He loves actors. If you are a good, hardworking, honest actor, he will teach, guide, support, challenge, and celebrate you." Peacock agrees with me that very often we over-intellectualize Shakespeare: "I personally believe that we do, but, as I've said, I believe it's visceral. It's athletic mentally, physically, and technically."

She advocates fitness ("You have to be rigorous in your taking all the elements in your possession") and once again she could be echoing Olivier because that paragon of actors tackled the great Shakespearean roles athletically, by a regimen of physical exercises, such as running, weight-lifting, and swimming. Olivier contended:

> To be fit should be one of an actor's first priorities. Daily exercise is of the utmost importance. The body is an instrument which must be finely tuned and played as often as possible. The actor should be able to control it from the tip of his head to his little toe. He must be able to send messages to any part of it with the speed and skill of a computer. We are living in a machine, a machine of great complexity, and in order to use it properly we must try to understand as

> much about it as possible. Perhaps part of an actor's course should
> include a few months of medical studies (Olivier 1986: 242-243).

Olivier was only joking about the prescription of medical studies, but he did insist on the importance of an actor knowing how the body works and how to keep this body supple and agile.

Peacock's voice can be silken or husky, subtle or bold. It can manage Congreve as skilfully as it engages easily with Coward, but hers is not an acting talent that is all voice. She can surprise an audience by a gesture or piece of business without making her inventiveness seem too carefully studied or worked out. A vivid manifestation came to the fore when she tackled the role of Lady Macbeth under John Wood's direction in 2004. She showed up for rehearsals three weeks late because she had been performing Regan for Plummer's Lear in New York. All the company was on pins and needles while awaiting her arrival.

When she did appear, she deliberately avoided Graham Abbey, who was to play the title role, because she didn't want to dilute the anticipated stage tension generated by the central couple. She knew her lines but didn't know some members of the cast. The director was working on crowd scenes when she showed up, so she went directly for costume fittings. That very afternoon some of the blocking was rehearsed, then there was a run with lighting by Gil Wechsler.

She had been informed that there was to be a big white cloth on stage for the sleepwalking scene. As that scene increased in intensity, she began to pull on the cloth relentlessly and ever more desperately—startling the rest of the cast and her director by her feverish spontaneity. Eventually she dragged the whole cloth off with her, crystallizing in the moment a dramatic epiphany of Lady Macbeth's disintegrating mind. Obviously, the action was not realism but a kind of metaphor for gathering up the white blindness of her encroaching madness. So, it represented her mind or the ground on which she had walked before losing both. The actress and the passion were one. Recalling this moment, she comments: "It was inspired by my engine running hot. It was a good feeling. There are some Shakespearean parts that have been very dangerous in my life. She was certainly one of them."

Acting at its highest necessarily requires a sense of danger— for the actor and for the audience as well. An audience never knows what a great actor is going to do from one moment to the next, whether it is a gesture, a tone, or a tiny or huge explosion of energy. Examples abound in the cases of Olivier, Vanessa Redgrave, Kim Stanley, Geraldine Page, Marlon Brando, Daniel Day Lewis, et cetera. Genius is nothing without risk, and the greatest actors are those who take the greatest risks. And by this I do not mean simply physical risks of business or choreography, such as Olivier's startling death fall in *Coriolanus* (directed by Peter Hall) when he was stabbed in the belly, fell forward, head first, from an upper rostrum where, somehow, his ankles were held firmly by Volscian soldiers and he was prevented from killing himself literally at every performance.

I mean the same actor's risk with makeup, accent, intonation, movement, and gesture as Othello (blacker than black in his negritude) or his seedy Archie Rice, gap-toothed, thickly made up with rouge and thickly-painted eyebrows, spontaneously creating a high arc of pain as he described the "beautiful fuss" he once heard made by a blues-singer in a bar, or his portrayal of Shylock as a Victorian outsider in Jonathan Miller's version of *The Merchant of Venice*, in which he hugged his dead wife's portrait while issuing heart-rending moans of lamentation over his daughter's betrayal, or the scene in which he performed a little, gleeful dance at the moment when Tubal told him Antonio's ships had gone down.

Lucy Peacock takes similar risks with roles—as with her wildly demented Agave or her virtuoso performances of four monologues in Robert Hewett's *The Blonde, the Brunette and the Vengeful Red-head*, in which she incarnated seven distinctively different characters at extremes of age, gender, and temperament. But while Lucy Peacock incarnates passion in all its blazingly dangerous colour and energy when she fully inhabits a role, she highlights Shakespeare's complex humanity. She treasures him because he tries to make acting easy or easier for actors who are smart enough to pick up his clues in a text: "For me, what's interesting is the built-in complexity. Sometimes it's not good to try and make sense of it all. You have to know some things, but you can also have things that you don't know, that you simply trust. You need to give everything the right value, give the image equal value to the thought."

She uses the metaphor of an engine and its forward momentum, and cautions: "If you try and manipulate something to fit your need to make sense of it, I think you're missing something. It's more valuable to offer yourself to the unknown because often something will be revealed—which would be humanity or the complexity of humanity."

When she teaches classes in acting, she says to her students: "You're going to take everything you know about the form of this speech, the grammar, the beats, the verbs, and the shape, and you're not going to think about it for this exercise. You're going to take everything that you know and put it through the *chaos* of the heart. Poof! That's what I think is fun. That's better than rock 'n' roll."

I suggest that success in this type of exercise also requires experience, to which she retorts: "It takes experience, but I can help them do that, and I can help them taste it. Takes me ninety minutes at the most for it to be in their heart and deep in their gut. And if they experience it once, they will want it again. It's addictive."

As for her own heart and gut, she eagerly awaits opportunities to bend gender in Shakespeare: "I've always wanted to play Richard III and Hamlet. I've done Lear or the map of Lear as a woman.

And I have played Grumio in *Shrew*, or Gruvio, as I used to call her. Given my experience and life's commitment to this language, why shouldn't I be allowed to do some of the great male parts? It would be interesting to explore what that side of the coin is—what the story is, what the muscle is. It's fun for those of us women who've been doing this for so long to explore previously uncharted territory."

Her remarks exemplify what can be termed "actress lib"— a rebellion against traditional male chauvinism in theatre, not excluding Shakespearean theatre. The theatre of Shakespeare's day, of course, had an understandable male bias: Female roles could be played only by boy-actors or young males trained to imperson- ate women. That historical limitation no longer applies to mod- ern theatre, where it is becoming increasingly possible to watch a Glenda Jackson or Janet McTeer, Diane D'Aquila or Seana McK- enna, Kelli Fox or Meryl Streep cross the gender boundary.

Shakespeare certainly provides an actress with the opportunity to use her stagecraft, and that can be equal to an actor's, for as Harriet Walter maintains: "It's as difficult for a man to say that verse as it is for a woman. There's as much mind and heart to link up, as much technique and emotion—all those challenges set by the verse" (Todd 17).

Peacock relishes the prospect of joining their ranks, though she has little reason to complain about her roles this season at Strat- ford where she plays the goddess Juno in *The Tempest*, Satan in Erin Shields' modernization of *Paradise Lost*, and Volumnia in *Coriolanus*. Goddess, demon, and demon-mother. Quite a gallery, which she jokingly represents as a stretch "from the highest of the high to the lowest of the low, even geographically."

Although a standout in all three roles, she blazes in Robert Lepage's brilliantly filmic *Coriolanus* that opens with a marvellous illusion of a talking bust of the eponymous character and narrates its story through projected *trompe l'oeil* imagery, live video, sliding diorama-like boxes and panels that expand or contract like equivalents of cinematic pans, tracking shots, close-ups, and letter-box effects.

Shakespeare, however, never gets obscured in the thrilling process, because the story is told clearly, vividly, colourfully by an ensemble headed by robustly vigorous André Sills (Coriolanus), supported by such expert versatile players as Graham Abbey (Aufidius), Tom McCamus (Menenius), Stephen Ouimette (Brutus), and Tom Rooney (Sicinius). There are two customary areas of dramatic focus in any production of this play: the Coriolanus-Aufidius conflict and the complicated mother-son relationship of Coriolanus and Volumnia. Both of these areas are highlighted in the Lepage production, though the first one is diluted in its homo-eroticism and by the staging of Coriolanus' death in a way that runs counter to Shakespeare's original.

The second, however, gleams with Lucy Peacock's charismatic genius. Without diminishing the role's acid comedy or brutal satire, she turns Volumnia into an amalgam of Lady Macbeth and "Mama Rose of Rome," to echo the label created by Jesse Green in his *New York Times* review (July 18, 2008). While she can be regarded as a demon stage-mother who is out to stage-manage her boy-man warrior's life, she is absolutely convinced of her own rectitude. It is no small irony when she accuses Coriolanus of being "too absolute" (3.2.39), because, in fact, she is absolute herself.

Peacock seizes on the point: "That's what I really appreciate about Volumnia: her blindness. She overreacts to his overreacting, but he's basically responding to his own nature which she has nurtured. She doesn't recognize that he is of her making and accuses him of the exact thing she is guilty of."

While the other women in the plot (Virgilia, her daughter-in-law, and Valeria, a friend) don't have many speaking lines, Volumnia speaks forcefully for herself. She has no husband to force her to be his "gracious silence," as Virgilia is to Coriolanus (2.1.175), nor would she, one suspects, ever be successfully made docile by a man. She rules her household as surely as she rules her son, whom she wants to turn into the greatest Roman who ever lived. She had sent him into battle when he was a teenager, and she thanks the gods that he has been wounded in war even as she counts his wounds. It is significant that she doesn't address him as "son" till Act 3, Scene 2, choosing to call him "my good soldier" instead (2.1.172). Indeed, she declares at one point that if her son were her own husband, she'd prefer him to find honour in battle than to show love in bed:

> If my son were my husband, I should freelier rejoice in that absence wherein he won honour than in the embracements of his bed where he would show most love. When yet he was but tender-bodied and the only son of my womb; when youth with comeliness pluck'd all gaze his way; when for a day of kings' entreaties a mother should not sell him an hour from her beholding; I, considering how honor would become such a person, that it was no better than picture-like to hang by th' wall, if renown made it not stir, was pleas'd to let him seek danger where he was like to find fame. To a cruel war I sent him, from whence he return'd, his brows bound with oak. I tell thee, daughter, I sprang not more in joy at first hearing he was a man-child than now in first seeing he had prov'd himself a man (1.3.2-17).

The language in the passage is as muscular as her conviction and ambition, and Peacock recognizes this while handling it deftly:

> It's very meaty language. It takes a lot of muscle. In most of Shakespeare's plays, if there is a connection to the thought or the rigour of the language, then it can sound naturalistic. I would certainly say by setting the play the way he did, Robert Lepage enhances that. There is a sophistication in the language, but I don't know if it is any more so than some other plays, like *As You Like It* or *King Lear*. Maybe when you approach these plays with more experience and skill and well-honed craft, the better you are at making it sound, seem, and feel

naturalistic, true, and real. It's still heightened language but it doesn't necessarily have to be heard as archaic or distancing.

The language fortifies the sense of Volumnia's huge status, not only as the mother of a heroic warrior but as a Roman woman who would do the state some service herself and through her son. As Tina Packer puts it: "[Volumnia] knows the contribution she has made to the state, and she doesn't mind whether she's at home sewing or in the street greeting people—her status is assured." Her son's wounds in battle are treasured, so, "whether it's the wounds her son has received, or the wings being pulled off butterflies by her grandson, or death by burning of the whole town, she can endure all that, mostly because she identifies with 'Rome.' It is her religion, her faith, her God—and to sacrifice for it is an honour" (Packer 174-75).

In other words, Volumnia could be called a fundamentalist for her belief in Rome, and her language channels the role's huge energy and scope, as Peacock acknowledges: "Volumnia is a force, no doubt about it. Because of the society that they live in, she lives out her own ambitions through him. If it wasn't for the way that this particular society is set up, she'd be the warrior. Even more important to her are the politics because she wants her son to be the politician. She's living out her fantasy through him." Rather like the Mama Rose of *Gypsy*, who tries to live out her own fantasy of stardom through her daughters, or like Lady Macbeth who initially begins wanting the kingdom for her husband and herself but who then loses her mind (Mama Rose does so, too) and spirals to her death.

Mama Rose and Lady Macbeth demonstrate extreme ferocity at times, and Volumnia exhibits similar ferocity in some of her speeches, most especially in the one when she casts decorum to the winds and conjures up images of brutal violence as she tries to impress upon her son his ruthless betrayal of Rome:

Think with thyself
How more unfortunate than all living women
Are we come hither; since that thy sight, which should
Make our eyes flow with joy, hearts dance with comforts,
Constrains them weep and shake with fear and sorrow,
Making the mother, wife, and child to see
The son, the husband, and the father tearing
His country's bowels out (5.3.96-103).

Combining aspects here of Juno and Bellona, Volumnia is as histrionic as she is conscientious, and the speech is meat for a hungry actress who has technique, intelligence, and passion working in finely calibrated unity.

Peacock also explores the affinity between Volumnia and Lady Macbeth, agreeing with my opinion that the two women use their powers to promote the masculine institutions of war and some other forms of aggressive superiority: "Yes, you have that absolutely right. Lady Macbeth, though, is more fragile emotionally than Volumnia. I don't see Volumnia doing a sleepwalking scene or some dramatic death scene. She would rise up out of the ashes, as she says in her last line: 'I am hush'd until our city be afire,/And then I'll speak a little' (5.3.181-182). I think she absolutely will. She'll be a phoenix arising or she'll move to Monaco and start some production company."

The joking tone is in accord with Peacock's bold exploration of comic aspects of Volumnia, a woman of brilliant mind and skill of persuasion. Volumnia says to Coriolanus: 'Thou art my warrior/I holp to frame thee' (5.3.63-64)." But her vehemence sometimes creates comedy because of particular circumstance: for instance, the way she tries to manipulate her son into playing a politician when required without his having to really mean what he says or does at the time (3.2). Coriolanus wonders why she would wish him to be "milder": "Would you have me,/False to my nature? Rather say, I play/The man I am" (3.2.14-16), to which she responds with adroit suasion:

> Because that now it lies you on to speak
> To th' people; not by your own instruction,
> Not by th' matter which your heart prompts you,
> But with such words that are but rooted in
> Your tongue, though but bastards, and syllables
> Of no allowance, to your bosom's truth.
> Now, this no more dishonours you at all
> Than to take in a town with gentle words,
> Which else would put you to your fortune and
> The hazard of much blood.
> I would dissemble with my nature where
> My fortunes and my friends at stake requir'd
> I should do so in honour (3.2.53-64).

A second significant example of satire emerges in a public way in 2.1 that Lepage sets in a bar where Volumnia bursts in on Sicinius and Brutus to glory in her son's wounds. Peacock enlarges the moment with fierce black comedy, celebrating how her son has taken over Corioli: "He hath in/this action outdone his former deeds doubly" (2.1.135-136). When noise from without is heard, she seals the impression of his being a warrior who has carried noisy celebration into the present, while leaving a town full of tears behind.

The actress approves enthusiastically of Lepage's staging of the scene because "it feels real, natural, and excellent that the two politicians are able to witness that moment which may or may not be the case in another setting." A similar moment, though more darkly dramatic, occurs in 4.2 when she is in a rather posh restaurant but still seething over Coriolanus' banishment from Rome: "Anger's my meat; I sup upon myself,/And so shall starve with feeding" (4.2.50-51).

Peacock galvanizes the scene in performance, and (in our interview) she pays a debt of thanks to her director: "The fact that it's so *public* is so perfect. Not all directors would necessarily go down that road with whom she might refer to as the rabble for witnesses.

It all feels correct because Lepage is one of the most interesting, exquisite storytellers I've ever worked with. His attention to detail is all about story, character, and relationship. It's instinctual with him. He doesn't force anything. He just *knows* that these details will make the story clearer, better, and more interesting."

I rank Peacock's Volumnia alongside that of Vanessa Redgrave, my favourite actress of all time. However, there is a world of difference between the two interpretations, defined, in part, by their differing medium of performance: the stage (albeit treated cinematically) in Peacock's case; and Ralph Fiennes' extraordinary film, in Redgrave's case. Physically and temperamentally, the two actresses are different, as well, with Redgrave being much the older, taller, inspired visionary, a contemporary Duse, who can startle and move an audience by a quiet inflection or subtle gesture; while Peacock goes for relentlessly driving forward-momentum, eschewing genteel, ladylike restraint that British actresses of a certain era were wont to display.

Redgrave, of course, is an exception—a true genius who often emanates fierce, rushing passion, and who often leaves an audience breathless with suspense or battered by her emotional attack. But the case of Volumnia crystallizes just how different two major actresses can be in their approaches to the same role. The differences were incarnated in the final confrontation of mother and son in 5.3, where Volumnia successfully petitions her stubborn son to spare Rome, something she values higher than herself or him. In the film, Redgrave kneels before Fiennes' Coriolanus, placing her hands on his knees, and surprising both the character and the actor playing him by her "unnerving simplicity," to use Fiennes' own words (Carson 224). Peacock's Volumnia, however, goes big, not embarrassed in the least to do so. She grabs André Sills' face, moves closer to look him in the eye, and utters words to play on his heart-strings:

> thou shalt no sooner
> March to assault thy country than to tread
> (Trust to't, thou shalt not) on they mother's womb
> That brought thee to this world (5.3.122-125).

Alas, Lepage's staging of this scene (which is Volumnia's final scene in Lepage's version) dilutes the effect this is supposed to have on Coriolanus. He moves Volumnia, Virgilia, Valeria, young Martius, and Attendants offstage, leaving Sills' man-boy to surrender ("O mother, mother, what have you done?") to empty air. When I raise this criticism of Lepage with Peacock, she delivers a diplomatic, open-ended answer:

> I won't say this is wrong or right. There is no wrong or right as long as the choice is truthfully playable. Initially, I thought, 'Oh, no, that's not right.' But why not? I think it's more interesting to *not* wrap it all up, so to have her exiting right there is interesting because she fundamentally abandons him in favour of Rome. I would be curious, however, to know what might happen if she heard him say, 'O mother, mother!/ What have you done?' (5.3.183-184). Would she be aware she has sent him to his death? In this version, she takes a huge risk by leaving the possibility of failure of saving Rome in her wake. It would be interesting to imagine the story of Volumnia after the fall, as it were, to visit her five years after the fact. Her son is dead, she sent him to it, but does she know this and have to live with it? Or does she re-invent herself without him?

Her utterance reveals her dynamic imagination. Her professed love of story comes to the fore in her proposed scenario. She really is an actress who uses the "chaos of the heart" to find a path in an all-too-human journey of painful yearning.

Notes

[1]A sidelight: I directed one of Lucy's sisters (Susan) in a Montreal high school English language production of Anouilh's *Antigone*, and David Peacock generously accepted my invitation to address a drama workshop (gratis) I ran for fellow-teachers at the same high school.

Ben Carlson as Hamlet in Hamlet *(Stratford Festival, 2008).*
(Photo: David Hou. Courtesy of the Stratford Festival)

Appendix A

List Of Interviews Conducted For This Book

Nancy Palk, Toronto, January 18, 2017

Joseph Ziegler, Toronto, January 31, 2017

Albert Schultz, Toronto, April 24, 2017

Joseph Ziegler, Stratford, July 20, 2017

Ben Carlson, Toronto, November 19, 2017

Tom McCamus, Mississauga, December 1, 2017

Chick Reid, Stratford, May 16, 2018

Juan Chioran, Stratford, May 16, 2018

Tim Carroll, Niagara-on-the-Lake, May 23, 2018

Tom Rooney, Stratford, June 2, 2018

Graham Abbey, Stratford, June 2, 2018

Lucy Peacock, Stratford, June 2, 2018

Moya O'Connell, Vancouver, June 19, 2018

Chris Abraham, Toronto, June 26, 2018 (phone interview)

Lucy Peacock, Stratford, August 25, 2018 (phone interview)

Select Bibliography

Ackroyd, Peter, ed. *A Brief Guide to William Shakespeare (without the boring bits)*. London: Robinson, 2010.

Barratt, Mark. *Ian McKellen (An Unofficial Biography)*. London: Virgin Books, 2005.

Bell, John. *On Shakespeare*. Sydney: Allen & Unwin, [2011] 2012.

Berry, Ralph. *On Directing Shakespeare: Interviews with contemporary directors*. London: Hamish Hamilton, 1989.

Billington, Michael. *The Modern Actor*. London: Hamish Hamilton,1973.

Bloom, Harold. *Shakespeare: The Invention of the Human*. New York: Riverhead Books, 1998.

Brockbank, Philip, ed. *Players of Shakespeare 1: Essays in Shakespearean Performance by twelve players with the Royal Shakespeare Company*. Cambridge: Cambridge University Press, [1985] 1990.

Carson, Susannah, ed. *Living with Shakespeare: Essays by Writers, Actors, and Directors*. New York: Vintage Books, 2013.

Cook, Judith. *Directors' Theatre (Sixteen Leading Directors on the state of Theatre in Britain Today)*. London: Hodder & Stoughton, 1989.

_____. *Shakespeare's Players*. London: Harrap, 1983.

Coveney, Michael. *Maggie Smith (A Bright Particular Star)*. London: Victor Gollancz Ltd., 1992.

Cox, Brian. *Salem to Moscow: An Actor's Odyssey*. London: Methuen, 1991.

Croall, Jonathan, ed. *Buzz Buzz! (Playwrights, Actors and Directors at the National Theatre)*. London: Methuen Drama, 2008.

Cushman, Robert. *Fifty Seasons at Stratford*. Toronto: McClelland and Stewart, 2002.

David, Richard. *Shakespeare in the Theatre*. Cambridge: Cambridge University Press, [1978] 1981.

Davies, Oliver Ford. *Performing Shakespeare*. London: Nick Hern Books, [2007] 2013.

Delgado, Maria M. & Paul Heritage, eds. *In Contact with the Gods? (Directors Talk Theatre)*. Manchester & New York: Manchester University Press, 1996.

Dickson, Andrew. *Worlds Elsewhere: Journeys around Shakespeare's Globe*. New York: Henry Holt and Company, 2015.

Donnellan, Declan. *The Actor and the Target*. (New Edition). London: Theatre Communications Group, 2006.

Dromgoole, Dominic. *Will & Me (How Shakespeare Took Over My Life)*. London: Penguin, 2007.

Edmonson, Paul, Paul Prescott and Erin Sullivan, eds. *A Year of Shakespeare (Re-Living the World Shakespeare Festival)*. London: Bloomsbury, 2013.

Elsom, John, ed. *Is Shakespeare Still Our Contemporary?* London and New York: Routledge, 1989.

Epstein, Norrie. *The Friendly Shakespeare*. New York: Penguin Books, 1993.

Fischlin, Daniel & Judith Nasby, eds. *Shakespeare: Made in Canada (Contemporary Canadian Adaptations in Theatre, Pop Media and Visual Arts)*. [Guelph] Macdonald Stewart Art Centre, 2007.

Garber, Marjorie. *Profiling Shakespeare*. New York and London: Routledge, 2008.

_____. *Shakespeare After All*. New York: Anchor Books, [2004] 2005.

_____. *Shakespeare and Modern Culture*. New York: Anchor Books, 2008.

_____. *Vested Interests: Cross-Dressing & Cultural Anxiety*. New York: HarperPerennial, 1993.

Garebian, Keith. *A Well-Bred Muse: Selected Theatre Writings 1978-1988*. Oakville: Mosaic Press, 1991.

_____. *William Hutt: A Theatre Portrait*. Oakville: Mosaic Press, 1988.

_____. *William Hutt: Soldier Actor*. Toronto: Guernica Editions, 2017.

_____, ed. *Masks and Faces*. Oakville: Mosaic Press, 1995.

Gay, Penny. *As She Likes It: Shakespeare's Unruly Women.* London and New York: Routledge, 1994.

Goddard, Harold C. *The Meaning of Shakespeare, Vol. 1.* Chicago & London: Phoenix Books (The University of Chicago Press), [1951] 1960.

Gussow, Mel. *Michael Gambon: A Life in Acting.* New York: Applause Theatre & Cinema Books, 2004.

Hytner, Nicholas. *Balancing Acts (Behind the Scenes at London's National Theatre).* New York: Alfred A. Knopf, 2017.

Introductions to Shakespeare (being the Introductions to the individual plays in the Folio Society Edition 1950-76). Foreword by Charles Ede. London: Michael Joseph, 1977.

Jackson, Russell and Robert Smallwood, eds. *Players of Shakespeare 2: Further Essays in Shakespearean Performance by players with the Royal Shakespeare Company.* Cambridge: Cambridge University Press, [1988] 1989.

_____. eds. *Players of Shakespeare 3: Further Essays in Shakespearian Performance by players with the Royal Shakespeare Company.* Cambridge University Press, 1993.

Jacobs, Gerald. *Judi Dench: A Great Deal of Laughter.* London: Weidenfeld and Nicolson, 1985.

Johnson, Paul. *Creators (From Chaucer and Dürer to Picasso and Disney).* New York: HarperCollins, 2006.

Kott, Jan. *Shakespeare Our Contemporary.* London: Methuen, 1964.

Maher, Mary Z. *Actor Nicholas Pennell: Risking Enchantment.* Baltimore: PublishAmerica: 2005.

_____. *Actors Talk About Shakespeare.* New York: Limelight Editions, 2009.

Martz, Fraidie and Andrew Wilson. *A Fiery Soul: The Life and Theatrical Times of John Hirsch.* Montreal: Vehicule Press, 2011.

O'Connor, Garry, ed. *Olivier: In Celebration*. London: Hodder & Stoughton, 1987.

Olivier, Laurence. *Confessions of an Actor*. London: Weidenfeld and Nicolson, 1982.

_____. *On Acting*. London: Weidenfeld and Nicolson, 1986.

Packer, Tina. *Women of Will (The Remarkable Evolution of Shakespeare's Female Characters)*. New York: Vintage Books, 2016.

Perloff, Carey. *Beautiful Chaos: A Life in the Theater*. San Francisco: City Lights Foundation, 2015.

Righter, Anne. *Shakespeare And the Idea of The Play*. Harmondsworth: Penguin, 1967.

Rodenburg, Patsy. *Shakespeare Speaking*. New York: Palgrave Macmillan, 2004.

Rosenbaum, Ron. *The Shakespeare Wars (Clashing Scholars, Public Fiascoes, Palace Coups)*. New York: Random House, 2006.

Rutter, Carol. *Clamorous Voices (Shakespeare's Women Today)*. London: The Women's Press, 1988.

Sales, Roger, ed. *Shakespeare in Perspective, Volume 1*. London: Ariel Books, 1984.

Schafer, Elizabeth. *Ms-Directing Shakespeare: Women Direct Shakespeare*. New York: St. Martin's Press, 2000.

Sher, Antony. *Beside Myself (An Autobiography)*. London: Arrow Books, [2001] 2002.

_____. *Year of the Fat Knight: The Falstaff Diaries*. London: Nick Hern Books, [2015] 2016.

Smallwood, Robert, ed. *Players of Shakespeare 4: Further Essays in Shakespearian Performance by players with the Royal Shakespeare Company*. Cambridge University Press, 1998.

Spivack, Bernard. *Shakespeare and the Allegory of Evil (The History of a Metaphor in Relation to His Villains)*. New York: Columbia University Press, [1958] 1964.

Taylor, Gary. *Reinventing Shakespeare (A Cultural History from the Restoration to the Present)*. London: The Hogarth Press, 1990.

Tillyard, E.M.W. *Shakespeare's History Plays*. Harmondsworth: Penguin Books, [1944] 1969.

Todd, Susan, ed. *Women and Theatre: Calling the Shots*. London: Faber and Faber, 1984.

Trewin, J.C. *Shakespeare on the English Stage 1900-1964*. London: Barrie and Rockliff, 1964.

Tynan, Kenneth. *A View of the English Stage*. St. Albans, Herts: Paladin, 1976.

_____. *Tynan on Theatre*. Harmondsworth: Penguin, 1964.

_____(ed.). *Othello: The National Theatre Production*. London: Rupert Hart-Davis, 1966.

Wain, John. *The Living World of Shakespeare (A Playgoer's Guide)*. Harmondsworth: Penguin Books, 1964.

Walter, Harriet. *Brutus and Other Heroines (Playing Shakespeare's Roles for Women)*. London: Nick Hern Books, 2016.

Wilson-Lee, Edward. *Shakespeare in Swahililand: In Search of a Global Poet*. New York: Farrar, Straus and Giroux, 2016.

Acknowledgements

My thanks go to all who granted me interviews for what I regard as a collaborative effort in the matter of producing a ground-breaking Canadian theatre book, and to the following for arranging and providing space for many of the interviews: Anita Gaffney and Marion Burr of the Stratford Festival; Laura Hughes of the Shaw Festival; and Cynammon Schreinert of Bard on the Beach, Vancouver. Brad Lepp of Soulpepper furnished me with a solo shot of Albert Schultz's Hamlet. Liza Giffen (Archives Director, Stratford Festival) was her usual efficient self in extending me courteous co-operation in the matter of selecting solos of various actors, making available to me the services of Stephanie Vaillant, who proved her mettle as digitalization archivist, and Christine Schindler, who found the photograph used on the book's cover, and who helped in clearing permissions with the actors and Equity for print use of the photographs. I also owe a debt of gratitude to my extraordinary friend Maria Heidler for reading the essays with a clear, strict eye and offering her always constructive editorial suggestions. I also thank the book's designer Errol F. Richardson for giving me a cover to cherish. Finally, thanks to the Ontario Arts Council for a Writers Reserve Grant, and, most importantly, to Connie McParland and Michael Mirolla of Guernica Editions, who continue to support my writing of both poetry and prose.

About the Author

Keith Garebian has been writing professionally about theatre since 1976 for numerous magazines, journals, tabloids, and anthologies. Winner of a Canada Council Senior Grant, numerous grants from the Ontario Arts Council, the William Saroyan Medal (Armenia), and three Mississauga Arts Council Awards for Writing, he has served on arts and theatre juries for the OAC. His production histories of classic Broadway musicals culminated in *The Making of 'Cabaret'* (2nd ed.) (Oxford University Press), and his authoritative biography, *William Hutt: Soldier Actor* (Guernica), has earned unanimous praise, thereby extending his international reputation. *Colours to the Chameleon* fulfills his ambition of celebrating some of the best contemporary Canadian actors and actresses as they discuss their various engagements with Shakespeare. His current project (in addition to completing a ninth collection of poetry) is a set of miniature essays on Theatre and Poetry, two of his greatest obsessions.

Selected Books in Print
by Keith Garebian

Blue: The Derek Jarman Poems (Signature Editions)
The Making of 'Cabaret' (Second Edition) (Oxford University Press)
Accidental Genius (The Pantheon of Modern American Poets) (Guernica)
Georgia and Alfred (Quattro)
Lerner and Loewe's 'My Fair Lady' (Routledge)
William Hutt: Soldier Actor (Guernica)
Poetry is Blood (Guernica)
Against Forgetting (Frontenac House)